STOCK MARKET
CRASHES

Predictable and Unpredictable
and What To Do About Them

World Scientific Series
in FINANCE vol. 13

STOCK MARKET CRASHES

Predictable and Unpredictable and What To Do About Them

William T. Ziemba
University of British Columbia, Canada
London School of Economics, UK

Sebastien Lleo
NEOMA Business School, France

Mikhail Zhitlukhin
Steklov Mathematical Institute, Moscow, Russia

World Scientific

NEW JERSEY · LONDON · SINGAPORE · BEIJING · SHANGHAI · HONG KONG · TAIPEI · CHENNAI · TOKYO

Published by

World Scientific Publishing Co. Pte. Ltd.

5 Toh Tuck Link, Singapore 596224

USA office: 27 Warren Street, Suite 401-402, Hackensack, NJ 07601

UK office: 57 Shelton Street, Covent Garden, London WC2H 9HE

British Library Cataloguing-in-Publication Data
A catalogue record for this book is available from the British Library.

World Scientific Series in Finance — Vol. 13
STOCK MARKET CRASHES
Predictable and Unpredictable and What to do About Them

Copyright © 2018 by World Scientific Publishing Co. Pte. Ltd.

ISBN 978-981-3222-60-1
ISBN 978-981-3222-61-8 (pbk)

Desk Editor: Lum Pui Yee

Typeset by Stallion Press
Email: enquiries@stallionpress.com

Printed in Singapore

Review Quotes

Stock market declines of ten percent or more are both costly and frequent. The authors share what they have learned about dodging these disasters, based on decades of research, data analysis and trading.

Edward O. Thorp, author of *A Man For All Markets* and the New York Times best seller, *Beat the Dealer.*

In my experience, one of the most important objectives stated by most investment managers is the preservation of investors' capital. Central to that objective is to avoid catastrophic losses due to major stock market declines or outright crashes. Hence, being able to predict crashes is a fundamental caveat to sound investment strategy. Probably more than anyone since the legendary works of Hyman Minsky, William Ziemba has provided the soundest, empirically based techniques, models and insights to investors to help them avoid and deal with major stock market declines. My own works, using fundamental models for predicting individual firm and sovereign defaults, complements well Bill Ziemba's important contributions.

Edward I. Altman, Max L. Heine Professor of Finance, Emeritus, New York University, Stern School of Business.

Stock Market Crashes: Predictable and Unpredictable is a well-documented account of research addressing the detection of stock market bubbles and the predictability of the timing of their eventual burst. Whereas the jury is still out, both practitioners and academics will benefit from reading this fascinating account by Professor Ziemba, an accomplished contributor to this quest.

George M. Constantinides, Leo Melamed Professor of Finance, Booth School of Business, University of Chicago.

Bill Ziemba has spent his professional life studying financial and other markets and their anomalies. His insights have been very valuable, time and again, for academic researchers and practitioners alike. A highly recommended read for anybody interested in financial markets.

Gerd Infanger, Stanford University and Infanger Investments, LLC.

William T Ziemba
Alumni Professor of Financial Modeling and Stochastic Optimization (Emeritus), University of British Columbia, Vancouver, BC and Distinguished Visiting Associate, Systemic Risk Centre, London School of Economics, UK
wtzimi@mac.com

assisted by

Sébastien Lleo
Finance Department, NEOMA Business School - Campus Reims, 59 rue Pierre Taittinger, 51100 Reims, France
sebastien.lleo@NEOMA-bs.fr

and

Mikhail Zhitlukhin
Steklov Mathematical Institute, Moscow, Russia
mikhailzh@mi.ras.ru

Dedication

Dedicated to the memory of stochastic programming colleagues Marida Bertocchi of the University of Bergamo, and Jitka Dupacova of Charles University in Prague

William T Ziemba, Bregamo, May 30, 2017

To Bill Z for unwavering support through the years, his thoughtful advice when I decided to pursue a PhD, and for the many adventures that he invited me to share with him.

And to Mark Davis, a gentleman, mathematician and mentor.

Sébastien Lleo

To Albert Shiryaev and Igor Evstigneev.

Mikhail Zhitlukhin

Preface

My greatest debt is to my two wonderful co-editors, Sebastien Lleo and Mikhail Zhitlukhin.

Special thanks goes to Keizo Nagatani who suggested me to interview to be the first Yamaichi Visiting Professor of Finance at the University of Tsukuba in 1988-89 where this all started. My colleagues in Japan, Mr Okada, Shigueri Ishi, Asaji Komatsu and others, were very helpful. So were my Frank Russell Colleagues, Chris Hensel, Doug Stone, David Myers, Andy Turner and David Carino and the Wilmott magazine gang, Paul Wilmott, Dan Tudbul and Beth Gongde. In the preparation of this book Sandra Schwartz and Rachel Ziemba were very helpful, so were Will Goetzmann, Robert Shiller, Robert Jarrow, Philip Protter, John Swetye and Mark Davis who either wrote chapters with us or supplied valuable materials that we could reference. Thanks to all of you.

William T Ziemba
London School of Economics
May 28, 2017

About the Authors

William T Ziemba is the Alumni Professor (Emeritus) of Financial Modeling and Stochastic Optimization in the Sauder School of Business, University of British Columbia where he taught from 1968–2006. His PhD is from the University of California, Berkeley. He currently teaches part time and makes short research visits to various universities. At present he is the Distinguished Visiting Research Associate, Systemic Risk Centre, London School of Economics. He has been a Visiting Professor at Cambridge, Oxford, London School of Economics, University of Reading and Warwick in the UK, at Stanford, UCLA, Berkeley, MIT, University of Washington and Chicago in the US, Universities of Bergamo, Venice and Luiss in Italy, the Universities of Zurich, Cyprus, Tsukuba (Japan), KAIST (Korea), and the National University and the National Technological University of Singapore. He has been a consultant to a number of leading financial institutions including the Frank Russell Company, Morgan Stanley, Buchanan Partners, RAB Hedge Funds, Gordon Capital, Matcap, Ketchum Trading, and in the gambling area to the BC Lotto Corporation, SCA Insurance, Singapore Pools, Canadian Sports Pool, Keeneland Racetrack, and some racetrack syndicates in Hong Kong, Manila and Australia. His research is in asset-liability management, portfolio theory and practice, security market imperfections, Japanese and Asian financial markets, hedge fund strategies, risk management, sports and lottery investments, and applied stochastic programming. His co-written practitioner paper on the Russell–Yasuda model won second prize in the 1993 Edelman Practice of Management Science Competition. He has been a futures and equity trader and hedge fund and investment manager since 1983. He has published widely in journals such as *Operations Research, Management Science, Mathematics of OR, Mathematical Programming, American Economic Review, Journal of Economic Perspectives, Journal of Finance, Journal of Economic Dynamics* and Control, JFQA, Quantitative Finance, Journal of Portfolio Management and Journal of Banking and Finance and in many books and special journal issues. Recent books include Applications of Stochastic Programming with S W Wallace, SIAMMPS (2005), Stochastic Optimization Models in Finance, 2nd edition with R G Vickson, World Scientific (2006) and Handbook of Asset and Liability Modeling, Volume 1: Theory and Methodology (2006) and Volume 2: Applications and Case Studies (2007) with S A Zenios, North Holland, Scenarios for Risk Management and Global Investment Strategies with Rachel Ziemba, Wiley (2007), Handbook of Investments: Sports and Lottery Betting Markets, with Donald Hausch, North Holland, 2008, Optimizing the Aging, Retirement and Pensions Dilemma with Marida Bertocchi and Sandra Schwartz (2010, 2015 (2nd edn.) and The Kelly Capital Growth Investment Criterion (2010), with legendary hedge fund trader Edward Thorp and Leonard MacLean, Calendar Anomalies and Arbitrage, The Handbook of Financial Decision Making (with Leonard MacLean) and Stochastic Programming (with Horand Gassman), published by World Scientific in 2012 and 2013. In progress is Handbook on the Economics of Wine (with O Ashenfelter, O Gergaud and K Storchmann) and the Handbook Futures Markets (with T Mallaris). He is the series editor for North Holland's Handbooks in Finance, World Scientific Handbooks in Financial Economics and Books in Finance, and previously was the CORS editor of INFOR and the department of finance editor of Management Science, 1982–1992. He has continued his columns in Wilmott and his 2013 book with Rachel Ziemba have the 2007–2013 columns updated with new material published by World Scientific. Ziemba, along with Hausch, wrote the famous Beat the Racetrack book (1984), which was revised into Dr Z's Beat the Racetrack (1987), which presented their place and show betting system and the Efficiency of Racetrack Betting Markets (1994, 2008) — the so-called bible of racetrack syndicates. Their 1986 book Betting at the Racetrack extends this efficient inefficient market approach to simple exotic bets. Ziemba is revising BATR into Exotic Betting at the Racetrack (World Scientific) which adds Pick 3, 4, 5, 6, etc., and provides updates to be out in 2018 with real bets he made across the world. Finally he has just completed Travels with Dr Z: The Adventures of a Modern Renaissance Academic in Investing and Gambling, a memoir and financial history of his investment activities over the last fifty years and Great Investment Ideas, which has all twelve of his applied investment papers published in the Journal of Portfolio Management. These hard to find papers cover many important topics including the evaluation of the greatest investors.

Sébastien Lleo is an Associate Professor in the Finance Department at NEOMA Business School in France and a tutor on the Certificate in Quantitative Finance at FitchLearning in the UK. He currently serves as Director of NEOMA's doctoral programs and is a member of the Steering Group of the CQF Institute. Sébastien was previously Research Associate at Imperial College London in the UK, worked in the investment industry in Canada and consulted on risk management and asset allocation projects in Canada and the UK.

He has published research on investment management, stochastic control, behavioural finance, and risk management. He also coauthored the book "Risk-Sensitive Investment Management" with Mark Davis. Sébastien presented his research at leading conferences and seminars in Europe, North America and Asia Pacific.

He holds a PhD in Mathematics from Imperial College London (UK), a MBA from University of Ottawa (Canada), and MSc in Management from NEOMA Business School (France). He is also a CFA Charterholder, a Certified Financial Risk Manager, a Professional Risk Manager, and a CQF alumnus.

Mikhail Zhitlukhin is a researcher at Steklov Mathematical Institute in Moscow, Russia and a lecturer at the Higher School of Economics, Moscow. His research interests are probability theory, stochastic processes and optimal control theory as well as their applications in finance and economics. He holds a PhD from Steklov Institute and the University of Manchester, UK.

Contents

Chapter 1

Introduction

Trying to predict stock market declines or crashes is important to all investors and especially to speculative investors and hedge funds. Avoiding them or dealing with them greatly improves portfolio performance. But it is hard to predict these declines. Moreover, to quote Peter Lynch:

> Far more money has been lost by investors preparing for corrections, or trying to anticipate corrections, than has been lost in corrections themselves.

Financial bubbles and crashes are certainly not new, and the most dramatic ones tend to leave a lasting memory. "The South Sea Bubble, a Scene in 'Change Alley in 1720'," reproduced in Figure 1.1, was painted by Edward Matthew Ward in 1847, nearly 130 years after the events but only a couple of years after another famous stock market bubble: Railway Mania.[1]

The academic literature on bubbles and crashes is well established, starting with the studies on bubbles by Blanchard and Watson (1982), Flood *et al.* (1986), Camerer (1989), Allen and Gorton (1993), Diba and Grossman (1988), Abreu and Brunnermeier (2003) and more recently Corgnet *et al.* (2015), Andrade *et al.* (2016) or Sato (2016). A rich literature on bubble and crash predictions has also emerged. We can classify most bubble and crash prediction models in three broad categories based on the type of methodology and variable used: fundamental models, stochastic models and sentiment-based models.

Fundamental models use fundamental variables such as stock prices, corporate earnings, interest rates, inflation or GNP to forecast crashes. The bond–stock earnings yield differential (BSEYD) measure (Ziemba and

---

[1] A note for art *amateurs*: the painting is housed at the Tate, in London.

Fig. 1.1. "The South Sea Bubble, a Scene in 'Change Alley in 1720' " by Edward Matthew Ward (1816–1879).

Schwartz, 1991; Lleo and Ziemba, 2012, 2015c, 2017) is the oldest model in this category, which also includes the CAPE (Lleo and Ziemba, 2017) and the ratio of the market value of all publicly traded stocks to the current level of the GNP (MV/GNP) that Warren Buffett popularized (Buffett and Loomis, 1999, 2001; Lleo and Ziemba, 2016b). Recently, Callen and Fang (2015) also found evidence that short interest is positively related to one-year ahead stock price crash risk.

Stochastic models construct a probabilistic representation of the asset prices. This representation can be either a discrete or a continuous time stochastic process. Examples include the local martingale model proposed by Jarrow and Protter (Jarrow *et al.*, 2010, 2011; Jarrow and Larsson, 2012; Protter, 2013; Jarrow, 2016; Protter, 2016), the disorder detection model proposed by Shiryaev, Zhitlukhin and Ziemba (Shiryaev, 2010a; Shiryaev *et al.*, 2014, 2015) and the earthquake model of Gresnigt *et al.* (2015). When it comes to actual implementation, the local martingale model and the disorder detection model share the same starting point: they assume that the evolution of the asset price $S(t)$ can be best described using a diffusion process:

$$dS(t) = \mu(t, S(t))S(t)dt + \sigma(t, S(t))S(t)dW(t), \quad S(0) = s_0, t \in \mathbb{R}^+,$$

where $W(t)$ is a standard Brownian motion on the underlying probability space. However, the two models look at different aspects of the evolution. The disorder detection model detects crashes by looking for a change in regime in the drift μ and volatility σ. The local martingale model detects bubbles by testing whether the process is a martingale or a strict local martingale.

Behavioral analyses, such as the recent work by Goetzmann *et al.* (2016), are the latest addition to the bubble and crash literature. The emphasis here is on the way individuals assess the probabilities of market crashes, and on the discrepancy between these subjective probability and the historical probabilities observed on the market.

In this book, we present models that have been shown to predict many large crashes averaging -25%. We also discuss how to deal with small declines in the -5% to -15% range. The S&P500 had 22 10%+ corrections over less than a year since the mid-1960s. Figure 1.2 shows the cycles of bull and bear markets on the Dow Jones Industrial Average (DJIA) from 1929 to 2016. In China, the Shanghai Composite Index had 22 such corrections since it opened 25 years ago, and the Shenzhen Composite Index, 21.

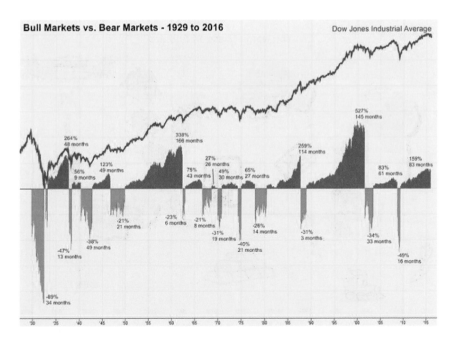

Fig. 1.2. Bull and Bear Markets on the Dow Jones Industrial Average (1929–2016).

Source: Yahoo!

The discussion proceeds by discussing when a bubble exists. A bubble exists when prices are trending just because they are trending up or down. The definition and identification of whether a particular market is a bubble or not is complex and is discussed in Appendix A.

1.1. How rare are bubbles?

In this book, we present evidence associated with trying to predict when a bubble exists, when it might burst and deflate and how to get out of bubble-like markets near the top. From Tulip Mania to the Mississippi Bubble, the South Sea Bubble. The 1929 Crash, the dotcom bubble and the housing bubble. Figure 1.3 is a visual reminder that bubbles and crashes have occured for a long time, all around the world. Goetzman in (2014) considers the questions on how rare are these bubbles and what happens to them. When they burst do they give back most or all of the gain in their rise to bubble status?

Goetzmann, using the 1900–2014, 21-country world equity market data from Dimson *et al.* (2014), found that bubbles are quite rare, the chance

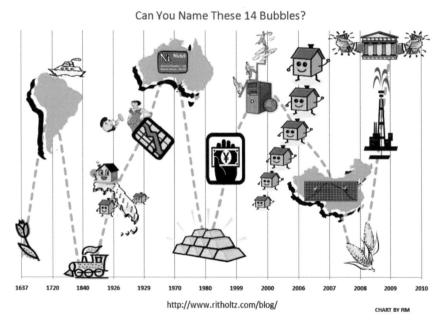

Fig. 1.3.   Around the world in 14 crashes.

that a market that doubles gives back its gain is only about 10%, markets are more likely to double again following a 100% doubling move, and that the probability of a crash conditional on a bubble-like boom is only slightly higher than the unconditional probability., namely 0.3–1.4% for various bubble definitions.

Goetzmann defines a boom as a 100% increase in (a) one year or (b) three years and defines a crash or drop of at least 50% (a) in the next year or (b) in the next five years. To be specific in 3470 market years there were 72 one year returns of 100%+ and 84 with returns less than −50% busts. Of the 72 booms, 6 (8.33%) doubled again versus an unconditional frequency of 0.18%, and 3 (4.1%) fell by a half or more versus an unconditional 0.09%. And of the 84 busts, 10 (13.16%) doubled versus 0.3% unconditional and 5 (0.50%) halved again versus 0.15% unconditional.

Over five years, there are a lot more doubling gains and halving loses. The results are in Table 1.1.

1.2. How many crashes and how deep are they going to be in the opinion of investors?

The data show that single-day large drops in equity prices are rare. But we have some large ones such as October 28, 1929, October 19, 1987 and September 11, 2001. These all occurred during a period of high volatility with prices rising and falling dramatically in the period before the big drop day. Table 1.2 lists the 10 largest 1-day declines in the S&P500 from 1928

Table 1.1.   Five year doubling and halving results.

		Probability	
	Count	Conditional	Unconditional
	3127		
Double or +	803		25.72%
Halve or +	197		6.31%
Years 100%+	72		2.13%
Doubles again in 1 year	19	26.39%	
Below half in 1 year	11	15.28%	
Years with −50% decline	75		2.21%
then doubles	27	36.00%	0.80%
then halves again	7	9.3%	0.21%

Source: Goetzmann (2014).

Table 1.2.   The 10 largest 1-day declines in the S&P500.

LARGEST ONE DAY DROPS EVER FOR THE S&P500. OCTOBER IS WELL REPRESENTED		
Date	S&P500	Change
19/10/87	224.84	−20.5%
28/10/29	22.74	−12.9%
29/10/43	20.43	−10.2%
5/11/29	20.61	−9.9%
18/10/37	10.76	−9.1%
5/10/31	8.82	−9.1%
15/10/08	907.84	−9.0%
1/12/08	816.21	−8.9%
20/7/33	16.57	−8.9%
29/9/08	1106.39	−8.8%

Source: UPI Research FactSet 11/10/16.

to 2016. One sees many large drops in october. Also, only three days had declines greater than 10%.

Goetzmann *et al.* (2016) show with surveys of high net worth individual and institutional investors over 26 years in the US 1989–2015 that these investors expect many more crashes than actually occur. They found that recent market declines and adverse market events and media reporting boost these probabilities. They also found that non-market related rare disasters yield higher investor subjective crash probabilities. The following question is asked:

> What do you think is the probability of a catastrophic stock market crash in the US like that of October 28, 1929 or October 19, 1987, in the next six months, including the case that a crash occurred in the other countries and spreads to the US? (An answer of 0% means that it cannot happen, an answer of 100% means it is sure to happen.
> Probability = _____%.)

The mean and median responses were an astounding 19% and 10%, respectively, about 10 times the actual frequency which was about 1.7% over the period October 23, 1925 to December 31, 2015.

Chapter 2 discusses the bond-stock earnings yield differential model (BSEYD) model which Ziemba devised in Japan in 1988 based on the 1987 US stock market crash. In the model, we use the long bond rate versus the earning yield which is the reciprocal of the trailing price earnings

(P/E)–ratio. When the difference is too high, a crash almost always occurs. By a crash, we mean a decline of 10% plus from the signal point within one year. We apply this to many markets including Japan and the US over a long period of time. Usually, the market rallies for a while past the signal date and then declines. The model has predicted many crashes. It also predicted two crashes where famed bubble George Soros shorted too soon and lost billions. The so-called FED model is the special case of the BSYED model when the difference between the long bond and the earnings yield on equities is zero.

In Chapter 3, we focus on the short window 2006–2009 crash period. The BSEYD model predicted the stock market crashes in Iceland which fell 95%, China where the market had a huge rally then fell below the signal point and the US which had a correct call on June 14, 2007 with the market falling from the 1500s to 666 in March 2009.

- Graphs show what happened. The US call was on June 14, 2007 with the S&P500 over 1500. Then it fell to 666 in early March 2009. Then a huge bull market more than tripled the S&P500, which is still going. We have simple graphs where two curves cross and one can be made a horizontal line for easy understanding.
- Ziemba was in Iceland in 2006 and the model was not in the danger zone for the index which is mostly banks acting as hedge funds. Small caps were in the danger zone in 2006. It took the Lehman September 2008 drop to crash Iceland.
- China was a strange one. The model worked but there was a big decline after a big rally. The decline was large starting from the start of the call. Also, we applied the BSEYD model to China in 2009 and 2015 so show those results too.

Ziemba showed Harry Markowitz the 2012 Lleo and Ziemba *Quantitative Finance* paper on the 2006–2009 crashes and he suggested that we do a larger 50-year study in the US and compare the BSEYD results with Shiller's high P/E models. In Chapter 4, we take this up. First, it is known from Ziemba's pension fund book with Bertocchi, Schwartz and Ziemba (2010, 2015) that high stock market return periods start with low P/Es and end with high P/Es. John Campbell and Robert Shiller found that over long periods P/E ratios do in fact predict future returns. We show how to use Campbell and Shiller's work on P/E ratio and the predictability of long-term returns to create a crash prediction measure: the high P/E measure. Next, we present a statistical procedure to test the accuracy of crash prediction models. We conclude this chapter with a test of the BSEYD and high P/E model on a 51-year period on the US market, starting on January 1, 1962, and ending on December 31, 2014 (12,846 daily data points). At the end of the chapter, we expand the analysis beyond the US market to look at the Chinese stock markets. Material in this chapter is based on Lleo and Ziemba (2016c) and (2017).

Chapter 5 presents other prediction models for the large crashes. The first is a behavioral finance model based on overconfidence measured by relative put and call prices. Normally, put prices greatly exceed call prices; however, when call prices exceed put prices, it is a crash signal. From 1985 to 2016, the model was in the danger zone six times and the sum of the S&P500 returns in the following quarter was −41.7%. It is rare for the irrational exuberance of the stock market to have calls worth more than puts and the last time this happened was in 2003. Since then, there have been no danger signals by this crash measure.

Another crash measure is Buffett's value of the stock market to the value of the economy. The measure originally proposed has no predictive value, but a modification using confidence limit ideas from the BSEYD research shows value in 8 of 11 situations. The Sotheby's stock price valuation measure is based on the idea that wealthy Sotheby clients sense the top is approaching and exit and this is when the stock price peaks. The measure did predict three major stock market crashes correctly. Finally, Goetzmann, *et al.* (2016) showed with surveys that investors expect more crashes than actually happen and Goetzmann (2014) showed that most bubbles do not result in crashes.

In Chapter 6, we discuss the very positive effect of the FED meetings. We updated the 2011 paper of Lucca and Moench, published in 2016, which shows the influence of the Fed Open Market meetings since they were publicized and announced in 1994. We used data 2011–2016 and small cap effects. We also discuss small cap dominance and presidential election effects. There is a small cap dominance with Democratic presidents. It is very powerful and in the 60–40 stock–bond portfolio Frank Russell (where Ziemba consulted) is beaten 20-1 by small cap with Democrats and bonds or high cap stocks with Republicans. The reason consulting firms like Frank Russell suggest 60-40 portfolios is that bonds rise when stocks are in a crash mode so portfolio variance is lower with this strategy compared with all equity portfolios. However, over long periods of time, the small cap, large cap or bond portfolio approach has much higher final wealth.

Zweig was the top Wall Street analyst, as evidenced by his $125 million New York Penthouse. Ziemba recalls his remarks before 1987 crash on Wall Street week. In Chapter 7, He and Swetye, a colleague, describe the approaches of the famous investor Marty Zweig in making buy/sell or entry/exit decisions in financial markets using Fed information. They applied Marty Zweig's FED-based prediction model applied to the 2015–2016 stock market. Zweig had developed and used his model from 1971 till his death in 2013. Momentum and FED movements are still working with his simple arithmetic model. Swetye and Ziemba focus on the general equity index market. John Reese has been using Zweig's methods for individual stocks and his experience is discussed. We know that FED policy is driving the 2009–2017 bull market, especially during FED meetings.

Zweig's models use many variables: prime rate, discount rate, reserve requirement, installment debt, the Value Line Index, and ratio of advancing stock volume to declining stock volume. Cumulative scores from the variables are tracked using two models: the Monetary and Momentum models. Decisions are based on thresholds for the cumulative scores combined into a "Super Model".

Chapter 8 discusses smaller declines in the 5–15% area that are largely unpredictable but are situations we can deal with. Although these markets are not bubbles, the use of investment strategies which weather volatile markets is clearly important. We discuss eight such declines and categorize them into three types. Namely, V-shaped (as in October 2014) when the market falls then quickly reverses, WWW-shaped (like August to October 2015) where the market goes down, up, down, etc. for an extended period and MMMWWW-shaped decline (as in January–February 2016 following the first FED rate increase) where the market falls sharply for a number of days then moves into an up, down, up, down situation like the WWW decline. We discuss procedures for dealing with each of these type declines. We discuss the effect of movements of the VIX volatility index to signal the end of declines such as the January–February and Brexit declines in 2016.

Chapter 9 discusses the Shiryaev and Zhitlukhin stopping rule model for exiting bubble-like markets. The model is based on mathematical finance concepts and only uses discrete time, prices assumed to be lognormal. It is developed in Appendix B. The key elements are briefly discussed in the text. The idea is to determine when the rate of increase in prices stops and becomes flat and then declines. Usually, markets fall faster than they rise but in bubble-like markets, the growth and decline rates are similar.

The exit time or stopping time is based on a decision that the market dynamics (mean, variance) are likely to change. A time-dependent threshold for a Shiryaev–Roberts statistic (calculated from estimated model price distribution parameters, alternative model parameter specifications, and a negative power utility) is determined and the exit time is the first passage time to the threshold. Applications are made to Apple computer stock in 2012, the NASDAQ 100 in 2000, the US 1987 and 1929 crashes and the Japanese stock market and golf course membership crash in 1989. We also discuss sensitivity tests of the model and entry as well as exits.

Chapter 10 shows how to include the crash predictions made by these models as scenarios in dynamics investment models.

The appendices discuss the following points:

Appendix A: Other bubble testing methodologies.
Appendix B: Mathematics of the Shiryaev and Zhitlukhin changepoint detection model.

Chapter 2

Discovery of the Bond–Stock Earnings Yield Differential Model

We discuss the bond–stock earnings yield differential (BSEYD) model starting from when Ziemba first used it in Japan in 1988–89 in various countries. The model has called many but not all crashes. Those have high interest rates in the most liquid long-term bonds relative to the trailing earnings-to-price ratio (EP ratio). In general, when the model is in the danger zone, there will almost always be a crash. The model called the 2000 and 2002 US crashes. A long horizon study for the US, Canada, Japan, Germany, and UK shows that being in the stock market when the bond–stock signal is not in the danger zone and in cash when it is in the danger zone provides a final wealth about double buy and hold in these five countries during 1975–2000 or 1980–2000.

2.1. Introduction

This chapter discusses the bond–stock earnings yield differential (BSEYD) crash prediction model that has worked well over time in the US, Japan and elsewhere. Other crash prediction models are discussed in later chapters and in Appendix A, which includes work by Sornette and Zhou (2002), Sornette (2009), and Yan *et al.* (2012a, b). Jarrow *et al.* (2011) discuss when a bubble exists; see Appendix A.1.4. Shirayev *et al.* (2014, 2015) discuss a stopping rule model to exit and enter *bubble type markets*; see Chapter 9 and Appendix B.

In May 1988, Ziemba was invited by Yamaichi Securities to interview to be the first Yamaichi Visiting Professor of Finance at the University of Tsukuba, a Japanese National University. Yamaichi wished to establish the study of finance, especially investments, in Japanese universities, which was not generally taught. They established a 5-year program with five such visiting professors in succession. His teaching at the university (investments, security market anomalies, futures and options) was supplemented with a

2-day a week consulting position in Tokyo, some 60 kilometers southwest of Tsukuba, with the research arm of Yamaichi Securities. At that time, Yamaichi Securities was the fourth largest securities firm in Japan and the sixth largest in the world. In his interview, Ziemba asked if he could study market imperfections (anomalies) and stock market crashes in two study groups with some of the young Yamaichi Research Institute employees who also came up to Tsukuba for his classes.

The proposal was accepted and each study group with about 10 eager young students proceeded by me giving lectures on the US experience and they helped investigate the Japanese situation. They focused on the postwar period 1948–1988 and much of what he learned appears in the book *Invest Japan*, Ziemba and Schwartz (1991) and the 1989–1993 research papers of Ziemba and Schwartz and Stone and Ziemba (1993). Ziemba and his wife also wrote the book *Power Japan* (1992) that discussed the Japanese economy. Sandra had a pretty good idea right away that the Japanese policies that led to astronomically high land and stock prices and massive trade surpluses would lead to disaster and they would eventually lose most of the money that they received from selling cars, stereos and the like. We made a list of prestige buildings that the Japanese overpaid for in the 1987–1989 era in *Power Japan*. Even at the height of their economic power in 1989, only 3% of Japanese assets were invested abroad.

The study groups started in August 1988 and ended a year later. Ziemba was asked to remain as a consultant for the fall of 1988 to complete a factor model discussed in Schwartz and Ziemba (2000) which was originally presented at a Berkeley Program in Finance meeting in Santa Barbara in September 1992. The factor model used anomaly ideas such as mean reversion, earnings surprise, momentum, price–earnings ratios (P/E), future earnings overprice, and value embedded in 30 variables to separate and rank stocks by their future mean return performance from best to worst for all the stocks on the Tokyo Stock Exchange first section which was about 86% of the total capitalization. The model, motivated by a similar model for the US by Jacobs and Levy (1988), was estimated yearly but updated monthly. The model performed well out of sample, so was useful for hedge fund long–short trading as well as long only investing. The hedge fund Buchanan Partners in London discovered the model which was discussed in *Invest Japan* when they bought the book and hired Ziemba to help them in their Japanese warrant trading which was largely long underpriced warrants and short overpriced stocks. Their trading was successful and the model, which was estimated using data during a stock market rise still worked when the decline came since variables such as earnings were the key drivers of the returns. An update of Japanese anomalies to 1994 appears in Comolli and Ziemba (2000); see also Ziemba (2012) for various US, Japanese and other anomalies.

2.2.   The bond–stock equity return crash danger model

In the crash study group, Ziemba came up with a simple model in 1988 with only a single variable, that being the difference between stock and bond rates of return.[1] The idea was that stocks and bonds compete for investment dollars and, when interest rates are low, stocks are favored and when interest rates are high, bonds are favored. The main thing that he wished to focus on is that when the measure, the difference between these two rates, the long bond yield minus the earnings yield (the reciprocal of the P/E ratio), was very large, then there was a high chance of a stock market crash. A crash was defined as a 10% fall in the index within 1 year from the start of the initial danger signal. The model explains the October 1987 crash. Indeed, that application is how the idea evolved. Table 2.1 and Fig. 2.1 show this. The boxes indicate that there is extreme danger in the stock market because 30-year government bond yields are very much higher than usual stock market yields measured by the reciprocal of the previous year's reported P/E ratio. These high interest rates invariably lead to a stock market crash. Here, the danger indicator moved across a statistical 95% confidence line in April. The market ignored this signal but did eventually crash in October 1987. There was a similar signal in the US S&P500 around April 1999 and then a crash that began in August 2000 and a weak stock market in 2001/2002 which is discussed below.

Returning to the story in Japan, in 1988–1989, Ziemba asked one of the young colleagues in the crash study group, Sugheri Ishi, to check the accuracy of the bond–stock prediction model in Japan. They found that

---

[1]This difference model is a generalization of the ratio model, known as the Fed model. Koivu, Pennanen and Ziemba (2005) study this model. Yardeni (1997) originally used the term "Fed model" to refer to a comment made by Fed Chairman Alan Greenspan during his Humphrey-Hawkins testimony on July 22, 1997. In lectures on a mean-variance modeling I have said Ishi got his US masters at the University that was the best using a mean-variance model. He studied with Steve Ross, who rented our house in the summer of 1976 while we were away, as the only Yale University finance professor so the variance was zero. Steve, who died recently, was a giant finance theorist and practitioner with Richard Roll, who invited me to teach in the UCLA finance department at UCLA so had a high mean. Yale now has a terrific finance group but has no one of the Ross's calibre.

Table 2.1. S&P500 index, P/E ratios, government bond yields and the
yield premium over stocks, January 1984–August 1988.

		S&P Index	PER	(a) 30 Yr G bd	(b) 1/pe (%)	(a) − (b)
1986	Jan	208.19	14.63	9.32	6.84	2.48
	Feb	219.37	15.67	8.28	6.38	1.90
	Mar	232.33	16.50	7.59	6.06	1.53
	Apr	237.98	16.27	7.58	6.15	1.43
	May	238.46	17.03	7.76	5.87	1.89
	Jun	245.30	17.32	7.27	5.77	1.50
	Jul	240.18	16.31	7.42	6.13	1.29
	Aug	245.00	17.47	7.26	5.72	1.54
	Sep	238.27	15.98	7.64	6.26	1.38
	Oct	237.36	16.85	7.61	5.93	1.68
	Nov	245.09	16.99	7.40	5.89	1.51
	Dec	248.60	16.72	7.33	5.98	1.35
1987	Jan	264.51	15.42	7.47	6.49	0.98
	Feb	280.93	15.98	7.46	6.26	1.20
	Mar	292.47	16.41	7.65	6.09	1.56
	Apr	289.32	16.22	9.56	6.17	3.39
	May	289.12	16.32	8.63	6.13	2.50
	Jun	301.38	17.10	8.40	5.85	2.55
	Jul	310.09	17.92	8.89	5.58	3.31
	Aug	329.36	18.55	9.17	5.39	3.78
	Sep	318.66	18.10	9.66	5.52	4.14
	Oct	280.16	14.16	9.03	7.06	1.97
	Nov	245.01	13.78	8.90	7.26	1.64
	Dec	240.96	13.55	9.10	7.38	1.72
1988	Jan	250.48	12.81	8.40	7.81	0.59
	Feb	258.10	13.02	8.33	7.68	0.65
	Mar	265.74	13.42	8.74	7.45	1.29
	Apr	262.61	13.24	9.10	7.55	1.55
	May	256.20	12.92	9.24	7.74	1.50
	Jun	270.68	13.65	8.85	7.33	1.52
	Jul	269.44	13.59	9.18	7.36	1.82
	Aug	263.73	13.30	9.30	7.52	1.78

Source: Ziemba and Schwartz (1991).

there were 20 10% plus crashes during the 40 years, 1949–1989. Whenever this measure was in the danger zone (that is, outside a 95% confidence band), there was a crash of 10% or more from the current level
within 1 year. This was 12 out of 12, a splendid prediction record. Not all
crashes had the measure in the danger zone, but whenever it was, there
was a crash with no misses. Some eight crashes occurred for other reasons.

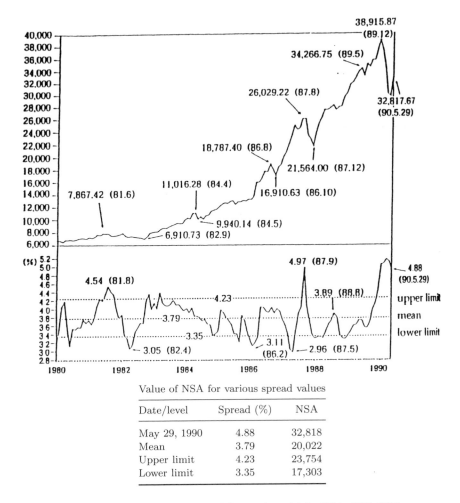

Fig. 2.1.   Bond and stock yield differential model for NSA, 1980–1990.
Source: Ziemba and Schwartz (1991).

Reinhart and Rogoff (2009) in their study of banking crises study some
such circumstances that lead to stock market crashes of both interest rate
and non-interest rate-driven types. See also the classic book of Kindleberger and Aliber (2011) and Lleo and Ziemba (2015a), who study hedge
funds and bank trading disasters, how they occur and how they could be
prevented.

So the measure was successful at predicting future crashes — but when
and how deep, there was no precise way to know. However, long-run mean

reversion suggests that the longer the bull run is and the more overpriced the measure is, the longer and deeper the decline will probably be. Then one can use the measure as part of an econometric system to estimate future scenarios.

Each time the spread exceeded the 4.23 cutoff (which was higher than 95% confidence), there was a crash. The measure was way in the danger zone in late 1989 and the decline (the 21st crash) began on the first trading day of 1990 with the Nikkei stock average (NSA) peaking at 38,916. See Fig. 2.1. It is too bad Yamaichi's top management did not listen to Iishi when Ziemba sent him up to explain our results in Japanese; there was much greater danger in the market then they thought in 1989. By 1995, Yamaichi Securities was bankrupt and ceased to exist in 1999.

The model also indicated that the valuation was still high as of May 29, 1990 at 4.88. Not much later, the 22nd crash began. Interestingly, at the bottom of the 22nd crash on October 1, 1990, the NSA was at 20,222, which was almost exactly the mean. Meanwhile, the same calculation on May 29, 1990, for the S&P500 is shown in Fig. 2.2. Indeed, it was cheap, that is, below the mean, since the September 1987 peak of 4.42. The May 29, 1990 value of 1.11 was, however, slightly above the mean level and the highest since the late fall of 1987.

Japan has had weak stock and land markets for over 20 years since the beginning of 1990. There are many factors for this that are political as well as economic. But the rising interest rates for eight full months until August 1990 is one of them. This extreme tightening of an overlevered economy was too much. Cheap and easily available money, which caused the big run-up in asset prices in the 1980s, turned into expensive and unavailable money in the 1990s. This has parallels to the 2007–2009 US situation where easy available money, not necessarily cheap, turned into unavailable cheap money.

Despite the terrible earthquake and tsunami in Japan in March 2011, many analysts considered the stock market finally a buy because of very low valuations. They were proved right in 2013 with a large rally caused more by a lower yen than high earnings or low interest rates. With very low interest rates that are close to zero, the BSEYD model was not in the danger zone. So the markets attractiveness is from its PE ratio relative to other assets and markets. There are various ways that one can compute the upper and lower limits, but experience has shown that with the various approaches, all of which use out of sample prior data, one usually has the same conclusion. In Figure 2.2, the limits are simply the trailing mean, plus

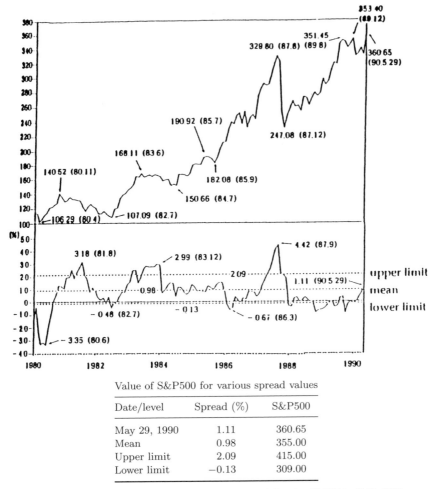

Value of S&P500 for various spread values

Date/level	Spread (%)	S&P500
May 29, 1990	1.11	360.65
Mean	0.98	355.00
Upper limit	2.09	415.00
Lower limit	−0.13	309.00

Fig. 2.2.   Bond and stock yield differential model for the S&P500, 1980–1990.
Source: Ziemba and Schwartz (1991).

or minus a standard deviation measure, so the one-sided limit has 95% of
the probability.[2]

_____

[2]Using a different index rather than the S&P500 has the same conclusion but slightly
different results. Berge *et al.* (2008) used the MSCI index. The danger zone was entered
in May 1987 and the correction occurred in October four months later. During June,
July and August investors kept rebalancing their portfolios from the bond to the equity
market (MSCI TRI + 13.87% over the quarter), then the equity market fell 31.80% in
the following quarter (September to November 1987) with the main decline in October.

Koivu, Pennanen and Ziemba (2005) study the Fed model using a dynamic vector equilibrium correction model with data from 1980 to 2003 in the US, UK and Germany and show that the Fed model had predictive power in forecasting equity prices, earnings and bond yields. The model has been successful in predicting market turns, but in spite of its empirical success and simplicity, the model has been criticized. First, it does not consider the role played by time-varying risk premiums in the portfolio selection process while it does consider a risk-free government interest rate as the discount factor of future earnings. The inflation illusion (the possible impact of inflation expectations on the stock market) as suggested by Modigliani and Cohn (1979) is not taken into consideration. Secondly, the model assumes the comparability of E/P ratios, a real quantity, with a nominal, bond-induced, interest rate (Campbell and Vuolteenaho, 2004; Asness, 2000, 2003; and Ritter and Warr, 2002 discuss these issues).

Consigli *et al.* (2009) propose a stochastic model of equity returns based on an extension of the model inclusive of a risk premium in which market corrections are endogenously generated by the bond–stock yield difference. The model accommodates both cases of prolonged yield deviations leading to a long series of small declines in the equity market and the case, peculiar of recent speculative bubbles, of a series of corrections over limited time periods. The inclusion of the yield differential as a key driver of the market correction process is tested and the model is validated with market data.

Furthermore, Lleo and Ziemba (2017) found that the BSEYD predicts crashes effectively despite ignoring inflation and comparing a real quantity, the PE ratio, with a nominal quantity, the bond yield. These findings appear to contradict the importance generally given to the effect of inflation. One possible explanation for this puzzle could lie in the "money illusion," a bias discussed in Behavioral Finance and first described by Irving Fisher (see Thaler, 1997). The "money illusion" bias suggests that portfolio managers either ignore or underweigh the impact of inflation on the 10-year Treasury yield and concentrate either on 2-year predictions or on the immediate decision to shift from stocks to bonds. Another possible explanation is that the magnitude of the impact of an equity market correction on an investor's wealth and utility often dwarfs the impact that inflation would have over 2 years. Portfolio managers might not ignore inflation, but they might regard it as a secondary factor. In any case, further research is required on this question.

Many of the critics focus on: (1) short-term predicability that we know is weak as does Giot and Petitjean (2008), (2) simply do not focus on the long-run value of the measure, or (3) dismiss it outright because of the real versus nominal versus real minor flaw as does Montier (2011). Consigli *et al.* (2009) use the model to estimate the current fair value of the S&P500. Of course, market and fair value can diverge for long periods. However, our concern is whether or not the model actually predicts stock market crashes, stock market rallies and good times to be in and out of stock markets. Berge *et al.* (2008) discuss the latter issue and found for five countries (US, Germany, Canada, UK and Japan) that the strategy to stay in the market when it is not in the danger zone and move to cash otherwise provides about double the final wealth with less variance and a higher Sharpe ratio than a buy and hold strategy. There is some limited predictability of stock market increases, but the evidence supports the good use of the model to predict crashes.

2.3.   The 2000–2003 crash in the S&P500

The S&P500 was 470.42 at the end of January 1995. It was about 750 in late 1996 at the time of Alan Greenspan's famous speech on irrational exuberance in the US stock market. It peaked at 1527.46 on March 24, 2000, fell to 1356.56 on April 4th, and then came close to this peak reaching 1520 on September 1st, the Friday before Labor Day. The bond–stock crash model was in the danger zone virtually all of 1999 and it got deeper in the danger zone as the year progressed as the S&P500 rose from 1229.23 at the end of December 1998 to 1460.25 at the end of December 1999. The P/E ratio was flat, increasing only from 32.34 to 33.29 while long bond yields rose from 5.47 to 6.69. The S&P500 fell to 1085 on September 7th prior to September 11, 2001.

Table 2.2 details this from January 1995 to December 1999. The spread reached three which was well in the 95% confidence danger band in April and rose to 3.69 in December 1999. The stage was set for a crash which did occur. Long-term mean reversion suggests that the 1996–2000 S&P500 values were too high relative to 1991–1995 and a linear interpolation of the latter period gives a value close to that in 2002.

The model for Japan was hard to interpret because there were high P/E ratios, but interest rates were close to zero, so one had a close to 0–0 situation, so the model did not apply to Japan in 1999. The model was not in the danger zone with return differences close to zero. We witnessed a dramatic fall in the S&P500 from its peak of 1527 in March 2000 to its September 17, 2000 low of 1085. Further declines occurred in 2001 and 2002. The lowest close to May 2003 was 768.63 on October 10, 2002. There

Table 2.2. Bond and stock yield differential model for the S&P500, 1995–1999.

Year	Month	S&P500 Index	a PER	b 30-yr gov't bond	c = 1/a return on stocks	b − c crash signal
1995	Jan	470.42	17.10	8.02	5.85	2.17
	Feb	487.39	17.75	7.81	5.63	2.18
	Mar	500.71	16.42	7.68	6.09	1.59
	Apr	514.71	16.73	7.48	5.98	1.50
	May	533.40	16.39	7.29	6.10	1.19
	Jun	544.75	16.68	6.66	6.00	0.66
	Jul	562.06	17.23	6.90	5.80	1.10
	Aug	561.88	16.20	7.00	6.17	0.83
	Sep	584.41	16.88	6.74	5.92	0.82
	Oct	581.50	16.92	6.55	5.91	0.64
	Nov	605.37	17.29	6.36	5.78	0.58
	Dec	615.93	17.47	6.25	5.72	0.53
1996	Jan	636.02	18.09	6.18	5.53	0.65
	Feb	640.43	18.86	6.46	5.30	1.16
	Mar	645.50	19.09	6.82	5.24	1.58
	Apr	654.17	19.15	7.07	5.22	1.85
	May	669.12	19.62	7.21	5.10	2.11
	Jun	670.63	19.52	7.30	5.12	2.18
	Jul	639.96	18.80	7.23	5.32	1.91
	Aug	651.99	19.08	7.17	5.24	1.93
	Sep	687.31	19.65	7.26	5.09	2.17
	Oct	705.27	20.08	6.95	4.98	1.97
	Nov	757.02	20.92	6.79	4.78	2.01
	Dec	740.74	20.86	6.73	4.79	1.94
1997	Jan	786.16	21.46	6.95	4.66	2.29
	Feb	790.82	20.51	6.85	4.88	1.97
	Mar	757.12	20.45	7.11	4.89	2.22
	Apr	801.34	20.69	7.23	4.83	2.40
	May	848.28	21.25	7.08	4.71	2.37
	Jun	885.14	22.09	6.93	4.53	2.40
	Jul	954.29	23.67	6.78	4.22	2.56
	Aug	899.47	22.53	6.71	4.44	2.27
	Sep	947.28	23.29	6.70	4.29	2.41
	Oct	914.62	22.67	6.46	4.41	2.05
	Nov	955.40	23.45	6.27	4.26	2.01
	Dec	970.43	23.88	6.15	4.19	1.96
1998	Jan	980.28	24.05	6.01	4.16	1.85
	Feb	1049.34	25.09	6.00	3.99	2.01
	Mar	1101.75	27.71	6.11	3.61	2.50
	Apr	1111.75	27.56	6.03	3.63	2.40
	May	1090.82	27.62	6.10	3.62	2.48
	Jun	1133.84	28.65	5.89	3.49	2.40

(*Continued*)

Table 2.2.   (*Continued*)

Year	Month	S&P500 Index	a PER	b 30-yr gov't bond	c = 1/a return on stocks	b − c crash signal
	Jul	1120.67	28.46	5.83	3.51	2.32
	Aug	97.28	27.42	5.74	3.65	2.09
	Sep	1017.01	26.10	5.47	3.83	1.64
	Oct	1098.67	27.41	5.42	3.65	1.77
	Nov	1163.63	31.15	5.54	3.21	2.33
	Dec	1229.23	32.34	5.47	3.09	2.38
1999	Jan	1279.64	32.64	5.49	3.06	2.43
	Feb	1238.33	32.91	5.66	3.04	2.62
	Mar	1286.37	34.11	5.87	2.93	2.94
	Apr	1335.18	35.82	5.82	2.79	3.03
	May	1301.84	34.60	6.08	2.89	3.19
	Jun	1372.71	35.77	6.36	2.80	3.56
	Jul	1328.72	35.58	6.34	2.81	3.53
	Aug	1320.41	36.00	6.35	2.78	3.57
	Sep	1282.70	30.92	6.50	3.23	3.27
	Oct	1362.92	31.61	6.66	3.16	3.50
	Nov	1388.91	32.24	6.48	3.10	3.38
	Dec	1469.25	33.29	6.69	3.00	3.69

Source: Berge and Ziemba (2001).

was a lower close of 666 in March 2009, just before the big rally into 2016. This decline was similar to previous crashes.

2.4. Using the BSEYD model for long-run investing

Berge and Ziemba (2003) and Berge *et al.* (2008) study this measure from 1970 and 1975 to 2000 in five major markets, namely the US, Germany, Canada, the UK, and Japan.

They compare four strategies for each of the time periods based on the length of the sample from previous data (either 5 or 10 years) to determine the distribution type (historical or assumed normally distributed), the fractile for entry (70, 75, 80 or 85%) and the fractile for exit (90 or 95%), the confidence limits.

The 5-year data intervals were used for the 1980–2005 calculations and 10 years for the 1975–2005 calculations. The results vary slightly by strategy, but the basic conclusions are the same. These results are summarized in Table 2.3 for strategies 1 and 5 that have 5 and 10 years prior historical

Table 2.3. Evaluation of the performance of the strategies 1 and 5 versus the market index in the US, Germany, Canada, UK and Japan from 1975 and 1980 to 2005.

Strategy	Number of Months in the Index	Overall Performance of the Strategies and the Stock Market				
		Mean Log Return	Standard Deviation	Sharpe Ratio	Mean Excess Return	Terminal Value
US 1	319 (85.75%)	0.01194	0.03933	0.17814	0.00162	8,480.41
US Index (1975–2005)	372 (100%)	0.01032	0.04347	0.12401		4,649.75
US 5	273 (87.5%)	0.01254	0.03887	0.19773	0.00224	5,009.00
US Index (1980–2005)	312 (100%)	0.0103	0.04389	0.12405		2,490.17
G 1	302 (81.18%)	0.00881	0.0515	0.09157	0.00068	2,652.80
German Index (1975–2005)	372 (100%)	0.00813	0.05864	0.06886		2,061.27
G 5	279 (89.42%)	0.00963	0.05836	0.09405	0.00123	2,014.62
German Index (1980–2005)	312 (100%)	0.0084	0.06201	0.0687		1,373.26
C 1	295 (79.3%)	0.00954	0.04243	0.08053	−0.0002	3,479.37
Canada Index (1975–2005)	372 (100%)	0.00974	0.04925	0.07337		3,743.49
C 5	273 (87.5%)	0.00937	0.04336	0.07839	0.00094	1,859.80
Canada Index (1980–2005)	312 (100%)	0.00843	0.04941	0.04977		1,387.23
UK 1	329 (88.44%)	0.01426	0.0502	0.14825	0.00102	20,163.11
UK Index (1975–2005)	372 (100%)	0.01324	0.05598	0.1147		13,787.40
UK 5	297 (95.19%)	0.01204	0.0442	0.12277	0.00101	4,275.28
UK Index (1980–2005)	312 (100%)	0.01103	0.04814	0.09179		3,121.47
J 1	222 (89.52%)	0.00612	0.05049	0.08427	0.00305	455.72
Japan Index (5/85–12/05)	248 (100%)	0.00307	0.05778	0.02085		213.88
J 5	172 (91.49%)	0.0012	0.0505	−0.00157	0.00168	125.35
Japan Index (5/90–12/05)	188 (100%)	−0.00048	0.05745	−0.03062		91.39

data, and 80% and 85% entry percentiles and 90% and 95% exit percentiles. All the results are in Berge *et al.* (2008) which also lists all the declines of 10%+ during this 20-year period.

The initial wealth starts at $100 (US), €100 (Germany), C$100 (Canada), £100 (UK), and ¥100 (Japan) and the terminal values are the gross performance using the strategy signals. The mean excess return is the average monthly excess return of the strategy over the stock market. In each country, the final wealth of the strategies exceeds (except for Canada) buy and hold for the stock market with some months in cash and a higher Sharpe ratio.

2.5. BSEYD and stock valuation

The Gordon (1959) growth model states that the price of a stock should be equal to the present value of its future dividends growing at a constant rate g, discounted at the cost of equity k:

$$P_t = \frac{D_{t+1}}{k - g}, \tag{2.1}$$

where P_t is the price at the end of period t, D_{t+1} is the dividend paid at time $t+1$. We can break down the dividend at time $t+1$ into the products of a measure of core (acyclical) earnings at time t, the payout ratio d and the growth rate g:

$$P_t = \frac{E_t d(1 + g)}{k - g}. \tag{2.2}$$

With some algebra, we obtain

$$k = g + \frac{(1 + g)d}{\gamma_t},$$

where we define $\gamma(t) = \frac{P_t}{E_t}$. These are nominal rates: we could for example deflate by the PPI to produce real rates. From Equation (2.2), we obtain the following definition for the earnings yield ρ_t:

$$\rho_t = \frac{E_t}{P_t} = \frac{k - g}{d(1 + g)}.$$

The cost of equity k, is the required return on the equity market, that is,

$$k_t = r_t + f_t,$$

where r_t is the yield on a government bond and f is the equity risk premium. Hence,

$$\text{BSEYD} = r_t - \rho_t$$

$$= \frac{1}{d(1+g)}(r_t[d(1+g) - 1] - f_t + g).$$

Further details of the connection between the BSEYD model and stock valuation is discussed in Section 1.2 of Chapter 4.

2.6.   Conclusion

The BSEYD has a remarkable track record of predicting major stock market crashes around the world over the past 50 years. The BSEYD draws its success form from two sources: the information contained by stock prices and earnings in relation to prevailing government bonds yields, and the signal construction which includes a time-varying probabilistic threshold.

Chapter 3

Prediction of the 2007–2009 Stock Market Crashes in the US, China and Iceland

We start this chapter with a deeper look at how crash prediction models such as the bond–stock earnings yield differential (BSEYD) work. Next, we explore the BSEYD's ability to predict crashes through a case study of the market meltdowns in China, Iceland, and the US in the 2007–2009 period. Historically, when the BSEYD measure is too high, meaning that long bond interest rates are too high relative to the trailing earnings over price ratio, there usually is a crash of 10% or more within four to twelve months. The BSEYD model did in fact predict all the three crashes. Iceland had a drop of fully 95%, China fell by two-thirds and the US by 57%. The material in this chapter is based on Lleo and Ziemba (2012).

3.1. How crash prediction models work

Equity market crash prediction models, such as the bond–stock earnings yield differential (BSEYD) model, work by generating a signal to indicate a downturn in the equity market at a given horizon H. This signal occurs whenever the value of a given measure crosses a threshold.

Given a crash prediction measure $M(t)$, a crash signal $S(t)$ occurs whenever

$$S(t) = M(t) - K(t) > 0, \qquad (3.1)$$

where $K(t)$ is a time-varying threshold for the signal. Three key inputs define the signal:

(1) the choice of a measure $M(t)$;
(2) the definition of threshold $K(t)$; and

(3) the specification of a time interval H between the occurrence of the signal and that of the crash.

3.1.1.   The measure $M(t)$

The measure is the pivotal component of crash prediction models. Its role is to assess relative market valuation in real-time.

At a conceptual level, the measure is a variable or a function of several variables. For the BSEYD, the measure is

$$\text{BSEYD}(t) = r(t) - \rho(t) = r(t) - \frac{E(t)}{P(t)}. \qquad (3.2)$$

where $r(t)$ is the current bond yield and $\rho(t)$ is the reciprocal of the P/E ratio.

Taking the logarithm, we can also define a logBSEYD measure as

$$\text{logBSEYD}(t) = \ln \frac{r(t)}{\rho(t)} = \ln r(t) - \ln \frac{E(t)}{P(t)}. \qquad (3.3)$$

Koivu *et al.* (2005) used the logBSEYD to predict returns. We will test its ability to predict equity market crashes in Chapter 4.

To successfully implement these measures, we need to specify precisely what each variable is. Do we compute the earnings based on their most current value or based on an historical average over a predetermined period? Do we use nominal (current dollar) or real (inflation-adjusted) earning? What measure of interest rates will we use? 30-year Treasury Bonds, 10-year Treasury notes, or seasoned corporate Bonds? With what credit rating? We will get back to this discussion in the next chapter. For now, we define the *BSEYD(t)* using current earnings and the 10-year Treasury yield.

3.1.2.   The threshold $K(t)$

We define the threshold as a confidence level. We start with a standard 95% one-tail confidence interval based on a Normal distribution. This definition is consistent with earlier works including Ziemba and Schwartz (1991) and Lleo and Ziemba (2012). A standard confidence level does not provide a robust threshold because the tails of the distribution of the measures may not be approximately Gaussian.

To address this problem, we also use Cantelli's inequality, a one-tailed version of Chebyshev's inequality, to derive a 'worst case' confidence level for heavily skewed or leptokurtic distributions (see Grimmett and Stirzaker, 2001, Problem 7.11.9). Cantelli's inequality relates the probability that the distance between a random variable X and its mean μ exceeds a number $k > 0$ of standard deviations σ to provide a robust confidence interval:

$$P\left[X - \mu \geq k\sigma\right] \leq \frac{1}{1 + k^2}.$$

Setting $\alpha = \frac{1}{1+k^2}$ yields

$$P\left[X - \mu \geq \sigma\sqrt{\frac{1}{\alpha} - 1}\right] \leq \alpha.$$

The parameter α provides an upper bound for a one-tailed confidence level on any distribution. Cantelli's inequality requires the true mean and standard deviation of the distribution. So the result only works approximately for estimated means and standard deviations.

We compute the sample mean and standard deviation of the distribution of the measures as a moving average and a rolling horizon standard deviation, respectively. The h-day moving average at time t, denoted by μ_t^h, and the corresponding rolling horizon standard deviation σ_t^h are

$$\mu_t^h = \frac{1}{h} \sum_{i=0}^{h-1} x_{t-i},$$

$$\sigma_t^h = \sqrt{\frac{1}{h-1} \sum_{i=0}^{h-1} (x_{t-i} - \mu_t^h)^2}.$$

Using rolling horizon means and standard deviations has the advantage of providing data consistency. In particular, rolling horizon mean and standard deviation are not overly sensitive to the starting date of the calculation. Most importantly, this construction addresses the in-sample versus out-sample problem by only using past data and predetermined parameters. To summarize, we compute the signal using: (1) a standard one-tail 95% standard confidence interval based on a normal distribution, and (2) an application of Cantelli's inequality. The horizon for the rolling statistics is $h = 252$. This horizon is short and can be used on most financial markets without requiring a long data history.

We select $\alpha = 95\%$ for the standard confidence interval. This choice is consistent with the crash prediction literature and can be traced to the first published work on the BSEYD (Ziemba and Schwartz, 1991). Looking at the statistical inference literature, $\alpha = 95\%$ is a natural choice for two-tailed tests: R.A. Fisher suggested the use of a two-tailed 5% significance level Fisher (see for example pp. 45, 98, 104, 117 in 1933). Pearson and Neyman insisted on the significance level to be selected *a priori*, before Neyman introduced the idea of a confidence interval (Neyman and Pearson, 1933; Neyman, 1934, 1937) first thought of by Pearson. Although Fisher later clarified that the level of significance needs to be selected in relation to the statistical problem under consideration (Fisher, 1955), the 5% significance/95% confidence has remained in widespread use ever since.

Another way to look at the choice of $\alpha = 95\%$ is in the context of the expert opinion literature (we refer the reader to Meyer and Booker, 2001; O'Hagan, 2006, for a up-to-date treatment). Here, we change our frame of reference from a classical frequentist approach, which assumes that that we are sampling repeatedly IID random variables, to subjective probabilities, and more specifically to the personal probability framework introduced by Ramsey, de Finetti and Savage (we refer the reader to the classic book by Savage, 1971). In this framework, the crash prediction model is subjective in nature and akin to an expert opinion. The confidence level α is properly defined as the subjective level of confidence in our measure's ability to predict "normal" market operations. Any departure above this level would indicate that we are outside of the confidence interval around our measure: a market disruption such as an equity market crash, is likely to happen. In the expert opinion literature, it is customary to ask for a two-tailed 90% confidence bound, translating into a one-tailed 95% confidence interval. This observation provides another motivation for our selection of α. Still, this discussion emphasizes the need to test how crash prediction models perform for various choices of α in order to ascertain whether they are robust to a misspecification or a change in confidence level.

We now turn our attention to Cantelli's inequality. There is no clear rule on how to select β, so we chose $\beta = 25\%$ to produce a slightly higher threshold than the standard confidence interval. In a normal distribution, we expect 5% of the observations to lie in the right tail, whereas Cantelli's inequality implies that the percentage of outliers in a distribution may be as high as 25%.

3.1.3. *The horizon H*

The last parameter we need to specify is the horizon between the signal and the crash identification date. The crash identification time is the date by which the S&P500 has declined by at least 10% in the last year (252 trading days). We define the local market peak as the highest level reached by the market index within 252 trading days before the crash.

Since we define an equity market crash as a 10% decline within a one-year period, we choose a two-year horizon ($H = 504$ trading days) between the signal and the crash identification date. This choice means that a signal could occur at any time between one trading day before the crash identification date (up to 251 days after the associated local market high), and 503 trading days before the crash identification date (up to 502 days before the associated local market high). Our choice of a 2-year horizon from signal to crash identification is closely linked to the definition of a crash. Reducing the horizon H may require us to reduce the timescale of our definition of a crash.

3.2. The Iceland 2008 crash

In July 2006, Ziemba was in Iceland speaking at the international INFORMS *Operations Research* conference and became interested in the economic situation there. Consider the long bond (10-year) versus earnings yield differentials for the US, the UK, Japan, France and Germany as of July 12, 2006 as shown in Table 3.1. Ziemba and Ziemba (2007) and Lleo and Ziemba (2012) discuss the Iceland bubble and subsequent crash.

Iceland is a small country with only about 300,000 people. From 2002 to 2007, the economy and asset prices rose dramatically, with much leveraging of investments, especially by the banks. This led to high interest rates of about 10% long-term and 16% short-term. Eventually, it all collapsed in the wake of the 2007–2009 worldwide financial crisis. And the decline was a massive crash of −95% in the equity index and a currency collapse. At the time, the 15 stocks in the index had weights of 26.5% all the way down to 1%, see Figure 3.1(a). The main point is that the three largest banks Kaupthing (26.5%), Lansbanki (13.0%) and Glitnir (12.3%) represented

Table 3.1.   Long bond (10 yr) versus earning yield differentials for major countries, July 12, 2006.

Index	S&P500 1259	FTSE200 5861	Nikkei225 15249	CAC40 4942	DAX30 5638
(A) P/E ratio	16.86	16.61	36.26	13.82	13.33
(B) Stock return (1/A)	5.93%	6.02%	2.76%	7.24%	7.50%
(C) Bond return (10 yr)	5.10%	4.67%	1.94%	4.10%	4.09%
(D) Crash signal (C−B)	−0.83	−1.35	−0.82	−3.14	−3.41

Source: Ziemba and Ziemba (2007).

Stock Market Crashes

Weights			Real rates of return		
Company	Fund	Index		Fund	Index
1 Kaupthing Banki hf.	27.2%	26.5%	2005	56.5%	54.5%
2 Landsbanki Islands hf.	13.1%	13.0%	2004	49.1%	47.2%
3 Glitnir Banki hf.	12.5%	12.3%	2003	42.7%	40.7%
4 Straumur Buróarás Fjárfes	8.9%	8.9%	2002	20.7%	19.2%
5 Actavis Banki hf.	10.1%	9.9%	2001	−16.4%	−16.6%
6 FL Banki hf.	6.3%	6.2%	2000	−16.7%	−17.2%
7 Bakkavör Group hf.	4.0%	4.1%	1999	36.7%	36.4%
8 Avion Group hf.	3.7%	3.7%	1998	6.3%	3.4%
9 Mosaic Fashions hf.	2.7%	2.6%	1997	9.0%	10.2%
10 Ossur hf.	2.2%	2.2%	1996	44.1%	57.3%
11 Tryggingamiðtöðinhf.	2.1%	2.0%	1995	33.4%	31.1%
12 Dagsbrún hf.	1.5%	1.5%			
13 Alfresca hf.	1.2%	1.2%			
14 FjárfestingafélagiðAtorka	1.0%	1.0%			
15 Grandi hf.	1.0%	1.0%			

(a)

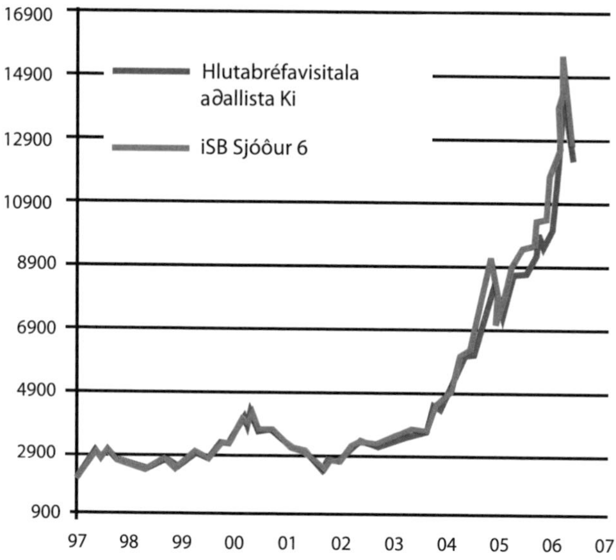

(b)

Fig. 3.1. The 15 stocks in the Iceland equity index and their growth in real terms from 1997–2006. (a) Stock market index. (b) The Iceland equity index and its growth in real terms from 1997 to 2006.

Source: Glitnir (2006).

more than half the market capitalization. In addition, Actavis Banki had 9.9%, and FL Banki a further 6.7%. So the banks are about two thirds of the index value. And index funds that track the market slightly overweight these banks to yield higher returns.

Figure 3.1(b) shows the dramatic rise of the stock market particularly since 2004. It also shows how quickly drops occur. However, the notable sharp sell-offs, have to a large extent been blips and there is a question whether these investments can continue to produce similar returns, and if not, whether that will prompt investors to seek other markets.

Table 3.2 provides two bond–stock measure calculations in 2006. The index measure was out of the danger zone. However, the non-financial sector was in the danger zones but its weight was not enough to pull down the whole market according to the script of the bond–stock crash measure. The low P/E plus the lower long-term interest rates (about 9%) but substantially below the 14.25% projected to 16% short rates made the market look risky. So did the parabolic increase of the index in real terms from 1997 to 2006 shown in Figure 3.1(b). But there was no signal yet for a crash.

Finally, the question of whether or not the BSEYD predicted the crash is studied in Figures 3.2(a), 3.2(b) and 3.2(c) which use 95% one-sided confidence intervals using moving averages. These graphs show that the crash was predicted in 2007. For Kaupthing, the danger zone was penetrated on September 28, 2007, two months after the July 18 peak and less than a month before the November 11 crash. Finally, for Glitnir, the signal was much earlier on October 10, 2006, some 13 months before the crash. Finally, for Lansbanki, the danger signal was on February 13, 2007. We focus on the largest banks because they led the market into the collapse. The smallest stocks were in the danger zone in 2006 as discussed in Ziemba and Ziemba (2007), but not the large banks then.

Table 3.2.   Bond–stock measure calculations in Iceland in 2006.

Index	16 non-fin	15 in index
A) P/E ratio		11.1
B) Stock Return (1/A)	6.13%	9.01%
C) Bond Return (5 yr)	11.00%	9.4%
D) Crash Signal (C−B)	4.87%	0.39%

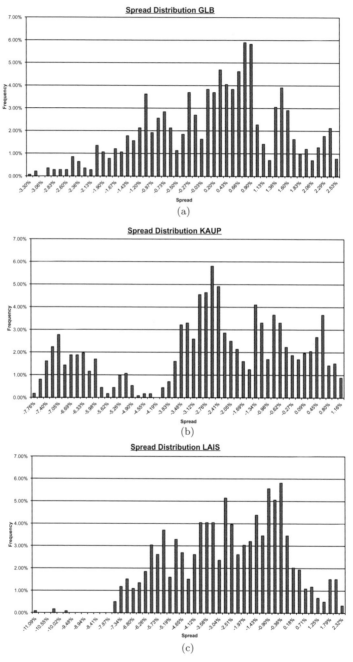

Fig. 3.2.   BSEYD Spread Distributions, Iceland. (a) Glitnir, MA. (b) Kaupthing, MA.
(c) Lansbanki, MA.

In summary, we make some comments on the crash signals for the three largest Icelandic banks.

Glitnir:

- Signal from September 15, 2003 until December 23, 2003: on October 12, 2004, the share price reached 11.90. By November 2, 2004, the share had gone down to 10, a 15.97% drop.
- Faint signal from November 17, 2004 until November 19, 2004 and December 6, 2004: on February 18, 2005, the share price fell to 11.60. By March 3, 2005, the share had gone down to 11.60, a 7.20% drop.
- Signal from November 22, 2005 until February 24, 2006 (with some interruptions): on October 12, 2004, the share price reached 22.60. By April 19, 2006, the share had gone down to 16.50, a 26.99% drop.
- Signal from October 17, 2006 (with P/E ratio of 22.30) until December 27, 2006: announces the market crash.
- Signal from December 28, 2007 until January 8, 2008.
- Signal from March 26, 2008 until April 10, 2008.

The crash signal analysis is basically according to the script except for the faint signal between November 17, 2004 until November 19, 2004 and December 6, 2004 for which we do not have a better explanation (See Figures 3.3(a), 3.3(b), 3.4(a) and 3.4(b).

Kaupthing:

- Signal from February 7, 2006 until February 24, 2006: on October 26, 2006, the share price reached 868. By November 28, 2006, the share had fallen to 785, a 9.56% drop.
- The market reaches its peak on July 18, 2007 and a crash occurred on November 11, 2007.
- Signal from September 28, 2007 until November 5, 2007.
- Signal from March 26, 2008 until April 4, 2008 (see Figures 3.3(c), 3.3(d), 3.4(c) and 3.4(d)).

Lansbanki:

- Signal from January 15, 2004 until March 4, 2004: on October 11, 2004, the share price reached 15.28. By November 2, 2004, the share has fallen to 10.85, a 28.98% drop.

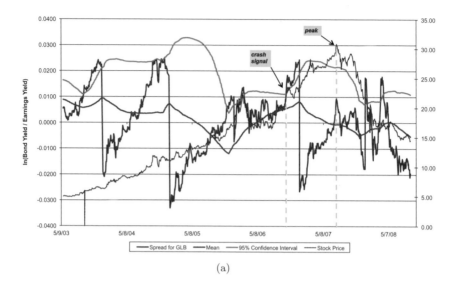

(a)

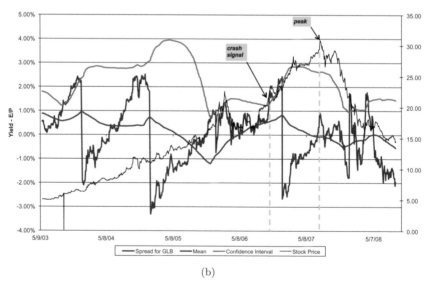

(b)

Fig. 3.3.   BSEYD Crash Indicators, Iceland. (a) BSEYD Chart (Indicator at 95% confidence): Glitnir. First crash signal occurs around October 17, 2006. The market reaches
its peak on July 20, 2007. (b) BSEYD Chart (Indicator using Cantelli's Inequality, 20%):
Glitnir. First crash signal occurs on October 17, 2006. The market reaches its peak on
July 20, 2007. (c) BSEYD Chart (Indicator at 95% confidence): Kaupthing. First signal occurs around October 2, 2007. The market reaches its peak on July 18, 2007 and
a crash occurred on November 11, 2007. (d) BSEYD Chart (Indicator using Cantelli's

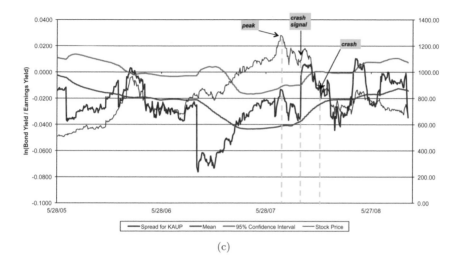

(c)

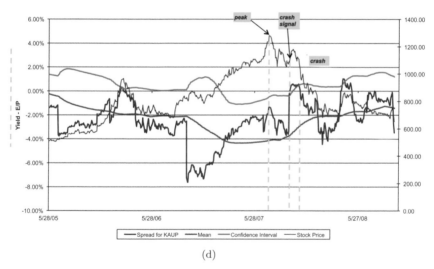

(d)

Fig. 3.3. (*Continued*). Inequality, 20%): Kaupthing. First crash signal occurs on October 2, 2007. The market reaches its peak on July 18, 2007 and a crash occurred on November 11, 2007. (e) BSEYD Chart (Indicator at 95% confidence): Lansbanki. First crash signal occurs around February 13, 2007. The market reaches its peak on October 17, 2007. (f) BSEYD Chart (Indicator using Cantelli's Inequality, 20%): Lansbanki. Faint crash signal throughout the first half of 2007. The market reaches its peak on October 17, 2007.

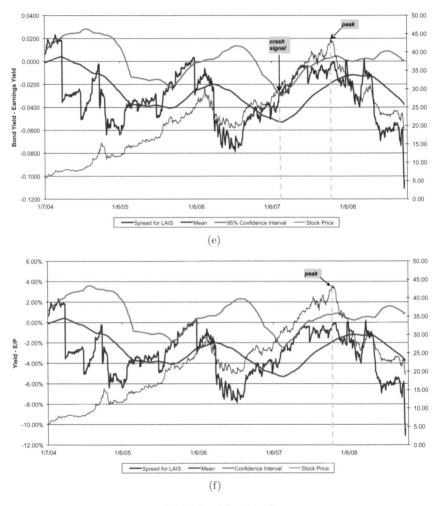

(e)

(f)

Fig. 3.3. (*Continued*)

- Signal from August 30, 2005 until December 29, 2005 (with minor interruptions): on February 16, 2006, the share price reached 30.56. By May 3,
  2006, the share has fallen to 20.05, a 34.39% drop.
- Signal from February 13, 2007 until March 13, 2007 and from March 30,
  2007 until the June 28, 2007: market crash signal.
- The market reaches its peak on October 17, 2007.

The crash model works out well for Lansbanki: the signal identifies the market crashes and two large declines. Although the signal could be clearer for Glitnir and Kaupthing, we do not observe any false positives (see Figures 3.3(c), 3.3 (f), 3.4(e) and 3.4(f)).

3.3.   The US 2007–2009 crash

We investigate whether or not the bond–stock measure did predict the US 2007–2009 crash, specifically the September 2008 to March 2009 period. There are numerous books concerning this period plus many articles and columns, even Ziemba has several in *Wilmott*.

Table 3.1 considers the measure in five major countries on July 12, 2006. None of these major markets were in the danger zone then. Table 3.3 for the S&P500 has the calculations for the years from 2006 to 2011 on trailing P/E ratios that are usually used for these calculations and for 2011 which uses Shiller's average inflation-adjusted earnings from the previous 10-years. Figures 3.7(a) and (b) show the S&P500 P/E ratios (Shiller's calculation method) and the 10-year Treasury bond yield.

Ex post it is clear that this stock market crash had a lot of components such as the first decline in aggregate US housing prices in more than 30 years, a subprime market collapsing because home buyers could not cover their mortgages, lots of suspect AAA rated tranches of securitized products build-out of these mortgages, followed by a credit squeeze with a large amount of counterparty credit risk. As a result, firms were unwilling to lend money to others, including supposedly sound financial institutions, which led to the collapse of many large and previously sound financial institutions, such as Bear Stearns, Freddie Mac, Fannie Mae and, the killer for the market, Lehman Brothers.

There are numerous books concerning this period plus many articles and columns, see, for example, Ziemba's several contributions in *Wilmott*. Starting in June 2007, Ziemba designed strategies and traded for an offshore BVI-based hedge fund group whose hedge funds had investments in Bear Stearns and in June 2007 asked for their money back. The process took three months and gave the fund manager a strong signal of danger. As an astute trader, he hedged and studied carefully the market situation through technical indicators that he has developed. Ziemba remembers his view formed in the summer of 2007 that "this is the big one" ... "eventually

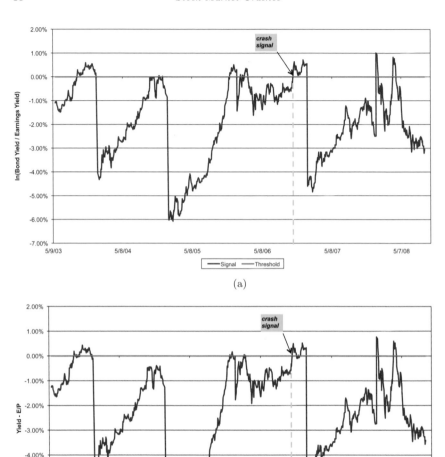

(a)

(b)

Fig. 3.4.   Crash Indicators, Iceland. (a) Crash Signal Indicator (based on 95% confidence): Glitnir. First crash signal occurs around October 17, 2006. The market reaches
its peak on July 20, 2007. (b) Signal Chart (Indicator using Cantelli's Inequality,
20%): Glitnir. First crash signal occurs on October 17, 2006. The market reaches its
peak on July 20, 2007. (c) Signal Chart (95% confidence): Kaupthing. First crash signal occurs around October 2, 2007. The market reaches its peak on July 18, 2007
and a crash occurred on November 11, 2007. (d) Signal Chart (Indicator using Cantelli's

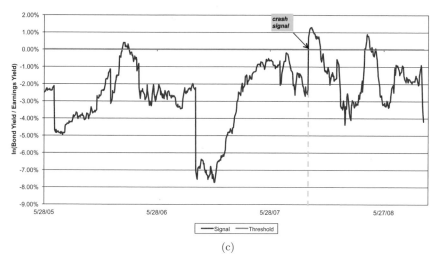

(c)

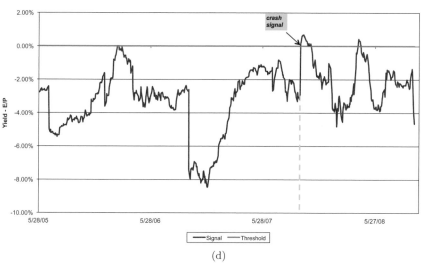

(d)

Fig. 3.4. (*Continued*). Inequality, 20%): Kaupthing. First crash signal occurs on October 2, 2007. The market reaches its peak on July 18, 2007 and a crash occurred on November 11, 2007. (e) Signal Chart (95% confidence): Lansbanki. First crash signal occurs around February 13, 2007. The market reaches its peak on October 17, 2007. (f) Signal Chart (Indicator using Cantelli's Inequality, 20%): Lansbanki. Faint crash signal throughout the first half of 2007. The market reaches its peak on October 17, 2007.

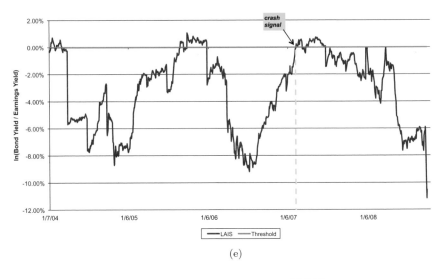

(e)

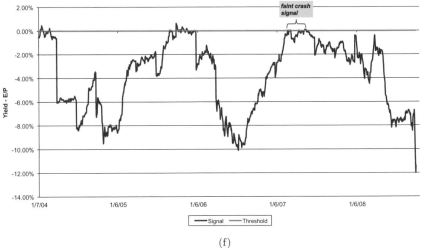

(f)

Fig. 3.4.   (*Continued*)

the market will go to 660 on the S&P500". In the fall of 2007, the S&P500
was about 1500, see Figure 3.5. So this was a rather bold call, but a private
one, and it turned out to be very accurate. Nouriel Roubini was boldly
predicting a serious financial meltdown starting in 2006, when the housing
market was beginning its decline; see Figure 3.6 (a) which gives the Case
Shiller Home Price Index as of July 24, 2008. There was a sharp decline

Table 3.3.   Bond–stock yield model calculations leading up to the 2007–2009 crisis in the S&P500.

Date	Long-Bond (10 years)	Trailing		
		P/E	1/PE, %	B-Y(pe)
Feb 2006	4.49	20.00	5.00	(0.56)
Jun 2007	5.15	17.00	5.98	(0.74)
Jun 2008	4.14	18.00	5.55	(1.41)
May 2009	3.70	33.30	3.00	0.70
May 2010	3.41	20.47	4.89	(1.48)
Feb 2011	3.59	23.83	4.20	(0.61)

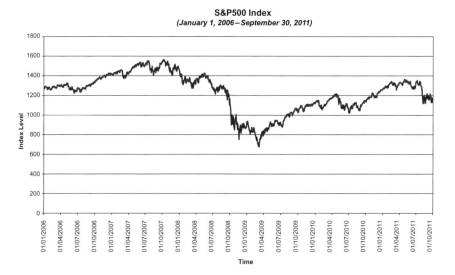

Fig. 3.5.   The S&P500, January 1, 2006 to June 30, 2012.

from 2005 to 2008. Figures 3.6(b) and 3.6(d) show the S&P Case Shiller index level and year-on-year change up until April 2012. Dropping real estate values have several depressive effects, such as homeowners can no longer use house price gains to fund consumption, foreclosures, etc. The March 2009 low closing was 676.53, with an intraday low of 660 on March 6. The subsequent rally has doubled the S&P500 to 1320.64 as of the end of June 2011. There is considerable discussion regarding whether or not this rally is low-interest-rate-related to the Fed's quantitative easing, or is

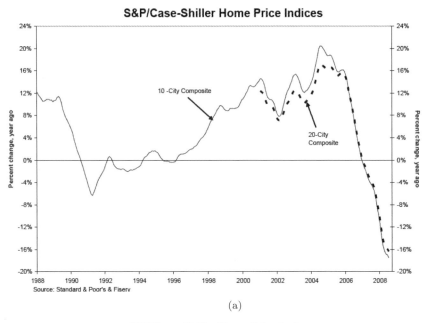

(a)

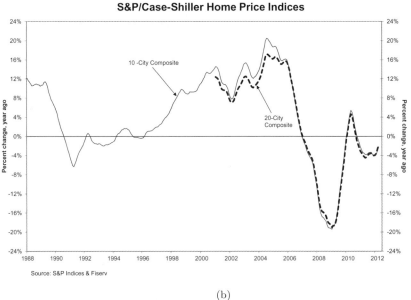

(b)

Fig. 3.6.   S&P/Case Shiller index. (a) Case Shiller Index: year-on-year percentage
(1988–2008). (b) S&P/Case Shiller Index: year-on-year percentage change (1988–2012).

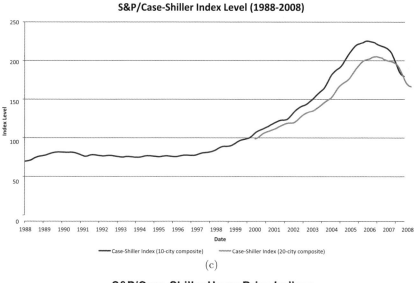

(c)

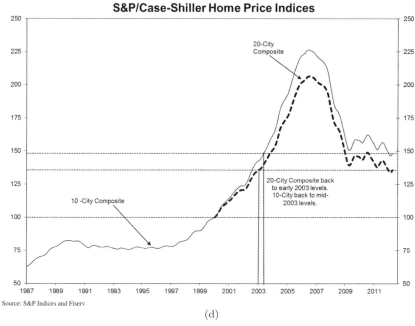

(d)

Fig. 3.6. (*Continued*). (c) S&P/Case Shiller Index level (1988–2008). (d) S&P/Case Shiller Index level (1987–2012).

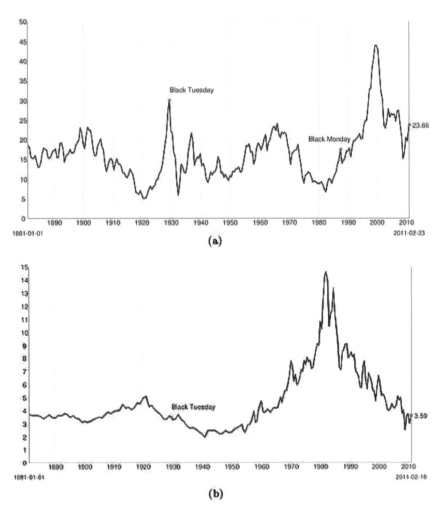

Fig. 3.7.   S&P500 and 10-year Treasury bond yields, January 1, 1881 to February 23, 2011. (a) S&P500 P/E ratios. (b) Treasury bond yield.

Source: Robert Shiller data.

the only game in town since real estate, bonds and cash look unattractive. This is a case when the BSEYD signaled the rise in stock prices. A volatile period followed the rally, with a drop in the level of the S&P500 in August and September 2009 followed by a stabilization in October.

Did the BSEYD model predict the US crash? Figures 3.8 and 3.9 show that it did on June 14, 2007. The BSEYD measure is not normally distributed: its distribution has fat tails, especially on the downside, as shown

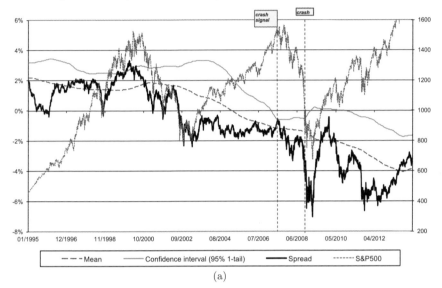

(a)

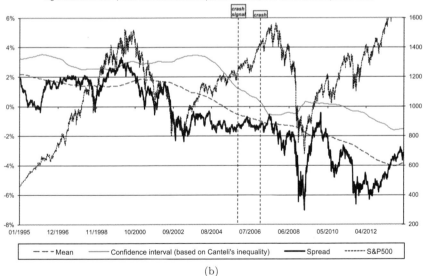

(b)

Fig. 3.8. Crash Indicators, US. (a) Crash Indicator (95% confidence: S&P500, MA. Signal occurs on June 14, 2007. The market reaches its peak on October 9, 2007. (b) Crash Indicator (Cantelli's Inequality): S&P500, MACI. Signal occurs on June 14, 2007. The market reaches its peak on October 9, 2007 and crashes in September 2008.

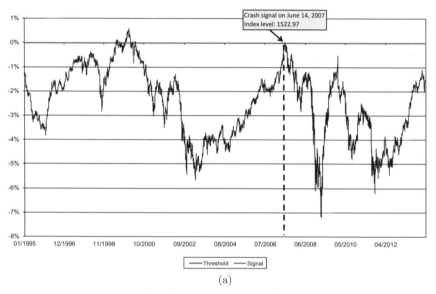

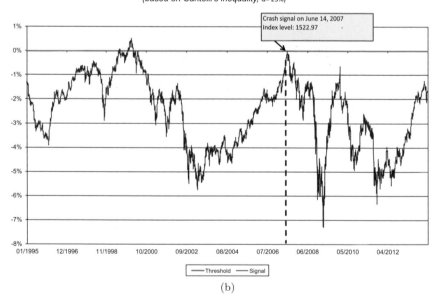

Fig. 3.9.   Signal occurs on June 14, 2007. (a) Based on a standard 1-tail 95% confidence level, moving average normal distribution assumption (b) Based on a standard 1-tail 95% confidence level, moving average Cantelli's inequality.

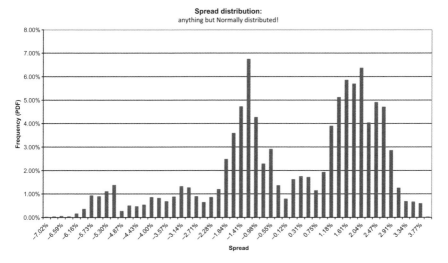

Fig. 3.10.   Spread distribution of the BSEYD measure on the S&P500.

Table 3.4.   Earnings revisions for 2008 and 2009, analysts estimates of earnings in dollars.

Date	Earnings	Date	Earnings
		...and estimates for 2009	
March 2007	92.00	March 20, 2008	81.52
December 2007	84.00	April 9, 2008	72.60
February 2008	71.20	June 25, 2008	70.13
June 1, 2008	68.93	September 10, 2008	48.52
July 25, 2008	72.00	August 29, 2008	64.44
September 30, 2008	60.00	February 1, 2009	42.00
October 15, 2008	54.82	February 20, 2009	32.41
February 20, 2009	26.23	April 10, 2009	28.51
April 10, 2009	14.88		

Source: Maudlin (2009).

in Figure 3.10. The 95% confidence graphs for the crash danger signal are shown in Figure 3.8(a). The Cantelli inequality version of the model, Figure 3.8(b), gives the danger signal on the same day, namely, June 14, 2007, see also Figures 3.9(a) and 3.9(b).

Let us go back to the BSEYD and consider Table 3.4 which was published in the Maudlin weekly newsletter, which had 1.5 million subscribers

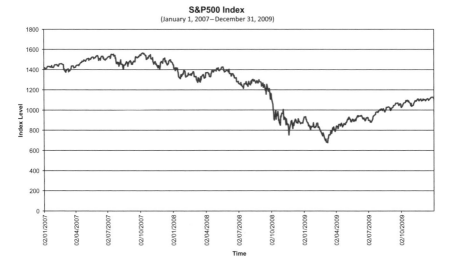

Fig. 3.11.   The S&P500, January 1, 2007 to December 31, 2012.

in May 2009, and discuss whether or not it called the September 2008 to
March 2009 crash. Figure 3.11 shows the S&P500 during this 2007–2009
period. Table 3.4 has the S&P500 2008 estimated earnings and 2009 forecast earnings. On July 25, 2008, the S&P500 earnings for 2008 were estimated to be 72.00, with the S&P500 at 1257.76, which gives a P/E ratio
of 17.47 — not high enough to signal the September 2008 to March 2009
crash. But by February 20, 2009, the 2008 earnings were estimated to be
only 26.23. With the S&P500 at 770.05 on that day the trailing P/E ratio
was 29.36 which gives a BSEYD value of $2.78 - (100/29.36) = -0.626$.

Shepherd (2008) estimates the S&P500 P/E ratio at 723 on July 28,
2009, four months into the rally that began in March 2009! The S&P500
was then 979.62, up nearly 50% from the March lows. This high P/E ratio
was based on reported real earnings from SEC 10Q filings. So what do
we conclude here? Our conclusion is in Figure 3.12. The BSEYD model
did not give any additional sell signals during 2008. The signal was on
June 14, 2007 with the index at 1522.97 and the crash occurred in various phases with closing peak of 1565.15 on October 9, 2007 and a closing
low of 676.53 on March 9, 2009, down some 56.8% from the peak. The
conclusions are similar: over the period January 1, 1995 to June 30, 2012,
two BSYED crash signals occurred, one in June 1999 and the other in
June 2007.

Fig. 3.12.   Crash Indicator (95% confidence): S&P500, January 1, 2007–June 30, 2012.

3.4.   The 2008 Shanghai stock index crash

Figure 3.13 shows the rise of the Shanghai stock index from January 2000 to June 2012. The market bottomed at 1011.50 on July 11, 2005. It then rose six-fold to peak at 6092.06 on October 16, 2007. Then there was a crash of 11.98% from 5180.51 to 4559.75 over the 2-day period January 21 and 22 followed by another 7.19% fall from 4761.69 to 4419.29 on January 28, 2008. Ultimately, the index fell to 1706.70 on November 4, 2008, a decline of over two-thirds from the peak and 23.09% and 29.93% from, respectively, the December 12, 2006 and December 25, 2006 BSEYD danger signals at 2218.95 and 2435.76.

Did the BSEYD model predict this crash? Figure 3.14 shows that the BSEYD measure is not normally distributed with fat right, and even fatter left, tails. The biggest declines are much larger than the biggest increases.

Figure 3.15 shows that the model did in fact predict the crash. See also the signals hitting the danger level in Figures 3.15(b) and 3.16. This is a typical application of the model. The signal goes into the danger zone, then the market continues higher, but within 4 to 12 months there is a crash of 10%+ from the value at the initial signal. In this case, the decline is much higher than 10%. Figure 3.15(a) uses a 95% confidence one-sided moving average interval using prior data out of sample. The danger signal occurred

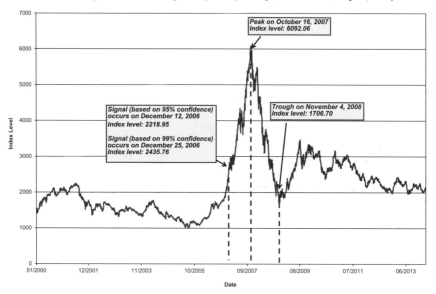

Fig. 3.13.   The Shanghai stock exchange composite index, January 2000 to February 25, 2014.

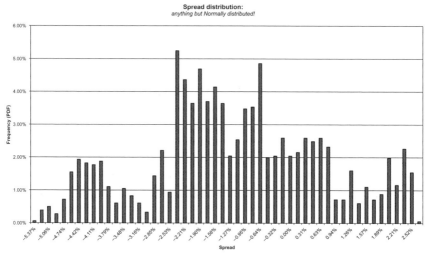

Fig. 3.14.   Spread distribution of the BSEYD measure on the Shanghai Stock Exchange Composite.

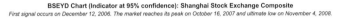

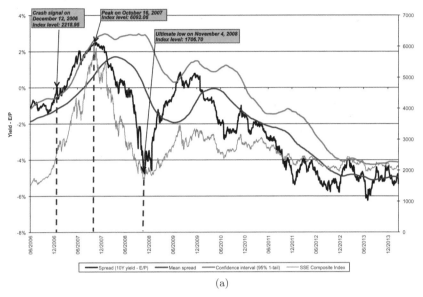

(a)

(b)

Fig. 3.15.   BSEYD crash indicator (95% one-sided moving average confidence interval): Shanghai Stock Exchange Composite. (a) the measure crosses the threshold on December 12, 2006 while the market reaches its peak on October 16th, 2007. (b) the signal (difference between the values of the measure and its threshold) moves decisively into positive territory on December 12, 2006.

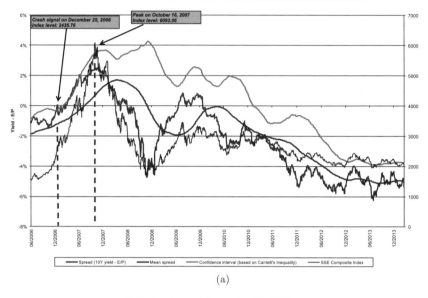

(a)

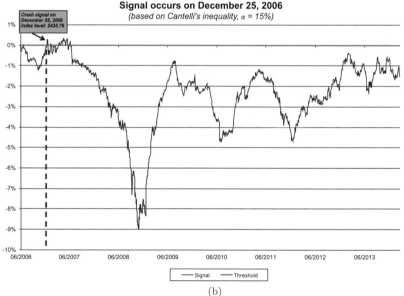

(b)

Fig. 3.16. BSEYD crash indicator (Cantelli's inequality): Shanghai Stock Exchange Composite. (a) Using Cantelli's equality, the measure crosses the threshold on December 25, 2006 while the market reaches its peak on October 16th, 2007. (b) the signal (difference between the values of the measure and its threshold) follows the pattern identified with the confidence interval.

on December 12, 2006, some ten months before the stock market peak with the index at 6092.06 on October 16, 2007. The ultimate fall was to 1706.70 on November 4, 2008 about 30% below the index value of 2218.95 or 2435.76 of the crash signals. These signals and the decline were a bit different from the usual case as it took almost two years to get the 10% plus crash and, in the meantime, the market almost tripled in value before the ultimate crash.

Chapter 4

The High Price–Earnings Stock Market Danger Approach of Campbell and Shiller versus the BSEYD Model

We show how to use Campbell and Shiller's work on price-to-earnings (P/E) ratio and the predictability of long-term returns to create a crash prediction measure: the high P/E measure. Next, we present a statistical procedure to test the accuracy of crash prediction models. We use this procedure to test the accuracy of the bond–stock earnings yield differential (BSEYD) and high P/E models on a 51-year period on the US market, starting on January 1, 1962, and ending on December 31, 2014 (12,846 daily data points). At the end of the Chapter, we expand the analysis beyond the US market to look at the two main Chinese stock markets: Shanghai and Shenzhen. Material in this chapter is based on Lleo and Ziemba (2017) and Lleo and Ziemba (2016c).

4.1. Exploring the predictability of long-term returns

4.1.1. From P/E to PE10

Financial market practitioners routinely use the price-to-earnings (P/E) ratio to gauge the relative valuation of stocks and stock markets, and the explanatory power with respect to stock over- and under-performance is well documented (Fama and French, 1992). Table 4.1 reports the evolution of the P/E–ratio over selected 20-year periods with high annual returns. In each period, the P/E ends 1.6 to 4.7 times higher than it started. Furthermore, there is a 90% correlation between the annual returns and the ending P/E ratio.

Table 4.1.   Evolution of the P/E over selected 20-year periods with
high annualized returns.

Beginning year	Ending year	Annual rate of return	Beginning P/E	Ending P/E
1975	1994	9.6%	10.9	20.5
1977	1996	9.7%	11.5	25.9
1942	1961	9.9%	12.2	20.5
1983	2002	10.9%	7.3	25.9
1978	1997	11.9%	10.4	31.0
1981	2000	12.8%	8.8	41.7
1979	1998	12.9%	9.4	36.0
1982	2001	13.0%	8.5	32.1
1980	1999	14.0%	8.9	42.1

Source: Bertocch *et al.* (2010).

In fact, Benjamin Graham and David Dodd were among the first to use
the P/E ratio to gauge the relative valuation of stocks, dedicating much of
Chapter XXXIX of *Security Analysis* to the subject (Graham and Dodd,
1934).

Graham and Dodd's book was a source of inspiration for John Campbell and Robert Shiller when they set out to question the predictability of
long-term equity returns. Campbell and Shiller (1988) proposed a vector-
autoregressive model relating the log return on the S&P500 with the log
dividend–price ratio, lagged dividend growth rate and average annual earnings over the previous 10 and 30 years. We can trace the use of average
earnings to Graham and Dodd: they advocated taking the average earnings
over 10 years to average out the effect that unique or specific economic or
business conditions might have on current earnings.

Campbell and Shiller started by performing a regression of the log
returns on the S&P500 over 1 year, 3 years and 10 years against each
of these variables and the average annual earnings over the previous 10
years. Continuing their study, they found that the R^2 of a regression of log
returns on the S&P500 over a 10-year period against the log of the P/E
ratio computed using average earnings over the previous 10 and 30 years is
significant.

Specifically, Campbell and Shiller define the one-period total return on
the stock as

$$h_{1t}^{\text{beg}} := \ln\left(\frac{P_{t+1}^{\text{beg}} + D_t}{P_t^{\text{beg}}}\right),$$

where, P_t^{beg} is the price of the stock at the beginning of period t and D_t is the dividend received during period t. Although Campbell and Shiller do not specify a present value or future value rule for the dividend, we will consider that all dividends received during period t are either carried or future valued to the end of period t, so that $D_t = D_t^{\text{end}}$. The i period total return on the stock is

$$h_{it}^{\text{beg}} := \sum_{j=0}^{i-1} h_{1,t+j}.$$

The regression in Campbell and Shiller (1988) is

$$h_{it}^{\text{beg}} = a + b \ln \left(\frac{P_t^{\text{beg}}}{\text{BSEYD}\overline{E}_{t,-n}^{\text{beg}}} \right) + \epsilon, \qquad (4.1)$$

where P_t is the level of the S&P500 index at time t and $\text{BSEYD}\overline{E}_{t,-n}^{\text{beg}}$ is the average of past annual earnings over the last n years, namely

$$\text{BSEYD}\overline{E}_{t,-n}^{\text{beg}} = \frac{1}{n} \sum_{i=0}^{n-1} E_{t-i}^{\text{beg}}.$$

The R^2 computed by Campbell and Shiller (1988) for $n = 30$ is 0.566, higher than the 0.401 computed for $n = 10$ and higher than the R^2 of regressions against the log dividend–price ratio and lagged dividend growth rate. Hence, the regression based on 30-year average earnings has a greater explanatory power than the regression based on 10 years of earnings, and than any other variable. To explain this difference, Shiller (1996) suggests that a 10-year average may still be sensitive to changes in the business cycle, whereas a 30-year average should be immune to short-term shifts in the business cycle.

Campbell and Shiller (1989) also conducted a Monte Carlo study to address the possibility of a small sample bias in their initial analysis. They found that the size of their sample did not provide a material explanation for their initial conclusions: the P/E ratio based on 30-year average earnings and on 10-year average earnings help explain the long-term performance of the S&P500.

These findings led Shiller to suggest the use of a Cyclically Adjusted P/E ratio (PE10), a P/E ratio using an 10-year average real (inflation-adjusted) earnings, to forecast the evolution of the equity risk premium (see Shiller, 2015).

4.1.2. *Relating P/E and stock valuation*

Campbell and Shiller do not explain how their empirical results fit with asset pricing theory. To fill this gap and provide a firm theoretical footing for their observations, we use the Gordon (1959) growth model to derive an approximate linear relation between the one-period log return on the S&P500 and the earnings yield.

On the assumptions of the Gordon Growth Model, and using standard notation, the price of a stock at time t equals

$$P_t^{\text{end}} = \frac{D_{t+1} + P_{t+1}^{\text{end}}}{1 + k},$$

where P_t^{end} is the price of the stock at the beginning of period t, and k is the cost of equity. This relation implies that the holding period return is linear in the current earnings yield

$$\frac{P_{t+1}^{\text{end}} + D_t}{P_t^{\text{end}}} = 1 + k - gd\rho_t,$$

where g is the constant growth rate of dividends, d is the dividend payout ratio and $\rho_t^{\text{end}} = \frac{E_t^{\text{end}}}{P_t^{\text{end}}}$. The logarithmic return is

$$h_{1t}^{\text{end}} = \ln\left(\frac{P_{t+1}^{\text{end}} + D_{t+1}}{P_t^{\text{end}}}\right) = \ln(1 + k) + \ln\left(1 - \frac{gd}{k}\rho_t^{\text{end}}\right).$$

We linearize this expression by performing a first-order Taylor expansion around $\rho_t = \bar{\rho}$, where $\bar{\rho}$ is the average long-term earnings yield

$$h_{1t}^{\text{end}} \approx a_0 - a_1\rho_t^{\text{end}}, \qquad (4.2)$$

where $a_0 := \ln(1 + k) + \ln\left(1 - \frac{gd}{1+k}\bar{\rho}\right) + \frac{gd}{1+k-gd\bar{\rho}}$ and $a_1 := \frac{gd}{1+k-gd\bar{\rho}}$.

Provided that the price at the end of period t and at the beginning of period $t+1$ are equal, that is $P_t^{\text{end}} = P_{t+1}^{\text{beg}}$, then it follows that $\rho_t^{\text{end}} = \rho_{t+1}^{\text{beg}}$ and

$$h_{1t}^{\text{beg}} = \ln\left(\frac{P_{t+1}^{\text{beg}} + D_t}{P_t^{\text{beg}}}\right) = \ln\left(\frac{P_t^{\text{end}} + D_t}{P_{t-1}^{\text{end}}}\right) = h_{1(t-1)}^{\text{end}} \qquad (4.3)$$

Therefore, the two models are equivalent, with a small notation change.

Equation (4.2) differs from the Campbell–Shiller regression model (4.1) in two important ways. First, the Campbell–Shiller model regresses log returns against log P/E while the Gordon model relates log returns to earning yield (no log). Second, the Campbell–Shiller model uses the P/E ratio whereas the Gordon model is based on the earnings yield. However, the impact of this second difference is minor. The properties of the logarithm imply that,

$$\ln\left(h_{it}\right) = a + b\ln\left(\frac{P_t}{\overline{E}_{t,-n}}\right) + \epsilon = a - b\ln\left(\frac{\overline{E}_{t,-n}}{P_t}\right) + \epsilon. \qquad (4.4)$$

Hence, only the regression slope changes sign. The significance of the model is not affected otherwise.

4.1.3. *Using the P/E ratio as a crash prediction model*

We saw in Chapter 3 that crash prediction models generate a signal to indicate a downturn in the equity market at a given horizon H. This signal SIGNAL(t) occurs whenever the value of a given measure $M(t)$ crosses a time varying threshold $K(t)$:

$$\text{SIGNAL}(t) = M(t) - K(t) > 0. \qquad (4.5)$$

The P/E ratio, calculated using either current earnings or using 10-year average earnings, provides the measure $M(t)$. The threshold $K(t)$ is either standard confidence interval around the measure based on 252-day rolling horizon statistics, or an upper bound derived from Cantelli's inequality.

4.2. A statistical test of accuracy for crash prediction models

Testing the accuracy of crash prediction models is a five-step process, starting from defining what we mean by equity market crash, to constructing a "hit" sequence, estimating the probability of a crash, performing a likelihood ratio test, and finally addressing small sample bias. We discuss each step in detail below.

Step 1: Define An Equity Market Crash

We define an equity market crash as a decline of at least 10% in the level of the S&P500 from peak to trough based on closing prices for the day, over a period of at most one year (252 trading days). A crash is formally identified on the day when the closing price crosses the 10% threshold. The crash identification algorithm is as follows:

(1) Identify all the local troughs in the data set. Today is a local trough if there is no lower closing price within $\pm d$ business days.

(2) Identify the crashes. Today is a crash identification day if all of the following conditions hold:

   (a) The closing level of S&P500 is down at least 10% from its highest level within the past year today, and the loss was less than 10% yesterday;

   (b) This highest level reached by the S&P500 prior to the present crash differs from the highest level corresponding to a previous crash;

   (c) This highest level occurred after the local trough that followed the last crash.

The objective of these rules is to guarantee that the crashes we identify are distinct. Two crashes are not distinct if they occur within the same larger market decline.

The choice of the parameter d is not as important as might initially appear. In practice, selecting d in the range $[1, 94]$, will still lead to the identification of the same 22 crashes. The difference is in the number of local troughs and the amplitude of the various crashes. As d increases past a value of 94 days, our algorithm identifies fewer crashes. For example, we identify 21 crashes for $d = 95$, 20 crashes for $d = 100$, and 15 crashes for $d = 200$.

In this paper, we pick $d = 90$ in order to capture the full amplitude of some of the crashes, such as the 56% market meltdown of 2008. In practice, this choice will not affect our statistical test, because the test is based on the number of crashes and crash identification dates. These numbers are the same whenever we select d in the interval $[1, 94]$.

Table 4.2 shows the 22 crashes that occurred between January 31, 1964 and December 31, 2014. We observe the October 1987 crash, the Russian currency default and LTCM in 1998, the dot.com collapse in 2000–2002 and the subprime crisis in 2007–2009. The average duration of a correction was 199 days, and the average decline was 20.3%.

Table 4.2 gives the crash identification date, defined as the date at which the decline from the previous local peak reaches 10%. With this information, we define a crash indicator sequence $C = \{C_t, t = 1, \ldots, T\}$, where C_t takes the value 1 if date t is a crash identification date and 0 otherwise, and the associated vector $c = (C_1, \ldots, C_t, \ldots C_T)$. Thus, the event "a crash is identified on day t" is represented as $\{C_t = 1\}$. This variable plays a leading role in the hypothesis test. We repeat this procedure for each day in our sample. The result is a binary sequence with "1" in 22 entries, one for each crash, and "0" everywhere else.

Table 4.2. The S&P500 index experienced 22 corrections between January 31, 1964 and December 31, 2014.

	Crash identification date	Peak date	S&P Index at Peak	Trough date	S&P Level at trough	Peak-to-trough decline (%)	Peak-to-trough duration (in days)
1	16–05–1966	09–02–1966	94.06	07–10–1966	73.2	22.2%	240
2	05–03–1968	25–09–1967	97.59	05–03–1968	87.72	10.1%	162
3	19–06–1969	29–11–1968	108.37	29–07–1969	89.48	17.4%	242
4	04–08–1971	28–04–1971	104.77	23–11–1971	90.16	13.9%	209
5	27–04–1973	11–01–1973	120.24	03–10–1974	62.28	48.2%	630
6	08–08–1975	15–07–1975	95.61	16–09–1975	82.09	14.1%	63
7	25–05–1977	21–09–1976	107.83	06–03–1978	86.9	19.4%	531
8	26–10–1978	12–09–1978	106.99	14–11–1978	92.49	13.6%	63
9	25–10–1979	05–10–1979	111.27	07–11–1979	99.87	10.2%	33
10	10–03–1980	13–02–1980	118.44	27–03–1980	98.22	17.1%	43
11	24–08–1981	28–11–1980	140.52	25–09–1981	112.77	19.7%	301
12	13–02–1984	10–10–1983	172.65	24–07–1984	147.82	14.4%	288
13	15–10–1987	25–08–1987	336.77	04–12–1987	223.92	33.5%	101
14	30–01–1990	09–10–1989	359.8	30–01–1990	322.98	10.2%	113
15	17–08–1990	16–07–1990	368.95	11–10–1990	295.46	19.9%	87
16	27–10–1997	07–10–1997	983.12	27–10–1997	876.99	10.8%	20
17	14–08–1998	17–07–1998	1186.75	31–08–1998	957.28	19.3%	45
18	29–09–1999	16–07–1999	1418.78	15–10–1999	1247.41	12.1%	91
19	14–04–2000	24–03–2000	1527.46	04–04–2001	1103.25	27.8%	376
20	26–11–2007	09–10–2007	1565.15	09–03–2009	676.53	56.8%	517
21	20–05–2010	23–04–2010	1217.28	02–07–2010	1022.58	16.0%	70
22	04–08–2011	29–04–2011	1363.61	03–10–2011	1099.23	19.4%	157

Step 2: Construct the Hit Sequence X

The construction process for the signal and hit sequence is crucial to ensure that the crash prediction models produce out of sample predictions free from look-ahead bias. It also eliminates data snooping by setting the parameters *ex ante* during the signal construction, with no possibilities of changing them when we construct the hit sequence. More importantly, the construction of the hit sequence removes the effect of autocorrelation, making it possible to test the accuracy of the measures using a standard likelihood ratio test.

While predicting returns is extremely difficult, earlier research suggests that it is possible to predict crashes based on a signal. To check this, we perform a simple and effective statistical significance test.

All crash prediction models have two components: (1) a signal which takes the value 1 or 0 depending on whether the measure has crossed the confidence level, and (2) a crash indicator which takes value 1 when an equity market crash occurs and 0 otherwise. From a probabilistic perspective, these components are Bernoulli random variables.

We start by computing the signal S_t for each day period t over our historical sample $t = 1, \ldots, T$. Next, we define a signal indicator sequence $S = \{S_t, t = 1, \ldots, T\}$. This sequence records the first day in a series of positive signals as the signal date and only counts distinct signal dates. Two signals are distinct if a new signal occurs more than 30 days after the previous signal. The objective is to have enough time between two series of signals to identify them as distinct. The signal indicator S_t takes the value 1 if date t is the starting date of a distinct signal and 0 otherwise. Thus, the event "a distinct signal starts on day t" is represented as $\{S_t = 1\}$. We express the signal indicator sequence as the vector $s = (S_1, \ldots, S_t, \ldots, S_T)$.

We denote by $C_{t,H}$ the indicator function returning 1 if the crash identification date of at least one equity market correction occurs between time t and time $t + H$. The relation between $C_{t,H}$ and C_t is

$$C_{t,H} := 1 - \prod_{i=1}^{H} (1 - C_{t+i}).$$

We identify the vector C_H with the sequence $C_H := \{C_{t,H}, t = 1, \ldots, T-H\}$ and define the vector $c_H := (C_{1,H}, \ldots, C_{t,H}, \ldots C_{T-H,H})$.

The accuracy of the crash prediction model is the conditional probability $P(C_{t,H} = 1 | S_t = 1)$ of a crash being identified between time t and time $t + H$, given that we observed a signal at time t. The higher the probability, the more accurate the model. We use maximum likelihood to estimate this probability and to test whether it is significantly higher than a random draw. We can obtain a simple analytical solution because the conditional random variable $\{C_{t,H} = 1|S_t = 1\}$ is a Bernoulli trial with probability $p = P(C_{t,H} = 1|S_t = 1)$.

To estimate the probability p, we change the indexing to consider only events along the sequence $\{S_t|S_t = 1, t = 1, \ldots T\}$ and denote by $X := \{X_i, i = 1, \ldots, N\}$ the "hit sequence" where $x_i = 1$ if the ith signal is followed by a crash and 0 otherwise. Here, N denotes the total number of signals, that is,

$$N = \sum_{t=1}^{T} S_t = \mathbf{1}'s,$$

where $\mathbf{1}$ is a vector with all entries set to 1 and v' denotes the transpose of vector v. The sequence X can be expressed in vector notation as $x = (X_1, X_2, \ldots, X_N)$.

Step 3: Estimate $p = P(C_{t,H}|S_t)$ Via Maximum Likelihood Methods

The likelihood function L associated with the observations sequence X is

$$L(p|X) := \prod_{i=1}^{N} p^{X_i}(1-p)^{1-X_i}$$

and the log likelihood function $\mathcal{L}$ is

$$\mathcal{L}(p|X) := \ln L(p|X) = \sum_{i=1}^{N} X_i \ln p + \left(N - \sum_{i=1}^{N} X_i\right) \ln(1-p)$$

This function is maximized for

$$\hat{p} := \frac{\sum_{i=1}^{N} X_i}{N} \tag{4.6}$$

so the maximum likelihood estimate of the probability $p = P(C_{t,H}|S_t)$ is the historical proportion of correct predictions out of all observations.

Step 4: Perform a Likelihood Ratio Test

We apply a likelihood ratio test to test the null hypothesis $H_0 : p = p_0$ against the alternative hypothesis $H_A : p \neq p_0$. The null hypothesis reflects the idea that the probability of a random, uninformed, signal correctly

predicting crashes is p_0. A significant departure above this level indicates
that the measure we are considering has some predictive value.

The likelihood ratio test is

$$\Lambda = \frac{L(p = p_0 | X)}{\max_{p \in (0,1)} L(p | X)} = \frac{L(p = p_0 | X)}{L(p = \hat{p} | X)}. \tag{4.7}$$

The statistic $Y := -2 \ln \Lambda$ is asymptotically χ^2-distributed with $\nu = 1$
degree of freedom. We reject the null hypothesis $H_0 : p = p_0$ and accept
that the model has some predictive power if $Y > c$, where c is the critical
value chosen for the test. We perform the test for the three critical values
3.84, 6.63 and 7.88 corresponding respectively to a 95%, 99% and 99.5%
confidence level.

A key advantage of this test is that it can be applied to all crash prediction models, whether based on fundamental variables (P/E, BSEYD or Fed
model) or on probabilistic models (Jarrow–Protter, Shiryaev–Zitlukhin–
Ziemba) and could apply more generally to any model designed to predict
a market event.

Step 5: Perform a Monte Carlo Study for Small Sample Bias

A limitation of the likelihood ratio test is that the χ^2 distribution is only
valid asymptotically. In our case, the number of correct predictions follows a binomial distribution with an estimated probability of success $\hat{p}$ and
N trials. Between January 31, 1964 and December 31, 2014, 22 crashes
occurred. As a result, the total number of signals N should also be low and
we will have a discrete empirical distribution of test statistics. The continuous χ^2 distribution might not provide an adequate approximation for this
discrete distribution: $\hat{p}$ might appear significantly different from p_0 under
a χ^2 distribution but not under the empirical distribution. This difficulty
is an example of small sample bias. Monte Carlo methods are the method
of choice to identify and correct small sample bias.

The Monte Carlo algorithm is as follows. Generate a large number
K of paths. For each path $k = 1, \ldots, K$, simulate N Bernoulli random variables with probability p_0 of obtaining a "success." Denote by
$X_k := \{X_i^k, i = 1, \ldots, N\}$ the realization sequence where $x_i^k = 1$ if the
ith Bernoulli variable produces a "success" and 0 otherwise. Next, compute the maximum likelihood estimate for the probability of success given
the realization sequence X_k as

$$\hat{p} := \frac{\sum_{i=1}^{N} X_i^k}{N},$$

and the test statistics for the path as

$$Y_k = -2\ln\Lambda_k = -2\ln\frac{L(p=p_0|X_k)}{\max_{p\in(0,1)} L(p_k|X_k)} = -2\ln\frac{L(p=p_0|X_k)}{L(p=\hat{p}_k|X_k)}.$$

Once all the paths have been simulated, we use all K test statistics $Y_k, k = 1,\ldots,K$ to produce an empirical distributions for the test statistic Y.

From the empirical distribution, we obtain critical values at a 95%, 99% and 99.5% confidence level against which we assess the crash prediction test statistics Y. The empirical distribution also enables us to compute a p-value for the crash prediction test statistics. Finally, we compare the results obtained under the empirical distribution to those derived using the asymptotic χ^2 distribution.

4.2.1. *Model-on-model significance test*

In addition to testing each crash prediction model separately, the likelihood ratio test also allows us to perform a pairwise model-on-model test to determine whether the accuracy p_i of a given model i, $i = 1,\ldots 32$ is significantly higher than the estimated accuracy $\hat{p}_j = \text{argmax}_{p_j\in(0,1)} L(p_j|X)$ of model j, $j = 1,\ldots 32, j \neq i$.

Treating $\hat{p}_j$ as fixed for the purpose of this test, we apply a likelihood ratio test to test the null hypothesis $H_0 : p_i = \hat{p}_j$ against the alternative hypothesis $H_A : p_i \neq \hat{p}_j$. A significant departure above this level indicates that model i contains more information than model j. Here, the likelihood ratio test is

$$\Lambda = \frac{L(p=\hat{p}_j|X)}{\max_{p_i\in(0,1)} L(p_i|X)} = \frac{L(p=\hat{p}_j|X)}{L(p=\hat{p}_i|X)}. \tag{4.8}$$

The statistic $Y := -2\ln\Lambda$ is still asymptotically χ^2-distributed with $\nu = 1$ degree of freedom. We reject the null hypothesis $H_0 : p_i = p_j$ and accept that model i has a higher predictive power than model j if $p_i > p_j$ and $Y > c$, where c is the critical value chosen for the test.

As we treat $\hat{p}_j$ as fixed, the test is not symmetric in i and j. The likelihood ratio only enables us to confirm whether p_i is significantly different from $\hat{p}_j$, but does not convey accurate statistical information about the significance of p_j relative to p_i.

4.2.2. *Robustness*

The question of robustness is critical for all empirical models. In our model, we distinguish two closely connected views of robustness: robustness with respect to the dataset (data robustness) and robustness with respect to the specific parameters of the model (model parameter robustness).

Addressing Data Robustness: Subperiod Study

Data robustness addresses the question of the sensitivity of model predictions when the underlying dataset changes. This is the more traditional view of robustness, and it is generally dealt with either by using an out-of-sample study or by analyzing the behavior of the model in several subperiods.

Measuring Parameter Robustness: Robust Likelihood Statistics

Though crucial, the question of robustness has mostly remained peripheral to the debate on the predictability of market downturns and crashes. To address this question, and quatify model specification robustness, we can use a robust version of the likelihood ratio and of the associated test statistics. Measuring the robustness of a crash prediction model using a robust likelihood ratio has significant advantages. First, the likelihood ratio provides a direct, objective measure of robustness that allows direct comparison between different model specifications and even different types of models. Second, we can use the robust test statistics to evaluate the significance of the model using a χ^2 distribution. The immediate benefit is that we can equate loss of robustness over a set of model parameters with loss of prediction significance. Third, the idea of robust likelihood ratio can be easily extended to account for small sample bias. We can use the Monte Carlo algorithm presented in an earlier section to compute the (standard) likelihood ratio under each specification and then select the lowest one as a robust likelihood ratio.

The robust likelihood ratio generalizes the (standard) likelihood ratio to account for the impact of the choice of parameters on the predictions of the model. Compared with the standard likelihood ratio, we need to enlarge the set of model parameters to consider both free parameters and model specifications. Free parameters are the parameters that we seek to estimate based on the model output, such as the success probability p. Model specifications are the set of parameters that specify the model: type of earnings, threshold calculation, type of bond yields.

Denoting by Ω the enlarged set of parameters, Θ the set of free parameters and $\mathcal{M}$ the set of model specifications, we have $\Omega = (\Theta, \mathcal{M})$. This enlarged formulation leads us to revisit the definition of likelihood function and likelihood ratio. The model specification $\mu \in \mathcal{M}$ directly affects the signal indicator sequence, the total number of signals and the probability of successfully predicting a crash. We denote the signal indicator sequence by $S^\mu := \{S_t^\mu, t = 1, \ldots, T\}$ and express the signal indicator sequence as a vector $s^\mu := (S_1^\mu, \ldots, S_t^\mu, \ldots, S_T^\mu)$. The total number of signals N^μ is

$$N^\mu = \sum_{t=1}^{T} S_t^\mu = \mathbf{1}'s^\mu,$$

and the probability of successfully predicting a crash is $p = P(C_{t,H} = 1 | S_t^\mu = 1)$. As a result the "hit sequence" $X^\mu := \{X_i^\mu, i = 1, \ldots, N\}$ where $x_i^\mu = 1$ if the ith signal is followed by a crash and 0 otherwise also depends on the model specification μ.

The likelihood function L associated with the observations sequence X^μ generated under model specification μ is

$$L(p|X, \mu) := \prod_{i=1}^{N^\mu} p^{X_i^\mu} (1-p)^{1-X_i^\mu}.$$

In our case, there is only one free parameter, the probability p, and as a result the set of free parameters Θ is effectively the interval $(0, 1)$. Maximizing the log likelihood function gives us an estimate of the maximum likelihood of successfully predicting crashes based on model specification μ

$$\hat{p}^\mu := \frac{\sum_{i=1}^{N^\mu} X_i}{N^\mu}. \tag{4.9}$$

The standard likelihood ratio under model specification μ and given the null hypothesis $H_0 : p = p_0$ is

$$\Lambda^\mu = \frac{L(p = p_0 | X, \mu)}{\max_{p \in (0,1)} L(p | X, \mu)} = \frac{L(p = p_0 | X, \mu)}{L(p = \hat{p}^\mu | X, \mu)}. \tag{4.10}$$

We define the robust likelihood ratio $\check{\Lambda}$ given the null hypothesis $H_0 : p = p_0 := \frac{1}{2}$ as the supremum over all possible model specifications of the standard likelihood ratio

$$\check{\Lambda} = \sup_{\mu \in \mathcal{M}} \Lambda^\mu = \sup_{\mu \in \mathcal{M}} \frac{L(p = p_0 | X, \mu)}{\max_{p \in (0,1)} L(p | X, \mu)}$$

$$= \sup_{\mu \in \mathcal{M}} \frac{L(p = p_0 | X, \mu)}{L(p = \hat{p}^\mu | X, \mu)}. \tag{4.11}$$

Higher robust likelihood ratios are indicative of a lower statistical significance. The associated robust test statistic is

$$\check{Y} := \inf_{\mu \in \mathcal{M}} Y^{\mu}$$

$$= \inf_{\mu \in \mathcal{M}} -2\ln \frac{L(p = p_0 | X, \mu)}{L(p = \hat{p}^{\mu} | X, \mu)}$$

$$= -2\ln \sup_{\mu \in \mathcal{M}} \frac{L(p = p_0 | X, \mu)}{L(p = \hat{p}^{\mu} | X, \mu)}. \qquad (4.12)$$

Because the test statistic for the (standard) likelihood ratio under specification μ, Y^{μ}, is asymptotically χ^2 distributed, the test statistic for robust likelihood ratio $\check{Y}$ is also asymptotically χ^2 distributed.

4.3.   Testing the predictive ability of the BSEYD and P/E

In this section, we test the predictions of 8 P/E-based models and 32 BSEYD-based models on the S&P500, over a 51-year period starting on January 31, 1964, and ending on December 31, 2014 (12,846 daily data points).

4.3.1.   *Prediction models*

The statistical procedure discussed above is model-dependent. We need to specify the model we are testing before performing the actual statistical test. Specifying the model requires defining the measure $M(t)$, the threshold $K(t)$ and the horizon H. We fix the horizon at two years, meaning $H = 504$ days.

   To compute the measure $M(t)$, we use both current earnings and average earnings over the past 10 years. This is consistent with the observation that the cyclicality of earnings matters. Graham and Dodd (1934), for example, suggest using 10 years of earnings in stock and company valuation. Although Campbell and Shiller tested their model using average earnings over 30 years, we consider only 10 years because our objective is to predict medium-term market downturns rather than long-term market returns. As a result, we do not want our measures to be immune from the movements of the business cycle. For the interest rates, we use the yield on either the 10-year U.S. Treasury Note, or seasoned corporate bonds rated Aaa or Baa by Moody's.

To define the threshold $K(t)$, we use both a standard confidence rule and Cantelli's inequality. Overall, this gives us four ways of computing the crash signals for the P/E and log P/E measure, based on the definition of earnings (current or 10-year average) and the type of confidence interval (standard or Cantelli). Taking also into consideration the type of interest rates used (yield on a 10-year Treasury Note or on a seasoned Aaa corporate bond), we have 12 ways of computing the crash signals for the BSEYD and logBSEYD measure.

Table 4.3 lists these 32 signal models. The P/E and log P/E measures serve as bases for our four models:

(1) P/E1 and log P/E1 use current earnings and a standard confidence level;
(2) P/E2 and log P/E2 use current earnings and Cantelli's inequality;
(3) P/E3 and log P/E3 use average earnings over 10 years and a standard confidence level;
(4) P/E4 and log P/E4 use average earnings over 10 years and Cantelli's inequality.

The BSEYD and logBSEYD measures are used in eight models each:

(1) BSEYD1 and logBSEYD1 use current earnings, a standard confidence level and yields on 10-year Treasury Notes;
(2) BSEYD2 and logBSEYD2 use current earnings, Cantelli's inequality;
(3) BSEYD3 and logBSEYD3 use average earnings over 10 years, a standard confidence level and yields on 10-year Treasury Notes;
(4) BSEYD4 and logBSEYD4 use average earnings over 10 years, a Cantelli's inequality and yields on seasoned Aaa corporate bonds;
(5) BSEYD5 and logBSEYD5 use current earnings, a standard confidence level and yields on seasoned Aaa corporate bonds;
(6) BSEYD6 and logBSEYD6 use current earnings, Cantelli's inequality and yields on seasoned Aaa corporate bonds;
(7) BSEYD7 and logBSEYD7 use average earnings over 10 years, a standard confidence level and yields on seasoned Aaa corporate bonds;
(8) BSEYD8 and logBSEYD8 are based on average earnings over 10 years, a Cantelli's inequality and yields on seasoned Aaa corporate bonds.
(9) BSEYD9 and logBSEYD9 use current earnings, a standard confidence level and yields on seasoned Baa corporate bonds;

Table 4.3. List of 16 Signal models tested.

Measure	Signal	Current earnings	Average earnings over 10 years	Confidence interval	Cantelli's inequality	Yield on 10-year Treasury Note	Yield on Aaa corporate bond	Yield on Baa corporate bond	Dataset start date	Dataset end date
P/E	P/E1	✓		✓					Jan. 1, 1962	Dec. 31, 2014
	P/E2	✓		✓	✓				Jan. 1, 1962	Dec. 31, 2014
	P/E3		✓	✓					Jan. 31, 1964	Dec. 31, 2014
	P/E4		✓	✓	✓				Jan. 31, 1964	Dec. 31, 2014
log P/E	logP/E1	✓		✓					Jan. 1, 1962	Dec. 31, 2014
	logP/E2	✓		✓	✓				Jan. 1, 1962	Dec. 31, 2014
	logP/E3		✓	✓					Jan. 31, 1964	Dec. 31, 2014
	logP/E4		✓	✓	✓				Jan. 31, 1964	Dec. 31, 2014
BSEYD	BSEYD1	✓		✓		✓			Jan. 1, 1962	Dec. 31, 2014
	BSEYD2	✓		✓	✓	✓			Jan. 1, 1962	Dec. 31, 2014
	BSEYD3		✓	✓		✓			Jan. 31, 1964	Dec. 31, 2014
	BSEYD4		✓	✓	✓	✓			Jan. 31, 1964	Dec. 31, 2014
	BSEYD5	✓		✓			✓		Jan. 4, 1983	Dec. 31, 2014
	BSEYD6	✓		✓	✓		✓		Jan. 4, 1983	Dec. 31, 2014
	BSEYD7		✓	✓			✓		Jan. 4, 1983	Dec. 31, 2014
	BSEYD8		✓	✓	✓		✓		Jan. 4, 1983	Dec. 31, 2014
	BSEYD9	✓		✓				✓	Jan. 2, 1986	Dec. 31, 2014
	BSEYD10	✓		✓	✓			✓	Jan. 2, 1986	Dec. 31, 2014
	BSEYD11		✓	✓				✓	Jan. 2, 1986	Dec. 31, 2014
	BSEYD12		✓	✓	✓			✓	Jan. 2, 1986	Dec. 31, 2014

logBSEYD	logBSEYD1						✓	✓	Jan. 1, 1962 – Dec. 31, 2014
	logBSEYD2					✓	✓		Jan. 1, 1962 – Dec. 31, 2014
	logBSEYD3			✓	✓				Jan. 31, 1964 – Dec. 31, 2014
	logBSEYD4			✓	✓		✓	✓	Jan. 31, 1964 – Dec. 31, 2014
	logBSEYD5	✓				✓			Jan. 4, 1983 – Dec. 31, 2014
	logBSEYD6	✓		✓	✓	✓	✓		Jan. 4, 1983 – Dec. 31, 2014
	logBSEYD7	✓		✓	✓	✓			Jan. 4, 1983 – Dec. 31, 2014
	logBSEYD8	✓				✓	✓		Jan. 4, 1983 – Dec. 31, 2014
	logBSEYD9	✓	✓	✓	✓	✓	✓	✓	Jan. 2, 1986 – Dec. 31, 2014
	logBSEYD10					✓		✓	Jan. 2, 1986 – Dec. 31, 2014
	logBSEYD11		✓	✓	✓			✓	Jan. 2, 1986 – Dec. 31, 2014
	logBSEYD12		✓	✓	✓			✓	Jan. 2, 1986 – Dec. 31, 2014

(10) BSEYD10 and logBSEYD10 use current earnings, Cantelli's inequality and yields on seasoned Baa corporate bonds;

(11) BSEYD11 and logBSEYD11 use average earnings over 10 years, a standard confidence level and yields on seasoned Baa corporate bonds;

(12) BSEYD12 and logBSEYD12 use average earnings over 10 years, a Cantelli's inequality and yields on seasoned Baa corporate bonds.

4.3.2. *Dataset*

We use daily S&P500, earnings and P/E data for the period January 31, 1964 to December 31, 2014. We obtained the data from Bloomberg and used Thomson DataStream to cross-reference and check them. The daily yields on the 10-year Treasury Note for the period January 1, 1962 to December 31, 2014, the daily yields on seasoned corporate bonds rated Aaa by Moody's for the period January 3, 1983 to December 31, 2014 and the daily yields on seasoned corporate bonds rated Baa by Moody's for the period January 2, 1986 to December 31, 2014 come from the Board of Governors of the Federal Reserve System.

Because our models require the simultaneous use of stock market prices, P/E ratios and bond market yields, we are limited by the shortest data series. The longest period for which we can test the accuracy of crash prediction models is 50 years and 11 months, starting January 31, 1964, if we use 10-year Treasury Note. It comprises 12,815 daily data points. The shortest period for which we can test the accuracy of crash prediction models is 29 years, starting January 2, 1986, if we use seasoned corporate bonds rated Baa.

4.3.3. *Signal time series*

We use daily data from January 31, 1964 to December 31, 2014, 12,815 observations, to construct the time series for all the P/E and logP/E models as well as the BSEYD and logBSEYD models based on 10-year Treasury yields. For the BSEYD and logBSEYD models computed with Aaa corporate yields, we use daily data from January 3, 1983 to December 31, 2014, 8,036 observations. Finally, for the BSEYD and logBSEYD models computed with Baa corporate yields, we use daily data from January 2, 1986 to December 31, 2014, 7,277 observations. The results are displayed in Figures 4.1–4.8. The line represents the evolution of the signal at time t, $SIGNAL(t)$: a crash signal occurs whenever the signal series crosses the threshold when $SIGNAL(t) > 0$.

Figure 4.1 presents the signal time series related to the P/E measure. Panel (a) shows the PE1 signal series, which is based on current earnings and standard confidence intervals. Panel (b) shows the PE2 signal series, which is based on current earnings and Cantelli's inequality. Panel (c) shows the PE3 signal series, which is based on average earnings and standard confidence intervals. Lastly, Panel (d) shows the PE4 signal series based on average earnings and Cantelli's inequality. PE1 and PE2 are nearly identical, and the same is true of PE3 and PE4.

Figure 4.2 presents the signal time series related to the logP/E measure. Panel (a) shows the lnPE1 signal series, which is based on current earnings and standard confidence intervals. Panel (b) charts the lnPE2 signal series, which is based on current earnings and Cantelli's inequality. Panel (c) shows the lnPE3 signal series, which is based on average earnings and standard confidence intervals. Lastly, Panel (d) shows the lnPE4 signal series, which is based on average earnings and Cantelli's inequality.

Figure 4.3 presents the signal time series related to the BSEYD measure computed with Treasury yields. Panel (a) shows the BSEYD1 signal series, which is based on current earnings and standard confidence intervals. Panel (b) shows the BSEYD2 signal series, which is based on current earnings and Cantelli's inequality. Panel (c) shows the BSEYD3 signal series, which is based on average earnings and standard confidence intervals. Lastly, Panel (d) shows the BSEYD4 signal series which is based on average earnings and Cantelli's inequality.

Figure 4.4 presents the signal time series related to the BSEYD measure based on corporate yields with a Aaa rating. Panel (a) shows the BSEYD5 signal series, which is based on current earnings and standard confidence intervals. Panel (b) shows the BSEYD6 signal series, which is based on current earnings and Cantelli's inequality. Panel (c) shows the BSEYD7 signal series, which is based on average earnings and standard confidence intervals. Lastly, Panel (d) shows the BSEYD8 signal series, which is based on average earnings and Cantelli's inequality.

Figure 4.5 presents the signal time series related to the BSEYD measure based on the yield of Baa-rated corporate bonds. Panel (a) shows the BSEYD9 signal series, which is based on current earnings and standard confidence intervals. Panel (b) shows the BSEYD10 signal series, which is based on current earnings and Cantelli's inequality. Panel (c) shows the BSEYD11 signal series, which is based on average earnings and standard confidence intervals. Lastly, Panel (d) shows the BSEYD12 signal series, which is based on average earnings and Cantelli's inequality.

Figure 4.6 presents the signal time series related to the logBSEYD models calculated using Treasury yields. Panel (a) shows the logBSEYD1 signal series, which is based on current earnings and standard confidence intervals. Panel (b) shows the logBSEYD2 signal series, which is based on current earnings and Cantelli's inequality. Panel (c) shows the logBSEYD3 signal series, which is based on average earnings and standard confidence intervals. Lastly, Panel (d) shows the logBSEYD4 signal series, which is based on average earnings and Cantelli's inequality.

Figure 4.7 presents the signal time series related to the logBSEYD models computed using the yields of Aaa-rated corporate bond. Panel (a) shows the logBSEYD5 signal series, which is based on current earnings and standard confidence intervals. Panel (b) shows the logBSEYD6 signal series, which is based on current earnings and Cantelli's inequality. Panel (c) shows the logBSEYD7 signal series, which is based on average earnings and standard confidence intervals. Lastly, Panel (d) shows the logBSEYD8 signal series, which is based on average earnings and Cantelli's inequality.

Figure 4.8 presents the signal time series related to the logBSEYD models computed with Baa corporate yields. Panel (a) shows the logBSEYD9 signal series, which is based on current earnings and standard confidence intervals. Panel (b) shows the logBSEYD10 signal series, which is based on current earnings and Cantelli's inequality. Panel (c) shows the logBSEYD11 signal series, which is based on average earnings and standard confidence intervals. Lastly, Panel (d) shows the logBSEYD12 signal series, which is based on average earnings and Cantelli's inequality.

The time series for all 32 signal models lead to similar conclusions: the signals are very noisy, exhibiting sharp, asymmetric changes. The positive signals, that is, when $\text{SIGNAL}(t) > 0$, indicate that a crash may occur. Signals based on the P/E and BSEYD measures are more visible than those based on the logP/E and logBSEYD measures. Similarly, the signal models based on current earnings generate more and clearer positive signals than those based on average earnings over 10 years.

The length and behavior of the data series make it difficult to calculate the relationship between signals and crashes. As a preliminary step to computing summary statistics of the joint behavior of signals and crashes, we construct the crash indicator sequence C_H and an indicator sequence of distinct signals S. We express both sequences as vectors with upto 12,815 entries, one for each date, depending on the period covered by the model. The entry C_t is "1" if a crash is identified on date t, and 0 otherwise while

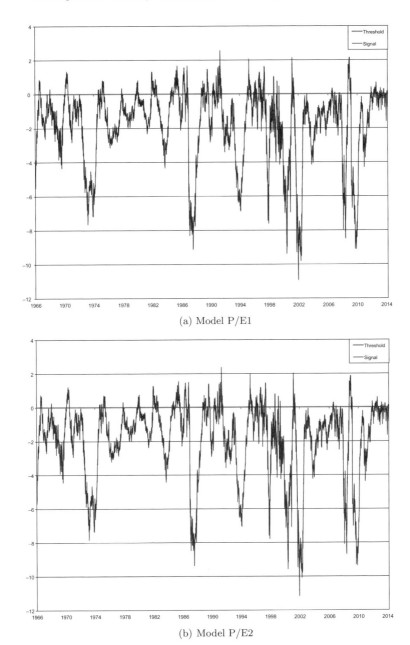

(a) Model P/E1

(b) Model P/E2

Fig. 4.1. Signal for Models P/E. This figure presents the signal time series related to the P/E measure. The jagged line is the signal at time t, SIGNAL(t). The horizontal line at 0 is the threshold for the signal: a crash signal occurs whenever the signal series crosses the threshold, meaning SIGNAL(t) > 0.

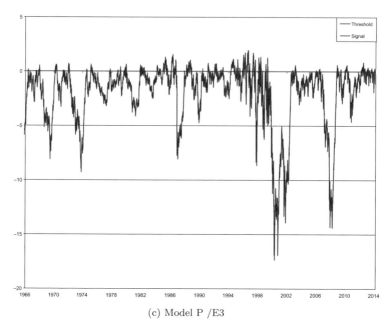

(c) Model P /E3

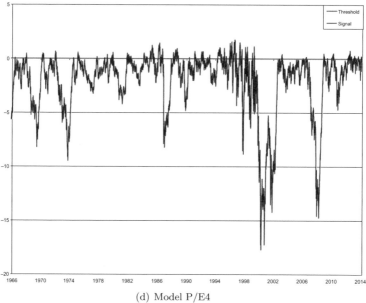

(d) Model P/E4

Fig. 4.1.   (*Continued*)

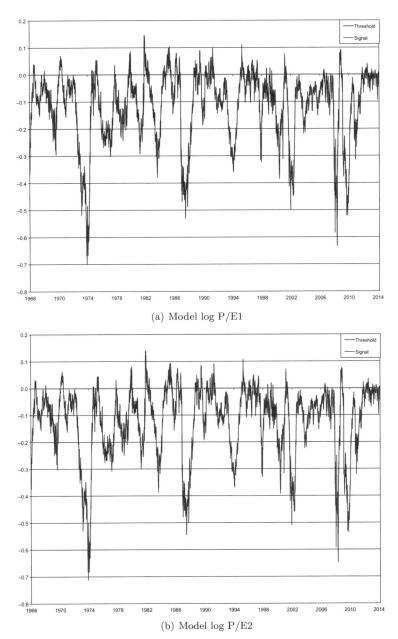

(a) Model log P/E1

(b) Model log P/E2

Fig. 4.2.   Signal for Models logP/E. The figure presents the signal time series related to the logP/E measure. The jagged line is the signal at time t, SIGNAL(t). The horizontal line at 0 is the threshold for the signal: a crash signal occurs whenever the signal series crosses the threshold, meaning SIGNAL(t) > 0.

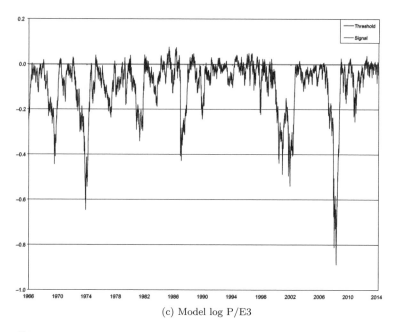

(c) Model log P/E3

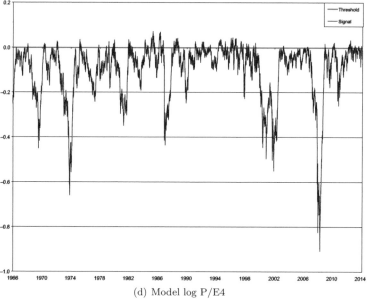

(d) Model log P/E4

Fig. 4.2.   (*Continued*)

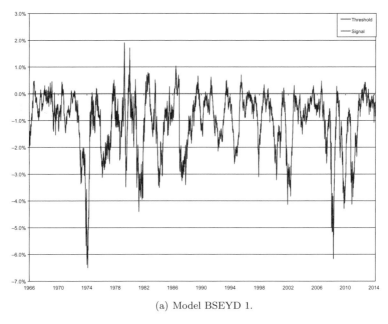

(a) Model BSEYD 1.

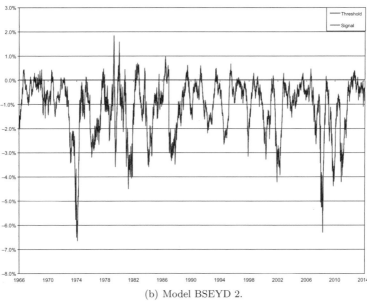

(b) Model BSEYD 2.

Fig. 4.3. Signal for Models BSEYD computed using the yield on Treasury notes. The figure shows the signal time series related to the BSEYD measure. The jagged line is the signal at time t, SIGNAL(t). The horizontal line at 0 is the threshold for the signal: a crash signal occurs whenever the signal series crosses the threshold, meaning SIGNAL(t) > 0.

Stock Market Crashes

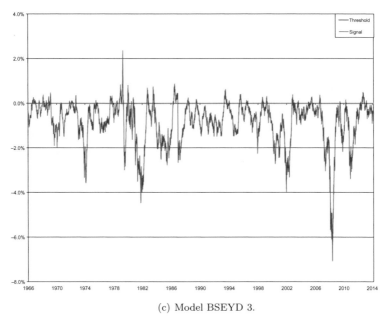

(c) Model BSEYD 3.

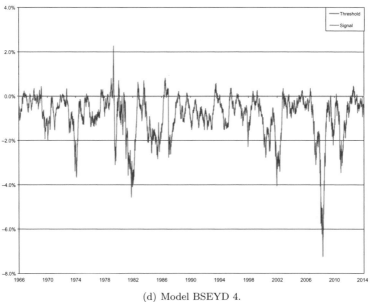

(d) Model BSEYD 4.

Fig. 4.3.   (*Continued*)

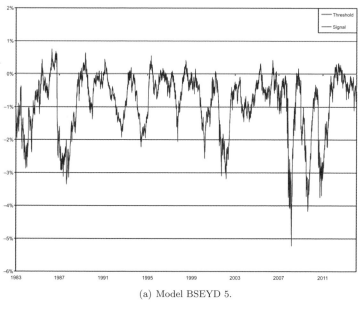

(a) Model BSEYD 5.

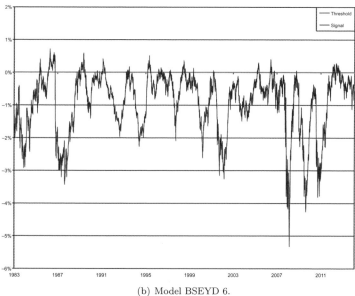

(b) Model BSEYD 6.

Fig. 4.4.   Signal for Models BSEYD computed using Aaa corporate bond yields. The figure shows the signal time series related to the BSEYD measure. The jagged line is the signal at time t, SIGNAL(t). The horizontal line at 0 is the threshold for the signal: a crash signal occurs whenever the signal series crosses the threshold, meaning SIGNAL(t) > 0.

Stock Market Crashes

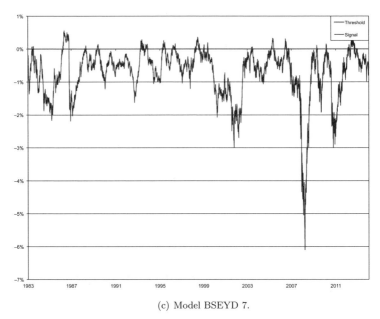

(c) Model BSEYD 7.

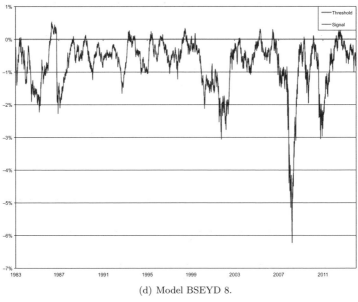

(d) Model BSEYD 8.

Fig. 4.4. (*Continued*)

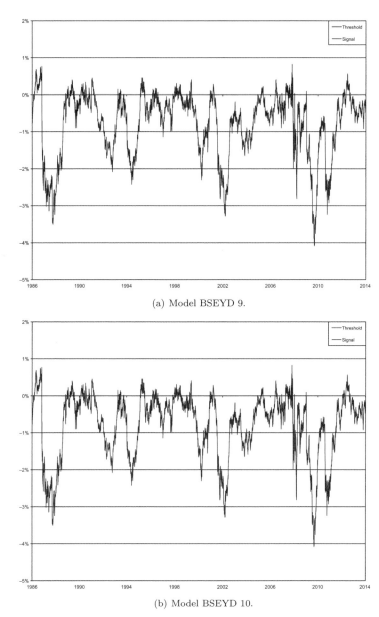

(a) Model BSEYD 9.

(b) Model BSEYD 10.

Fig. 4.5. Signal for Models BSEYD computed using Baa corporate bond yields. The figure shows the signal time series related to the BSEYD measure. The jagged line is the signal at time t, SIGNAL(t). The horizontal line at 0 is the threshold for the signal: a crash signal occurs whenever the signal series crosses the threshold, meaning SIGNAL(t) > 0.

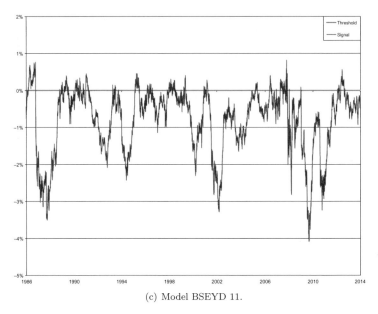

(c) Model BSEYD 11.

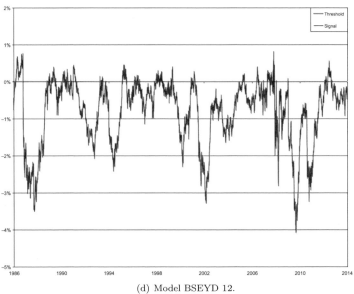

(d) Model BSEYD 12.

Fig. 4.5.   (*Continued*)

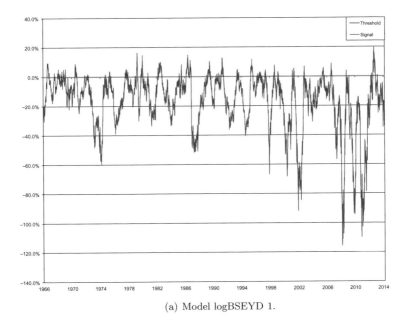

(a) Model logBSEYD 1.

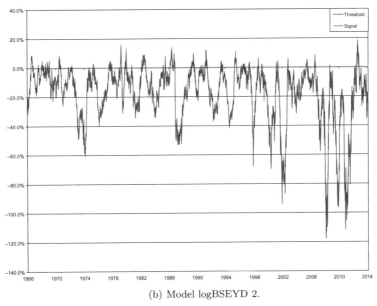

(b) Model logBSEYD 2.

Fig. 4.6. Signal for Models logBSEYD computed using the yield on Treasury notes. The figure shows the signal time series related to the logBSEYD measure. The jagged line is the signal at time t, SIGNAL(t). The horizontal line at 0 is the threshold for the signal: a crash signal occurs whenever the signal series crosses the threshold, meaning SIGNAL(t) > 0.

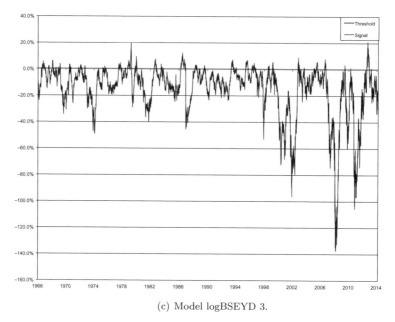

(c) Model logBSEYD 3.

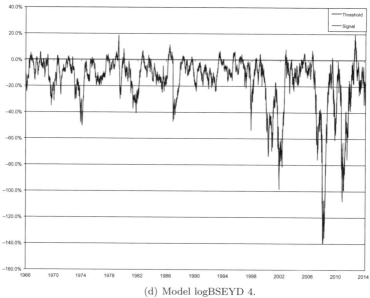

(d) Model logBSEYD 4.

Fig. 4.6. (*Continued*)

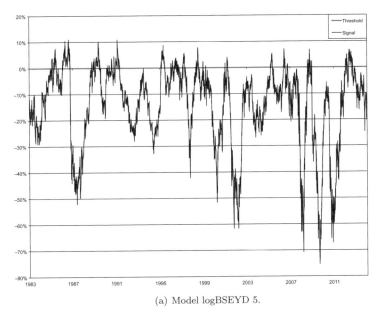

(a) Model logBSEYD 5.

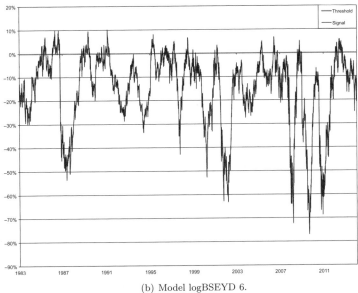

(b) Model logBSEYD 6.

Fig. 4.7.   Signal for Models logBSEYD computed using Aaa corporate bond yields. The figure shows the signal time series related to the logBSEYD measure. The jagged line is the signal at time t, SIGNAL(t). The horizontal line at 0 is the threshold for the signal: a crash signal occurs whenever the signal series crosses the threshold, meaning SIGNAL(t) > 0.

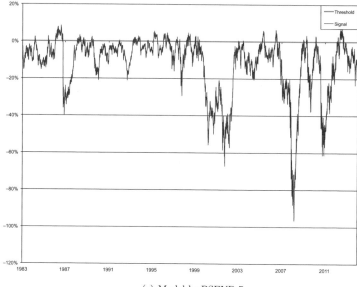

(c) Model logBSEYD 7.

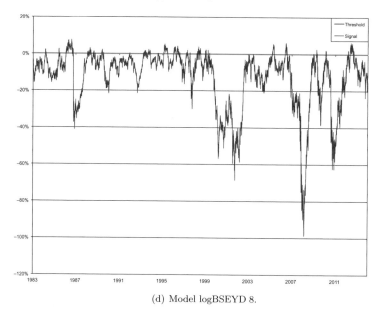

(d) Model logBSEYD 8.

Fig. 4.7.   (*Continued*)

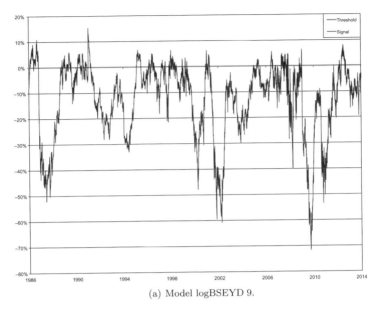

(a) Model logBSEYD 9.

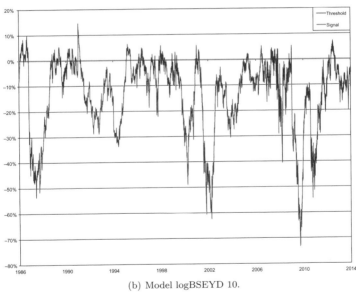

(b) Model logBSEYD 10.

Fig. 4.8. Signal for Models logBSEYD computed using Baa corporate bond yields. The figure shows the signal time series related to the logBSEYD measure. The jagged line is the signal at time t, SIGNAL(t). The horizontal line at 0 is the threshold for the signal: a crash signal occurs whenever the signal series crosses the threshold, meaning SIGNAL(t) > 0.

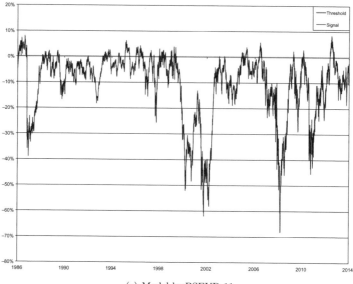

(c) Model logBSEYD 11.

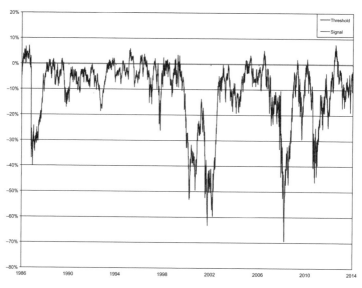

(d) Model logBSEYD 12.

Fig. 4.8.   (*Continued*)

the entry S_t is "1" if date t corresponds to the start date of a new and distinct signal, and 0 otherwise.

Now we compute the total number of *distinct* signals N as

$$N = \sum_{t=1}^{T} S_t = \mathbf{1}'s.$$

Table 4.4, Column 2, shows that over the full period (1964–2014), the total number of signals ranges from 36 for the P/E2 and logP/E2 model to 55 for the P/E3 model. P/E and logP/E models using average earnings (P/E3, P/E4, logP/E3 and logP/E4) generate between 20% and 50% more signals than models based on current earnings (P/E1, P/E2, logP/E1 and logP/E2). On the other hand, BSEYD and logBSEYD models based on current earnings generate slightly more signals than models using average earnings. Over the shorter period 1983–2014, models BSEYD5–8 generated between 18 and 24 signals while the models logBSEYD5–8 yielded between 20 and 27 signals. Finally, models BSEYD9–12 generated between 16 and 23 signals while the models logBSEYD9–12 produced between 21 and 22 signals over the shortest period 1986–2014.

The total number of distinct signals tells only a small part of the story. In particular, it does not directly measure the accuracy of the crash prediction models. As a first measure of accuracy, we compute the number of correct predictions n, which is defined as a tally of the crashes identified no more than $H = 504$ days after a positive signal:

$$n = \sum_{t=1}^{T} C_{t,H} = \mathbf{1}'c_H$$

We will later use it to compute a percentage of correct predictions. For models computed over the full period (1964–2014), Table 4.4, Column 3, shows that the number of correct predictions reaches a high of 37 for the P/E3 and a low of 24 for the P/E2 model. This statistic allows multiples signals for the same crash. The BSEYD and P/E models based on current earnings generated between 24 and 29 correct predictions, while the P/E models based on average earnings generated between 35 and 37 correct predictions, albeit out of a much larger number of signals. BSEYD and logBSEYD calculated with Treasury yields are consistent, with respective averages of 29 and 32.25 successful predictions. Over the shorter period (1983–2014), the BSEYD models based on Aaa corporate yields produced between 12 and 15 correct predictions while the logBSEYD models generated between 13 and 17 correct predictions. The BSEYD models based on

Table 4.4.   Proportion of correct and incorrect predictions for each signal model.

Signal Model (1)	Total number of signals (2)	Number of correct predictions (3)	Proportion of correct predictions (%) (4)	Number of incorrect predictions (5)	Proportion of incorrect predictions (%) (6)
PE1	37	25	67.57%	12	32.43%
PE2	36	24	66.67%	12	33.33%
PE3	55	37	67.27%	18	32.73%
PE4	49	35	71.43%	14	28.57%
lnPE1	37	25	67.57%	12	32.43%
lnPE2	36	25	69.44%	11	30.56%
lnPE3	50	34	68.00%	16	32.00%
lnPE4	44	31	70.45%	13	29.55%
BSEYD1	38	29	76.32%	9	23.68%
BSEYD2	39	28	71.79%	11	28.21%
BSEYD3	40	30	75.00%	10	25.00%
BSEYD4	39	29	74.36%	10	25.64%
BSEYD5	24	15	62.50%	9	37.50%
BSEYD6	22	14	63.64%	8	36.36%
BSEYD7	18	12	66.67%	6	33.33%
BSEYD8	19	12	63.16%	7	36.84%
BSEYD9	23	14	60.87%	9	39.13%
BSEYD10	19	11	57.89%	8	42.11%
BSEYD11	16	12	75.00%	4	25.00%
BSEYD12	16	11	68.75%	5	31.25%
lnBSEYD1	47	34	72.34%	13	27.66%
lnBSEYD2	44	33	75.00%	11	25.00%
lnBSEYD3	42	32	76.19%	10	23.81%
lnBSEYD4	39	30	76.92%	9	23.08%
lnBSEYD5	20	13	65.00%	7	35.00%
lnBSEYD6	21	14	66.67%	7	33.33%
lnBSEYD7	27	17	62.96%	10	37.04%
lnBSEYD8	26	17	65.38%	9	34.62%
lnBSEYD9	22	15	68.18%	7	31.82%
lnBSEYD10	22	14	63.64%	8	36.36%
lnBSEYD11	22	15	68.18%	7	31.82%
lnBSEYD12	21	16	76.19%	5	23.81%

Baa corporate yields produced between 11 and 14 correct predictions while the logBSEYD models produced between 14 and 16 correct predictions over the period 1986–2014.

Combining the total number of distinct signals and the number of correct predictions gives us a second measure of accuracy: the proportion of correct predictions, defined as the ratio $\frac{n}{N}$. This measure enables us to compare the accuracy of the various models directly. It also gives us an estimate of $p = P(C_{t,H} = 1|S_t = 1)$, the probability of correctly predicting a crash. Table 4.4, Column 4, shows that the BSEYD and logBSEYD models based on Treasury yields are consistently more than 70% accurate over the entire period 1964–2014. With the exception of P/E4 and logP/E4, the P/E and logP/E measures are between 65% and 70% accurate. The BSEYD and logBSEYD measures based on Aaa corporate bonds are between 62.50% and 66.67% accurate, while the BSEYD and logBSEYD measures based on Baa corporate bonds fluctuate between 57.89% and 76.19% accuracy.

The last two columns in Table 4.4 report the number of incorrect predictions $N - n$, that is, the number of signals that were not followed by a crash, and the proportion of incorrect crashes, that is, the percentage of false positive given by the signal and computed as $\frac{N-n}{N}$.

4.3.4. *Crash prediction test*

Although the proportion of correct signals computed in Table 4.4 is generally high, the central question is whether it is significantly different from the accuracy p_0 of an uninformed signal. We construct this uniformed signal by picking a day at random between January 31, 1964 and December 31, 2014 and checking whether a crash is identified within 252 days. This is the same rule used to compute the accuracy of our other measures: P/E, logP/E, BSEYD and logBSEYD. The probability p_0 is therefore the probability that a crash will be identified within 252 days of a randomly selected day. To compute p_0 empirically, we tally the number of days that are at most 252 days before a crash identification date and divide by the total number of days in the sample. For the entire period January 31, 1964 to December 31, 2014, we find that $p_0 = 39.85\%$. We can confirm this number heuristically. Given that 22 distinct crashes occurred, then at most $252 \times 22 = 5,544$ days in our sample fall within 252 days prior to a crash identification date. Because there are 12,815 days in the dataset, the heuristic probability is $\frac{5,544}{12,815} = 43.26\%$, just slightly higher than the empirical probability. The difference between the heuristic and empirical probability is due to the fact that in reality, equity market corrections are not spread evenly through the period. In fact, corrections might occur in quick succession, as was the case in the late 1990s when three crashes occurred within less than two years.

Table 4.5 reports the uninformed probability p_0 for all five periods considered in our study: the full period; Subperiod 1 from January 31, 1964 to December 31, 1981; Subperiod 2 from January 4, 1982 to December

Table 4.5.   Empirical probability p_0.

	Full dataset: Jan. 31, 1964–Dec. 31, 2014	Subperiod 1: Jan. 31, 1964–Dec 31, 1981	Subperiod 2: Jan. 4, 1982–Dec 31st, 2014	Aaa dataset: Jan. 3, 1983–Dec 31, 2014	Baa dataset: Jan. 2, 1986–Dec 31, 2014
Number of days in the period	12,815	4,484	8,320	8,067	7,308
Number of days less 252 days prior to a crash identification date	5,107	2,613	2,494	2,494	2,242
Empirical probability p_0	39.85%	58.27%	29.98%	30.92%	30.68%

31st, 2014, the period from January 3, 1983 to December 31, 2014 used for Aaa bonds; and the period January 2, 1986 to December 31, 2014 for Baa bonds. The empirical uninformed probability p_0 fluctuates from a high of 58.27% over the first subperiod to a low of 29.98% over the second subperiod. The empirical probabilities over subperiod 2, the Aaa dataset and the Baa dataset are within a narrow 30–31% range.

Because the empirical proportion of correct signals computed in Table 4.4 corresponds to the maximum likelihood estimate $\hat{p}$ of signal accuracy, we can evaluate its significance using a likelihood ratio test applied to the test statistics

$$-2\ln\Lambda = -2\ln\frac{L(p=p_0|X)}{L(p=\hat{p}|X)},$$

where p_0 is the empirical probability reported in Table 4.5.

Table 4.6 shows the maximum likelihood estimate of the signal $\hat{p}$ in Column 4, the likelihood for $\hat{p}$ in Column 5, followed by the likelihood ratio Λ in Column 6, the estimated test statistics $-2\ln\Lambda$ in Column 7 and the p-value. The estimated test statistic is asymptotically χ^2-distributed with 1 degree of freedom. The degree of significance and the p-value indicated in Table 4.6 are based on this distribution. The critical values at the 95%, 99% and 99.5% confidence level are respectively 3.84, 6.63 and 7.87. We find that all the measures except BSEYD10 are significant at a 99.5% level. BSEYD10, a measure computed using Baa corporate bonds, current earnings and Cantelli's inequality is significant at a 95% level and has a p-value of 1.44%.

Table 4.6. Maximum likelihood estimate and likelihood ratio test: uninformed prior.

Signal Model	Total number of signals	Number of correct predictions	ML Estimate $\hat{p}$	$L(\hat{p})$	Likelihood ratio Λ	Test statistics $-2\ln\Lambda$	p-value
PE1	37	25	67.57%	7.50E-11	0.0031	11.5744***	0.07%
PE2	36	24	66.67%	1.12E-10	0.0052	10.5318***	0.12%
PE3	55	37	67.27%	7.91E-16	0.0002	16.8358***	0.00%
PE4	49	35	71.43%	1.86E-13	0.0000	20.0039***	0.00%
lnPE1	37	25	67.57%	7.50E-11	0.0031	11.5744***	0.07%
lnPE2	36	25	69.44%	2.38E-10	0.0016	12.8682***	0.03%
lnPE3	50	34	68.00%	2.44E-14	0.0003	16.1408***	0.01%
lnPE4	44	31	70.45%	2.52E-12	0.0002	16.8448***	0.00%
BSEYD1	38	29	76.32%	9.25E-10	0.0000	20.9073***	0.00%
BSEYD2	39	28	71.79%	8.40E-11	0.0003	16.3034***	0.01%
BSEYD3	40	30	75.00%	1.70E-10	0.0000	20.3806***	0.00%
BSEYD4	39	29	74.36%	2.28E-10	0.0001	19.1244***	0.00%
BSEYD5	24	15	62.50%	1.27E-07	0.0063	10.1190***	0.15%
BSEYD6	22	14	63.64%	5.46E-07	0.0069	9.9454***	0.16%
BSEYD7	18	12	66.67%	1.06E-05	0.0078	9.6971***	0.18%
BSEYD8	19	12	63.16%	3.71E-06	0.0154	8.3431***	0.39%
BSEYD9	23	14	60.87%	2.06E-07	0.0117	8.8913***	0.29%
BSEYD10	19	11	57.89%	2.42E-06	0.0499	5.9940*	1.44%
BSEYD11	16	12	75.00%	1.24E-04	0.0013	13.2951***	0.03%
BSEYD12	16	11	68.75%	4.83E-05	0.0075	9.7846***	0.18%
lnBSEYD1	47	34	72.34%	9.18E-13	0.0000	20.3449***	0.00%
lnBSEYD2	44	33	75.00%	1.80E-11	0.0000	22.4187***	0.00%
lnBSEYD3	42	32	76.19%	9.73E-11	0.0000	22.9420***	0.00%
lnBSEYD4	39	30	76.92%	7.08E-10	0.0000	22.2148***	0.00%
lnBSEYD5	20	13	65.00%	2.38E-06	0.0074	9.8012***	0.17%
lnBSEYD6	21	14	66.67%	1.57E-06	0.0035	11.3133***	0.08%
lnBSEYD7	27	17	62.96%	1.87E-08	0.0029	11.7151***	0.06%
lnBSEYD8	26	17	65.38%	5.21E-08	0.0015	13.0279***	0.03%
lnBSEYD9	22	15	68.18%	1.06E-06	0.0015	13.0563***	0.03%
lnBSEYD10	22	14	63.64%	5.46E-07	0.0064	10.1063***	0.15%
lnBSEYD11	22	15	68.18%	1.06E-06	0.0015	13.0563***	0.03%
lnBSEYD12	21	16	76.19%	9.87E-06	0.0001	18.4227***	0.00%

Notes: *significant at the 5% level;
**significant at the 1% level;
***significant at the 0.5% level.

In addition to testing the measures against an uninformed signal with prediction probability p_0, we also test the measures to see whether they generate an accurate prediction more than half the time. To this end, we perform a likelihood ratio test against the arbitrary probability $p = \frac{1}{2}$ using the test statistics

$$-2\ln\Lambda = -2\ln\frac{L(p=\frac{1}{2}|X)}{L(p=\hat{p}|X)}.$$

Table 4.7 has the same structure as Table 4.6: the maximum likelihood estimate of the signal $\hat{p}$ is reported in Column 4, the likelihood for $\hat{p}$ is in

Table 4.7. Maximum likelihood estimate and likelihood ratio test: arbitrary 50% threshold.

Signal Model	Total number of signals	Number of correct predictions	ML Estimate $\hat{p}$	$L(\hat{p})$	Likelihood ratio Λ	Test statistics $-2\ln\Lambda$	p-value
PE1	37	25	67.57%	7.50E-11	0.0970	4.6665*	3.08%
PE2	36	24	66.67%	1.12E-10	0.1302	4.0776*	4.35%
PE3	55	37	67.27%	7.91E-16	0.0351	6.7008**	0.96%
PE4	49	35	71.43%	1.86E-13	0.0096	9.2980***	0.23%
lnPE1	37	25	67.57%	7.50E-11	0.0970	4.6665*	3.08%
lnPE2	36	25	69.44%	2.38E-10	0.0611	5.5907*	1.81%
lnPE3	50	34	68.00%	2.44E-14	0.0364	6.6278**	1.00%
lnPE4	44	31	70.45%	2.52E-12	0.0225	7.5842**	0.59%
BSEYD1	38	29	76.32%	9.25E-10	0.0039	11.0758***	0.09%
BSEYD2	39	28	71.79%	8.40E-11	0.0217	7.6648**	0.56%
BSEYD3	40	30	75.00%	1.70E-10	0.0053	10.4650***	0.12%
BSEYD4	39	29	74.36%	2.28E-10	0.0080	9.6625***	0.19%
BSEYD5	24	15	62.50%	1.27E-07	0.4686	1.5160	21.82%
BSEYD6	22	14	63.64%	5.46E-07	0.4366	1.6573	19.80%
BSEYD7	18	12	66.67%	1.06E-05	0.3608	2.0388	15.33%
BSEYD8	19	12	63.16%	3.71E-06	0.5139	1.3314	24.86%
BSEYD9	23	14	60.87%	2.06E-07	0.5782	1.0957	29.52%
BSEYD10	19	11	57.89%	2.42E-06	0.7883	0.4757	49.04%
BSEYD11	16	12	75.00%	1.24E-04	0.1233	4.1860*	4.08%
BSEYD12	16	11	68.75%	4.83E-05	0.3157	2.3059	12.89%
lnBSEYD1	47	34	72.34%	9.18E-13	0.0077	9.7232***	0.18%
lnBSEYD2	44	33	75.00%	1.80E-11	0.0032	11.5115***	0.07%
lnBSEYD3	42	32	76.19%	9.73E-11	0.0023	12.1189***	0.05%
lnBSEYD4	39	30	76.92%	7.08E-10	0.0026	11.9296***	0.06%
lnBSEYD5	20	13	65.00%	2.38E-06	0.4009	1.8280	17.64%
lnBSEYD6	21	14	66.67%	1.57E-06	0.3044	2.3786	12.30%
lnBSEYD7	27	17	62.96%	1.87E-08	0.3994	1.8357	17.55%
lnBSEYD8	26	17	65.38%	5.21E-08	0.2862	2.5019	11.37%
lnBSEYD9	22	15	68.18%	1.06E-06	0.2257	2.9769	8.45%
lnBSEYD10	22	14	63.64%	5.46E-07	0.4366	1.6573	19.80%
lnBSEYD11	22	15	68.18%	1.06E-06	0.2257	2.9769	8.45%
lnBSEYD12	21	16	76.19%	9.87E-06	0.0483	6.0595*	1.38%

Notes: *significant at the 5% level;
**significant at the 1% level;
***significant at the 0.5% level.

Column 5, followed by the likelihood ratio Λ in Column 6, the estimated test statistics $-2\ln\Lambda$ in Column 7 and the p-value. The estimated test statistic is asymptotically χ^2-distributed with 1 degree of freedom and the critical values at the 95%, 99% and 99.5% confidence level are respectively 3.84, 6.63 and 7.87.

The accuracy of the P/E and logP/E measures is not particularly consistent, although all the measures are significantly different from $p_0 = \frac{1}{2}$ at least at a 95% confidence level. On the other hand, seven out of eight BSEYD and logBSEYD measures computed with the yield of Treasury Notes over the full period are significant at a 99.5% confidence level. BSEYD3 misses the 99.5% mark by a narrow margin: it is in fact significant at a 99.44% level. With the exception of BSEYD11 and logBSEYD11, the BSEYD models computed using Aaa and Baa bond yields are not significant. A possible explanation for the low significance is the shorter data history. The data robustness analysis in Section 4.4 partly resolves this issue and permits a more objective comparison across all models.

4.3.5. *Monte Carlo study for small sample bias*

In addition to performing the likelihood ratio test using the χ^2 distribution, we carry out a likelihood ratio test based on empirical distributions obtained through Monte Carlo simulations. Table 4.8 reports the total number of signals, calculated as the sum of all the entries of the indicator sequence S and the maximum likelihood estimate, $\hat{p}$, which is the probability of correctly predicting a crash and is estimated by maximizing the likelihood function of the model. These statistics are identical to those reported in Table 4.9.

Columns 4–6 in Table 4.8 present the critical values at a 95%, 99% and 99.5% confidence level for the empirical distribution generated using $K = 10{,}000$ Monte Carlo simulations. These values are not uniform across all models as they depend directly on the total number of signals generated by each model. Column 7 and 8 report, respectively, the test statistics equal to $-2\ln\Lambda = -2\ln\frac{L(p=p_0|X)}{L(p=\hat{p}|X)}$ and $-2\ln\Lambda = -2\ln\frac{L(p=\frac{1}{2}|X)}{L(p=\hat{p}|X)}$. The level of significance indicated is based on the empirical distribution. Column 8 and 10 report the p-value, defined as the probability of obtaining a test statistic higher than that actually observed assuming that the null hypothesis is true, for each of the models under its empirical distribution.

The Monte Carlo study confirms our observations regarding the likelihood ratio test using the χ^2 distribution. All the measures but one (BSEYD10) are significant at 99.5% level when assessed against the

Table 4.8. Monte Carlo likelihood ratio test.

Signal model	Total number of signals	ML Estimate $\hat{p}$	Critical Value: 95% confidence	Critical Value: 99% confidence	Critical Value: 99.5% confidence	Test statistics $-2\ln\Lambda(p_0)$	Empirical p-value	Test statistics $-2\ln\Lambda(1/2)$	Empirical p-value
PE1	37	67.57%	3.9737	7.4726	7.4882	11.5744***	0.13%	4.6665*	4.88%
PE2	36	66.67%	3.6064	6.8973	8.4455	10.5318***	0.11%	4.0776†	7.07%
PE3	55	67.27%	3.8139	6.4684	8.0932	16.8358***	0.00%	6.7008*	1.31%
PE4	49	71.43%	3.8255	6.6871	7.4286	20.0039***	0.00%	9.2980***	0.32%
lnPE1	37	67.57%	3.9737	7.4726	7.4882	11.5744***	0.07%	4.6665†	5.21%
lnPE2	36	69.44%	3.6064	6.6033	8.4455	12.8682***	0.00%	5.5907*	2.87%
lnPE3	50	68.00%	4.0703	6.6821	7.2064	16.1408***	0.00%	6.6278*	1.43%
lnPE4	44	70.45%	3.8617	6.6068	8.2601	16.8448***	0.00%	7.5842*	1.09%
BSEYD1	38	76.32%	33.6670	6.5886	8.0916	20.9073***	0.00%	11.0758***	0.16%
BSEYD2	39	71.79%	3.5249	6.6587	8.7070	16.3034***	0.00%	7.6648***	0.94%
BSEYD3	40	75.00%	3.9147	7.2228	8.3259	20.3806***	0.00%	10.4650***	0.00%
BSEYD4	39	74.36%	4.3417	6.6587	7.4412	19.1244***	0.00%	9.6625***	0.42%
BSEYD5	24	62.50%	4.4920	7.2008	7.6647	10.1190***	0.24%	1.5160	31.56%
BSEYD6	22	63.64%	3.5721	6.0855	9.7455	9.9454***	0.22%	1.6573	28.62%
BSEYD7	18	66.67%	3.9728	7.1985	7.1985	9.6971***	0.27%	2.0388	24.03%
BSEYD8	19	63.16%	4.4836	7.8270	7.8270	8.3431***	0.45%	1.3314	36.01%
BSEYD9	23	60.87%	3.9346	6.5576	8.8913	8.8913**	0.53%	1.0957	40.72%
BSEYD10	19	57.89%	4.3978	7.7190	7.7190	5.9940*	2.27%	0.4757	65.05%

BSEYD11	16	75.00%	4.4686	6.8590	9.7846	13.2951***	0.00%	4.1860†	7.47%
BSEYD12	16	68.75%	4.4686	6.8590	6.8590	9.7846***	0.44%	2.3059	21.26%
lnBSEYD1	47	72.34%	3.4037	7.3643	7.4161	20.3449***	0.00%	9.7232***	0.38%
lnBSEYD2	44	75.00%	3.8617	6.6068	8.2601	22.4187***	0.00%	11.5115***	0.12%
lnBSEYD3	42	76.19%	3.7950	6.5932	8.2873	22.9420***	0.00%	12.1189***	0.08%
lnBSEYD4	39	76.92%	3.4819	6.6587	7.4412	22.2148***	0.00%	11.9296***	0.00%
lnBSEYD5	20	65.00%	4.9574	7.1706	8.4614	9.8012***	0.18%	1.8280	26.80%
lnBSEYD6	21	66.67%	4.1581	6.1486	9.1011	11.3133***	0.14%	2.3786	18.67%
lnBSEYD7	27	62.96%	3.7521	6.9972	8.9292	11.7151***	0.13%	1.8357	24.40%
lnBSEYD8	26	65.38%	4.0936	5.8557	8.3464	13.0279***	0.04%	2.5019	16.65%
lnBSEYD9	22	68.18%	3.5580	5.9791	7.5500	13.0563***	0.00%	2.9769	13.70%
lnBSEYD10	22	63.64%	4.7166	6.9162	6.9162	10.1063***	0.07%	1.6573	28.62%
lnBSEYD11	22	68.18%	3.5580	5.9791	7.5500	13.0563***	0.00%	2.9769	13.57%
lnBSEYD12	21	76.19%	4.2590	6.2718	8.9793	18.4227***	0.00%	6.0595*	2.46%

Notes: † significant at the 10% level;
* significant at the 5% level;
** significant at the 1% level;
*** significant at the 0.5% level.

uninformed probability p_0. The significance of the measures varies more when we use the arbitrary probability $p = \frac{1}{2}$. The BSEYD and logBSEYD measures computed with Treasury yields on the full dataset perform best: they are all significant at a 99.5% level. The significance of the P/E and log P/E measures vary from 90% for P/E2 and logP/E1 to 99.5% for P/E4. With the exception of BSEYD11 and logBSEYD12, the BSEYD and logBSEYD measures based on a shorter timescale are not significant.

4.3.6. *Measure-on-measure significance test*

Next, we compare the accuracy of the two measures using a pair-wise measure-on-measure test. Table 4.9 reports the test statistics $-2\ln\frac{L(p=\hat{p}_j|X)}{L(p=\hat{p}_i|X)}, i = 1, \ldots 32, j = 1, \ldots, 32, j \neq i$ for all 992 pairs of models. Table 4.10 is a heat map of the measure-on-measure significance test, based on the $p - value$. A darker background indicates a lower p-value, while a white background is indicative of a p-value above 20%.

We find that the measures based on corporate yields and shorter timescale, in particular BSEYD5, BSEYD6, BSEYD8, BSEYD9 and BSEYD10, are significantly less accurate than the other measures. However, this is possibly a reflection of the short timescale used to estimate these measures. On the other hand, the accuracy of those measures estimated using the full dataset, is not significantly different, even with 22 crashes and nearly 51 years of data.

4.4. Robustness

Data Robustness

We test the robustness of the crash prediction models with respect to a change in the underlying data over two subperiods:

(1) *Subperiod 1*: January 31, 1964 to December 31, 1981;
(2) *Subperiod 2*: January 1, 1982 to December 31, 2014.

Small sample bias is an important consideration here because of the limited amount of crash-related data available for each subperiod. For Subperiod 1, we have access to all statistics for the P/E and logP/E models as well as the BSEYD and logBSEYD models calculated using Treasury yields. For Subperiod 2, we have statistics for all 32 models, with a caveat: data for the BSEYD and logBSEYD models based on corporate yields start on January 1, 1983.

Table 4.9.   Test statistics for the measure-on-measure test. The table reports the test statistics $-2\ln\frac{L(p=\hat{p}_j|X)}{L(p=\hat{p}_i|X)}$ for all 992 pairs of models.

	Signals	Correct	p	L(p)	p	PE 1	PE 2	PE 3	PE 4	lnPE 1	lnPE 2	lnPE 3	lnPE 4	BSEYD 1	BSEYD 2	BSEYD 3	BSEYD 4	BSEYD 5	BSEYD 6	BSEYD 7	BSEYD 8
						67.57%	66.67%	67.27%	71.43%	67.57%	69.44%	68.00%	70.45%	76.32%	71.79%	75.00%	74.36%	62.50%	63.64%	66.67%	63.16%
PE 1	37	25	67.57%	7.50E-11	67.57%	0.0000	0.0136	0.0136	0.0015	0.2635	0.0607	0.0032	0.1455	1.4568	0.3175	1.0288	0.8504	0.4137	0.2513	0.0136	0.3149
PE 2	36	24	66.67%	1.12E-10	66.67%	0.0133	0.0000	0.0000	0.3880	0.0133	0.1288	0.0292	0.2425	1.7136	0.4521	1.2508	1.0552	0.2711	0.1447	0.0000	0.1932
PE 3	55	37	67.27%	7.91E-16	67.27%	0.0022	0.0091	0.0060	0.4531	0.0022	0.1207	0.0133	0.2623	2.3092	0.5391	1.6497	1.3735	0.5448	0.3192	0.0091	0.4071
PE 4	49	35	71.43%	1.86E-13	71.43%	0.3408	0.5133	0.3936	0.0000	0.3408	0.0921	0.2701	0.0225	0.6200	0.0032	0.3236	0.2155	1.7331	1.3334	0.5133	1.4957
lnPE 1	37	25	67.57%	7.50E-11	67.57%	0.2635	0.0585	0.0585	0.0780	0.0000	0.0348	0.0000	0.0175	1.4568	0.3175	1.0288	0.8504	0.4137	0.2513	0.0136	0.3149
lnPE 2	36	25	69.44%	2.38E-10	69.44%	0.0585	0.1268	0.0403	0.2816	0.0585	0.0000	0.0487	0.1236	0.8866	0.0966	0.5667	0.4389	0.7625	0.5386	0.1268	0.6284
lnPE 3	50	34	68.00%	2.44E-14	68.00%	0.0043	0.0403	0.0121	0.2059	0.0043	0.0487	0.0000	0.1236	1.7844	0.3467	1.2369	1.0104	0.4193	0.2900	0.0403	0.5142
lnPE 4	44	31	70.45%	2.52E-12	70.45%	0.1701	0.2900	0.1701	0.4618	0.1701	0.1236	0.1236	0.0000	0.7946	0.0387	0.4671	0.3411	1.2290	0.9119	0.2900	1.0400
BSEYD 1	38	29	76.32%	9.25E-10	76.32%	1.4033	1.6886	1.4940	0.4618	1.4033	0.8872	1.2749	0.6547	0.0000	0.3974	0.0387	0.0776	3.3118	2.8206	1.6886	3.0230
BSEYD 2	39	28	71.79%	8.40E-11	71.79%	1.0559	1.4749	1.3717	0.0026	1.0559	0.1031	0.2640	0.0340	0.4236	0.0000	0.2080	0.1317	1.1657	0.4749	1.3133	1.3008
BSEYD 3	40	30	75.00%	1.70E-10	75.00%	1.3133	1.3133	1.1373	0.9284	1.3133	1.0559	0.9416	0.4101	0.0000	0.2079	0.0000	0.0085	2.2800	2.3643	1.3133	2.5557
BSEYD 4	39	29	74.36%	2.38E-10	74.36%	1.0863	1.0863	0.9284	0.1677	1.0863	0.6042	0.7542	0.2936	0.0378	0.1291	0.0085	0.0000	2.0442	2.0442	1.0863	2.2205
BSEYD 5	24	15	62.50%	1.27E-07	62.50%	0.2744	0.2744	0.2427	0.8889	0.2744	0.4588	0.3247	0.6974	2.2802	0.9677	1.8287	1.6305	0.0000	0.0133	0.1839	0.0045
BSEYD 6	22	14	63.64%	5.46E-07	63.64%	0.1522	0.1522	0.1298	0.6242	0.1522	0.5255	0.1883	0.4723	1.7727	0.6875	1.3946	1.2299	0.0122	0.0000	0.0896	0.0022
BSEYD 7	18	12	66.67%	1.06E-05	66.67%	0.0066	0.0066	0.0030	0.1940	0.0066	0.3388	0.0146	0.1212	0.8568	0.2261	0.6254	0.5276	0.1355	0.0723	0.0000	0.0966
BSEYD 8	19	12	63.16%	3.71E-06	63.16%	0.1650	0.1650	0.1432	0.6058	0.1650	0.0644	0.1998	0.4660	1.6439	0.6637	1.3043	1.1559	0.0035	0.0019	0.1036	0.0000
BSEYD 9	23	14	60.87%	2.06E-07	60.87%	0.3390	0.3390	0.3390	1.1819	0.3390	0.3420	0.5193	0.9629	2.7056	1.2709	2.2193	2.0039	0.0259	0.0753	0.3390	0.0513
BSEYD 10	19	11	57.89%	2.42E-06	57.89%	0.6341	0.6341	0.7286	1.5827	0.6341	0.7621	0.8516	1.3484	3.1283	1.6766	2.6458	2.4296	0.1694	0.2654	0.6341	0.2223
BSEYD 11	16	12	75.00%	1.24E-04	75.00%	0.5253	0.5253	0.4549	0.1027	0.5253	0.2417	0.3766	0.1641	0.0151	0.0832	0.0000	0.0035	1.1320	0.9457	0.5253	1.0223
BSEYD 12	16	11	68.75%	4.83E-05	68.75%	0.0316	0.0316	0.0160	0.0553	0.0316	0.0036	0.0042	0.0221	0.4752	0.0718	0.3172	0.2528	0.2736	0.1849	0.0316	0.2202
lnBSEYD 1	47	34	72.34%	9.18E-13	72.34%	1.1615	1.4447	1.2511	0.5646	1.1615	0.1893	0.4177	0.0813	0.3965	0.0069	0.1734	0.0988	1.6039	1.6039	1.4447	1.7773
lnBSEYD 2	44	33	75.00%	1.80E-11	75.00%	1.4447	1.4447	1.2511	0.2825	1.4447	0.6647	1.0358	0.4512	0.0416	0.2287	0.0000	0.0095	2.6007	2.6007	1.4447	2.8113
lnBSEYD 3	42	32	76.19%	9.73E-11	76.19%	1.5055	1.8166	1.6044	0.4840	1.5055	0.9442	1.3656	0.6923	0.0004	0.4147	0.0321	0.0751	3.5914	3.0536	1.8166	3.3252
lnBSEYD 4	39	30	76.92%	7.08E-10	76.92%	1.6548	1.9670	1.7543	0.6021	1.6548	1.0839	1.5136	0.8225	0.0080	0.5275	0.0783	0.1376	3.7192	3.1920	1.9670	3.4095
lnBSEYD 5	20	13	65.00%	2.38E-06	65.00%	0.0594	0.0248	0.0464	0.3891	0.0594	0.1816	0.0814	0.2768	1.2947	0.4367	0.9900	0.8587	0.0538	0.0162	0.0248	0.0294
lnBSEYD 7	21	14	66.67%	1.57E-06	66.67%	0.0077	0.0000	0.0035	0.2263	0.0077	0.0751	0.0170	0.1414	0.9996	0.2637	0.7296	0.6155	0.1581	0.0844	0.0000	0.1127
lnBSEYD 8	27	17	62.96%	1.87E-08	62.96%	0.2554	0.1638	0.2231	0.9011	0.2554	0.5161	0.3070	0.6975	2.4029	0.9852	1.9128	1.6983	0.0025	0.0053	0.1638	0.0004
lnBSEYD 9	26	17	65.38%	5.21E-08	65.38%	0.0559	0.0191	0.0417	0.4481	0.0559	0.1974	0.0806	0.3115	1.5747	0.5064	1.1928	1.0289	0.0933	0.0346	0.0191	0.0559
lnBSEYD 9	22	15	68.18%	1.06E-06	68.18%	0.0038	0.0229	0.0083	0.1112	0.0038	0.0164	0.0003	0.0538	0.7522	0.1384	0.5170	0.4200	0.3101	0.2003	0.0229	0.2438
lnBSEYD 10	22	14	63.64%	5.46E-07	63.64%	0.1522	0.0896	0.1298	0.6242	0.1522	0.3388	0.1883	0.4723	1.7727	0.6875	1.3946	1.2299	0.0122	0.0000	0.0896	0.0022
lnBSEYD 11	22	15	68.18%	1.06E-06	68.18%	0.0038	0.0229	0.0083	0.1112	0.0038	0.0164	0.0003	0.0538	0.7522	0.1384	0.5170	0.4200	0.3101	0.2003	0.0229	0.2438
lnBSEYD 12	21	16	76.19%	9.87E-06	76.19%	0.7527	0.9083	0.8022	0.2420	0.7527	0.4721	0.6828	0.3462	0.0002	0.2074	0.0160	0.0375	1.7957	1.5268	0.9083	1.6376

(Continued)

Table 4.9. (*Continued*)

	Signals	Correct	p	L(p)	p	BSEYD 9 60.87%	BSEYD 10 57.89%	BSEYD 11 75.00%	BSEYD 12 68.75%	lnBSEYD 1 72.34%	lnBSEYD 2 75.00%	lnBSEYD 3 76.19%	lnBSEYD 4 76.92%	lnBSEYD 5 65.00%	lnBSEYD 6 66.67%	lnBSEYD 7 62.96%	lnBSEYD 8 65.38%	lnBSEYD 9 68.18%	lnBSEYD 10 63.64%	lnBSEYD 11 68.18%	lnBSEYD 12 76.19%
PE 1	37	25	67.57%	7.50E-11	67.57%	0.7139	1.4607	1.0288	0.0239	0.4077	1.0288	1.4123	1.6839	0.1085	0.0136	0.3428	0.0787	0.0064	0.2513	0.0064	1.4123
PE 2	36	24	66.67%	1.12E-10	66.67%	0.5184	1.1650	1.2508	0.0719	0.5575	1.2508	1.6658	1.9566	0.0443	0.0000	0.2150	0.0263	0.0378	0.1447	0.0378	1.6658
PE 3	55	37	67.27%	7.91E-16	67.27%	0.9687	2.0388	1.6497	0.0554	0.6820	1.6497	2.2408	2.6577	0.1262	0.0091	0.4459	0.0874	0.0208	0.3192	0.0208	2.2408
PE 4	49	35	71.43%	1.86E-13	71.43%	2.3917	3.8476	0.3236	0.1663	0.0202	0.3236	0.5873	0.7925	0.9194	0.5133	1.5643	0.8158	0.2427	1.3334	0.2427	0.5873
lnPE 1	37	25	67.57%	7.50E-11	67.57%	0.7139	1.4607	1.0288	0.0239	0.4077	1.0288	1.4123	1.6839	0.1085	0.0136	0.3428	0.0787	0.0064	0.2513	0.0064	1.4123
lnPE 2	36	25	69.44%	2.38E-10	69.44%	1.1479	2.0413	0.5667	0.0081	0.1478	0.5667	0.8527	1.0618	0.3194	0.1268	0.6668	0.2675	0.0266	0.5386	0.0266	0.8527
lnPE 3	50	34	68.00%	2.44E-14	68.00%	1.0954	2.1579	1.2369	0.0130	0.4569	1.2369	1.7273	2.0766	0.2006	0.0403	0.5555	0.1530	0.0008	0.4193	0.0008	1.7273
lnPE 4	44	31	70.45%	2.52E-12	70.45%	1.7613	2.9628	0.4671	0.0601	0.0772	0.4671	0.7593	0.9786	0.5911	0.2900	1.0944	0.5126	0.1062	0.9119	0.1062	0.7593
BSEYD 1	38	29	76.32%	9.25E-10	76.32%	4.0788	5.6661	0.0355	1.0656	0.3099	0.0355	0.0003	0.0078	2.2789	1.6886	3.1073	2.1356	1.2226	2.8206	1.2226	0.0003
BSEYD 2	39	30	76.92%	8.40E-11	76.92%	2.0417	3.2257	0.2080	0.1715	0.0058	0.2080	0.3995	0.5512	0.8193	0.4749	1.3578	0.7320	0.2398	1.1657	0.2398	0.3995
BSEYD 3	40	30	75.00%	1.70E-10	75.00%	3.5648	5.1058	0.0000	0.7578	0.1444	0.0000	0.0309	0.0818	1.8566	1.3133	2.6356	1.7236	0.8954	2.3643	0.8954	0.0309
BSEYD 4	39	29	74.36%	2.28E-10	74.36%	3.1558	4.5965	0.0085	0.5923	0.0807	0.0085	0.0709	0.1409	1.5789	1.0863	2.2943	1.4577	0.7132	2.0442	0.7132	0.0709
BSEYD 5	24	15	62.50%	1.27E-07	62.50%	0.0269	0.2112	1.8287	0.4225	1.0921	1.8287	2.2345	2.5100	0.0653	0.1839	0.0022	0.4577	0.3471	0.0133	0.3471	2.2345
BSEYD 6	22	14	63.64%	5.46E-07	63.64%	0.0713	0.3020	1.3946	0.2606	0.7880	1.3946	1.7343	1.9664	0.0179	0.0896	0.0043	0.0295	0.2047	0.0000	0.2047	1.7343
BSEYD 7	18	12	66.67%	1.06E-05	66.67%	0.2592	0.5825	0.6254	0.0359	0.2788	0.6254	0.8329	0.9783	0.0221	0.0000	0.1075	0.0132	0.0189	0.0723	0.0189	0.8329
BSEYD 8	19	12	63.16%	3.71E-06	63.16%	0.0421	0.2188	1.3043	0.2686	0.7555	1.3043	1.6094	1.8173	0.0281	0.1036	0.0003	0.0412	0.2155	0.0019	0.2155	1.6094
BSEYD 9	23	14	60.87%	2.06E-07	60.87%	0.0000	0.0841	2.2193	0.6390	1.4105	2.2193	2.6566	2.9512	0.1696	0.3390	0.0429	0.2033	0.5471	0.0753	0.5471	2.6566
BSEYD 10	19	11	57.89%	2.42E-06	57.89%	0.0700	0.0000	2.6458	0.9897	1.8226	2.6458	3.0800	3.3695	0.4105	0.6341	0.2058	0.4575	0.8840	0.2654	0.8840	3.0800
BSEYD 11	16	12	75.00%	1.24E-04	75.00%	1.4259	2.0423	0.0000	0.3031	0.0578	0.0000	0.0124	0.0377	0.7426	0.5253	1.0543	0.6894	0.3581	0.9457	0.3581	0.0124
BSEYD 12	16	11	68.75%	4.83E-05	68.75%	0.4295	0.7992	0.3172	0.0000	0.1005	0.3172	0.4586	0.5606	0.1007	0.0316	0.2355	0.0814	0.0024	0.1849	0.0024	0.4586
lnBSEYD 1	47	34	72.34%	9.18E-13	72.34%	2.7200	4.2222	0.1734	0.2884	0.0000	0.1734	0.3710	0.5329	1.1559	0.7029	1.8503	1.0421	0.3842	1.6039	0.3842	0.3710
lnBSEYD 2	44	33	75.00%	1.80E-11	75.00%	3.9213	5.6163	0.0000	0.8336	0.1588	0.0000	0.0340	0.0900	2.0423	1.4447	2.8992	1.8960	0.9849	2.6007	0.9849	0.0340
lnBSEYD 3	42	32	76.19%	9.73E-11	76.19%	4.4319	6.1733	0.0321	1.1379	0.3209	0.0321	0.0000	0.0126	2.4611	1.8166	3.3675	2.3045	1.3087	3.0536	1.3087	0.0000
lnBSEYD 4	39	30	76.92%	7.08E-10	76.92%	4.5391	6.2267	0.0783	1.2824	0.4249	0.0783	0.0116	0.0000	2.6079	1.9670	3.5000	2.4528	1.4560	3.1920	1.4560	0.0116
lnBSEYD 5	20	13	65.00%	2.38E-06	65.00%	0.1453	0.4222	0.9900	0.1283	0.5134	0.9900	1.2636	1.4523	0.0000	0.0248	0.0359	0.0013	0.0918	0.0162	0.0918	1.2636
lnBSEYD 6	21	14	66.67%	1.57E-06	66.67%	0.3024	0.6796	0.7296	0.0419	0.3252	0.7296	0.9717	1.1413	0.0258	0.0000	0.1254	0.0153	0.0220	0.0844	0.0220	0.9717
lnBSEYD 7	27	17	62.96%	1.87E-08	62.96%	0.0500	0.2882	1.9128	0.4084	1.1185	1.9128	2.3532	2.6529	0.0488	0.1638	0.0000	0.0692	0.3301	0.0053	0.3301	2.3532
lnBSEYD 8	26	17	65.38%	5.21E-08	65.38%	0.2260	0.6107	1.1928	0.1346	0.6006	1.1928	1.5355	1.7727	0.0017	0.0191	0.0660	0.0000	0.0924	0.0346	0.0924	1.5355
lnBSEYD 9	22	15	68.18%	1.06E-06	68.18%	0.5073	0.9847	0.5170	0.0033	0.1848	0.5170	0.7276	0.8780	0.0994	0.0229	0.2626	0.0771	0.0000	0.2003	0.0000	0.7276
lnBSEYD 10	22	14	63.64%	5.46E-07	63.64%	0.0713	0.3020	1.3946	0.2606	0.7880	1.3946	1.7343	1.9664	0.0179	0.0896	0.0043	0.0295	0.2047	0.0000	0.2047	1.7343
lnBSEYD 11	22	15	68.18%	1.06E-06	68.18%	0.5073	0.9847	0.5170	0.0033	0.1848	0.5170	0.7276	0.8780	0.0994	0.0229	0.2626	0.0771	0.0000	0.2003	0.0000	0.7276
lnBSEYD 12	21	16	76.19%	9.87E-06	76.19%	2.2160	3.0866	0.0160	0.5690	0.1604	0.0160	0.0000	0.0063	1.2306	0.9083	1.6837	1.1523	0.6544	1.5268	0.6544	0.0000

Table 4.10. Heat map for the measure-on-measure test. The table reports a heat map of the measure-on- measure significance test, based on the *p – value*. A darker background indicates a lower *p-value*. A white background is indicative of a *p*-value above 20%.

Model	Signals	Correct	p	L(p)	λp	PE 1	PE 2	PE 3	PE 4	lnPE 1	lnPE 2	lnPE 3	lnPE 4	BSEYD 1	BSEYD 2	BSEYD 3	BSEYD 4	BSEYD 5	BSEYD 6	BSEYD 7	BSEYD 8
						67.57%	66.67%	67.27%	71.43%	67.57%	69.44%	68.00%	70.45%	76.32%	71.79%	75.00%	74.36%	62.50%	63.64%	66.67%	63.16%
PE 1	37	25	67.57%	7.50E-11	7.50E-11	100.00%	100.00%	96.95%	60.77%	100.00%	80.53%	95.51%	70.29%	22.74%	57.31%	31.04%	35.65%	52.01%	61.62%	90.72%	57.47%
PE 2	36	24	66.67%	1.12E-10	1.12E-10	90.83%	100.00%	93.83%	53.34%	90.72%	71.97%	86.43%	62.24%	19.05%	50.13%	26.34%	30.43%	60.26%	70.37%	100.00%	66.02%
PE 3	55	37	67.27%	7.91E-16	7.91E-16	96.28%	92.39%	100.00%	50.09%	96.28%	72.83%	90.81%	60.86%	12.86%	46.28%	19.90%	24.12%	46.05%	57.21%	92.39%	52.35%
PE 4	49	35	71.43%	1.86E-13	1.86E-13	55.93%	47.37%	53.04%	100.00%	55.93%	76.16%	60.33%	88.08%	43.10%	95.46%	56.95%	64.25%	18.80%	24.82%	47.37%	22.13%
lnPE 1	37	25	67.57%	7.50E-11	7.50E-11	100.00%	90.72%	96.95%	60.77%	100.00%	80.53%	95.51%	70.29%	22.74%	57.31%	31.04%	35.65%	52.01%	61.62%	90.72%	57.47%
lnPE 2	36	25	69.44%	2.38E-10	2.38E-10	80.89%	72.17%	78.00%	79.35%	80.53%	100.00%	85.20%	89.47%	34.64%	75.59%	45.16%	50.77%	38.25%	46.30%	72.17%	42.80%
lnPE 3	50	34	68.00%	2.44E-14	2.44E-14	94.79%	91.26%	91.26%	59.57%	94.79%	85.20%	100.00%	70.58%	18.16%	55.60%	26.61%	31.48%	41.66%	51.73%	84.09%	47.33%
lnPE 4	44	31	70.45%	2.52E-12	2.52E-12	68.00%	59.02%	65.00%	88.67%	68.00%	88.09%	72.52%	100.00%	37.27%	84.41%	49.43%	55.92%	26.76%	33.96%	59.02%	30.78%
BSEYD 1	38	29	76.32%	9.25E-10	9.25E-10	23.62%	19.38%	22.16%	49.68%	23.62%	34.62%	25.89%	41.84%	100.00%	52.85%	85.05%	78.05%	6.88%	9.31%	19.38%	8.21%
BSEYD 2	39	28	71.79%	8.40E-11	8.40E-11	56.81%	49.08%	54.21%	95.96%	56.81%	74.82%	60.74%	85.38%	51.52%	100.00%	64.83%	71.67%	22.10%	28.03%	49.08%	25.41%
BSEYD 3	40	30	75.00%	1.70E-10	1.70E-10	30.41%	25.18%	28.62%	61.23%	30.41%	43.70%	33.19%	52.19%	84.58%	64.84%	100.00%	92.58%	9.25%	12.41%	25.18%	10.99%
BSEYD 4	39	29	74.36%	2.28E-10	2.28E-10	35.49%	29.73%	33.53%	68.22%	35.49%	49.82%	38.52%	58.79%	77.58%	71.94%	92.65%	100.00%	11.58%	15.28%	29.73%	13.62%
BSEYD 5	24	15	62.50%	1.27E-07	1.27E-07	60.04%	66.80%	62.22%	34.58%	60.04%	46.85%	56.88%	40.37%	13.10%	32.53%	17.63%	20.16%	100.00%	90.81%	66.80%	94.68%
BSEYD 6	22	14	63.64%	5.46E-07	5.46E-07	69.65%	76.47%	71.86%	42.95%	69.65%	56.05%	66.43%	49.19%	18.30%	40.70%	23.76%	26.74%	90.81%	100.00%	76.47%	96.29%
BSEYD 7	18	12	66.67%	1.06E-05	1.06E-05	93.51%	100.00%	100.00%	65.96%	93.51%	79.97%	90.38%	72.77%	35.46%	63.45%	42.91%	46.76%	87.20%	96.55%	100.00%	75.59%
BSEYD 8	19	12	63.16%	3.71E-06	3.71E-06	68.46%	74.76%	74.51%	43.64%	68.46%	56.49%	65.49%	49.48%	19.98%	41.52%	25.34%	28.23%	95.27%	74.76%	74.76%	100.00%
BSEYD 9	23	14	60.87%	2.06E-07	2.06E-07	49.94%	56.04%	51.90%	27.70%	49.94%	38.27%	47.11%	32.65%	10.00%	25.96%	13.63%	15.69%	87.20%	78.38%	56.04%	82.08%
BSEYD 10	19	11	57.89%	2.42E-06	2.42E-06	37.80%	42.59%	39.33%	20.84%	37.80%	28.82%	35.61%	24.56%	7.69%	19.54%	10.38%	11.91%	68.06%	60.65%	42.59%	63.73%
BSEYD 11	16	12	75.00%	1.24E-04	1.24E-04	51.58%	46.86%	50.00%	74.86%	51.58%	62.30%	53.94%	68.54%	90.21%	77.30%	100.00%	95.30%	28.73%	33.08%	46.86%	31.20%
BSEYD 12	16	11	68.75%	4.83E-05	4.83E-05	91.93%	85.89%	89.94%	81.42%	91.93%	95.20%	94.86%	88.18%	49.06%	78.88%	57.33%	61.51%	60.09%	66.72%	85.89%	63.89%
lnBSEYD 1	47	34	72.34%	9.18E-13	9.18E-13	47.84%	40.18%	45.24%	88.96%	47.84%	66.35%	51.81%	77.55%	52.89%	93.36%	67.71%	75.33%	15.43%	20.53%	40.18%	18.25%
lnBSEYD 2	44	33	75.00%	1.80E-11	1.80E-11	28.11%	22.94%	26.33%	59.51%	28.11%	41.49%	30.88%	50.18%	83.83%	63.25%	100.00%	92.22%	7.77%	10.68%	22.94%	9.36%
lnBSEYD 3	42	32	76.19%	9.73E-11	9.73E-11	21.98%	16.08%	20.53%	48.66%	21.98%	33.12%	24.26%	40.44%	98.48%	51.96%	85.78%	78.41%	5.81%	8.06%	17.77%	7.03%
lnBSEYD 4	39	30	76.92%	7.08E-10	7.08E-10	19.83%	16.08%	18.53%	43.78%	19.83%	29.78%	21.86%	36.44%	92.87%	46.77%	77.96%	71.07%	5.38%	7.40%	16.08%	6.48%
lnBSEYD 5	20	13	65.00%	2.38E-06	2.38E-06	80.75%	87.49%	82.95%	53.28%	80.75%	67.00%	77.54%	59.88%	25.52%	60.76%	31.97%	35.41%	81.65%	89.88%	87.49%	86.39%
lnBSEYD 6	21	14	66.67%	1.57E-06	1.57E-06	92.99%	100.00%	95.29%	63.43%	92.99%	74.40%	89.62%	70.69%	31.74%	70.99%	39.30%	43.27%	69.09%	77.14%	68.57%	73.71%
lnBSEYD 7	27	17	62.96%	1.87E-08	1.87E-08	61.33%	64.57%	63.67%	34.25%	61.33%	47.25%	57.95%	40.36%	20.95%	47.67%	16.66%	19.25%	96.03%	94.21%	100.00%	98.33%
lnBSEYD 8	26	17	65.38%	5.21E-08	5.21E-08	81.31%	89.00%	83.82%	50.33%	81.31%	65.69%	77.65%	57.68%	38.58%	70.99%	27.48%	31.04%	76.00%	85.25%	89.00%	81.31%
lnBSEYD 9	22	15	68.18%	1.06E-06	1.06E-06	95.08%	87.97%	92.74%	73.87%	95.08%	89.81%	98.54%	81.65%	18.30%	40.70%	23.76%	26.74%	57.76%	65.44%	87.97%	62.15%
lnBSEYD 10	22	14	63.64%	5.46E-07	5.46E-07	69.65%	76.47%	71.86%	42.95%	69.65%	56.05%	66.43%	49.19%	18.30%	40.70%	23.76%	26.74%	91.22%	100.00%	76.47%	96.29%
lnBSEYD 11	22	15	68.18%	1.06E-06	1.06E-06	95.08%	87.97%	92.74%	73.87%	95.08%	89.81%	98.54%	81.65%	18.30%	40.70%	23.76%	26.74%	57.76%	65.44%	87.97%	62.15%
lnBSEYD 12	21	16	76.19%	9.87E-06	9.87E-06	38.56%	34.06%	37.04%	62.28%	38.56%	49.20%	40.86%	55.63%	98.92%	64.88%	89.92%	84.64%	18.02%	21.66%	34.06%	20.07%

p-value scale: 0% ▓▓▓▓▒▒▒░░ >20%

(Continued)

Table 4.10. (Continued)

Model	Signals	Correct	p	L(p)	p	BSEYD 9	BSEYD 10	BSEYD 11	BSEYD 12	lnBSEYD 1	lnBSEYD 2	lnBSEYD 3	lnBSEYD 4	lnBSEYD 5	lnBSEYD 6	lnBSEYD 7	lnBSEYD 8	lnBSEYD 9	lnBSEYD 10	lnBSEYD 11	lnBSEYD 12
						60.87%	57.89%	68.75%	75.00%	72.34%	75.00%	76.19%	65.00%	76.92%	66.67%	62.96%	65.38%	68.18%	63.64%	68.18%	76.19%
PE 1	37	25	67.57%		7.50E-11	39.81%	22.68%	87.71%	31.04%	52.31%	31.04%	23.47%	19.44%	19.44%	90.72%	55.82%	77.91%	93.62%	61.62%	93.62%	23.47%
PE 2	36	24	66.67%		1.12E-10	47.15%	28.04%	78.86%	45.53%	70.06%	45.16%	35.58%	30.28%	57.20%	72.17%	64.29%	87.12%	84.59%	70.37%	84.59%	19.68%
PE 3	55	37	67.27%		7.91E-16	32.50%	15.33%	81.39%	19.90%	40.89%	19.90%	13.44%	10.30%	72.24%	92.39%	50.43%	76.75%	88.52%	57.21%	88.52%	13.44%
PE 4	49	35	71.43%		1.86E-13	12.20%	4.98%	68.34%	56.95%	88.69%	56.95%	44.35%	37.33%	33.76%	47.37%	21.10%	36.64%	62.22%	24.82%	62.22%	44.35%
lnPE 1	37	25	67.57%		7.50E-11	39.81%	22.68%	87.71%	31.04%	52.31%	31.04%	23.47%	19.44%	19.44%	90.72%	55.82%	77.91%	93.62%	61.62%	93.62%	23.47%
lnPE 2	36	25	69.44%		2.38E-10	28.40%	15.31%	92.82%	45.16%	70.06%	45.16%	35.58%	30.28%	57.20%	72.17%	41.42%	60.50%	87.03%	46.30%	87.03%	35.58%
lnPE 3	50	34	68.00%		2.44E-14	29.53%	14.18%	90.91%	26.61%	49.91%	26.61%	18.88%	14.96%	65.42%	84.09%	45.61%	69.57%	97.80%	51.73%	97.80%	18.88%
lnPE 4	44	31	70.45%		2.52E-12	18.45%	8.52%	80.63%	49.43%	78.12%	49.43%	38.36%	32.26%	44.20%	59.02%	29.55%	47.40%	74.46%	33.96%	74.46%	38.36%
BSEYD 1	38	29	76.32%		9.25E-10	4.34%	1.73%	30.19%	85.05%	57.78%	85.05%	98.55%	92.94%	13.11%	19.38%	7.79%	14.39%	26.89%	9.31%	26.89%	98.55%
BSEYD 2	39	28	71.79%		8.40E-11	15.30%	7.20%	67.88%	64.83%	93.94%	64.83%	52.74%	45.78%	36.54%	49.08%	24.39%	39.22%	62.43%	28.03%	62.43%	52.74%
BSEYD 3	40	30	75.00%		1.70E-10	5.90%	2.38%	38.40%	100.00%	70.40%	100.00%	86.05%	77.49%	17.30%	25.18%	10.45%	18.92%	34.40%	12.41%	34.40%	86.05%
BSEYD 4	39	29	74.36%		2.28E-10	7.57%	3.20%	44.15%	92.65%	77.64%	92.65%	79.00%	70.74%	20.89%	29.73%	12.99%	22.73%	39.84%	15.28%	39.84%	79.00%
BSEYD 5	24	15	62.50%		1.27E-07	86.97%	64.58%	51.57%	17.63%	29.60%	17.63%	13.50%	11.31%	79.84%	66.80%	96.26%	76.78%	55.58%	90.81%	55.58%	13.50%
BSEYD 6	22	14	63.64%		5.46E-07	78.94%	58.26%	60.97%	23.76%	51.55%	23.76%	18.79%	16.08%	89.36%	76.47%	94.78%	86.37%	65.10%	100.00%	65.10%	18.79%
BSEYD 7	28	18	61.07%		1.06E-05	61.07%	63.99%	60.43%	25.34%	38.47%	25.34%	20.46%	17.76%	45.95%	74.30%	98.60%	90.87%	89.07%	78.80%	89.07%	36.14%
BSEYD 8	19	12	63.16%		3.71E-06	83.75%	77.18%	10.38%	13.50%	23.50%	13.63%	10.31%	8.58%	68.04%	56.04%	83.59%	65.20%	64.25%	78.38%	64.25%	20.46%
BSEYD 9	23	14	60.87%		2.42E-06	100.00%	63.99%	23.24%	10.38%	13.63%	10.38%	9.11%	7.93%	74.30%	74.76%	98.60%	83.91%	45.55%	60.65%	45.55%	10.31%
BSEYD 10	19	11	57.89%		2.42E-06	79.13%	100.00%	10.38%	13.30%	10.38%	13.50%	7.93%	6.64%	65.01%	42.59%	65.01%	40.64%	34.71%	33.08%	34.71%	7.93%
BSEYD 11	16	11	68.75%		1.12E-04	23.24%	15.30%	100.00%	57.33%	81.01%	100.00%	91.15%	85.65%	52.17%	46.86%	65.01%	49.88%	96.10%	66.72%	96.10%	91.15%
BSEYD 12	16	11	68.75%		4.83E-05	51.22%	37.13%	57.33%	100.00%	75.12%	57.33%	49.83%	45.40%	75.10%	85.89%	62.75%	77.54%	54.95%	66.72%	96.10%	49.83%
lnBSEYD 1	47	34	72.34%		9.18E-13	9.91%	3.99%	67.71%	67.71%	100.00%	69.02%	54.25%	46.54%	28.23%	40.18%	17.38%	30.73%	53.53%	20.53%	53.53%	54.25%
lnBSEYD 2	44	33	75.00%		1.80E-11	4.77%	1.78%	85.78%	100.00%	69.02%	100.00%	85.37%	76.42%	15.30%	22.94%	8.86%	16.85%	32.10%	10.68%	32.10%	85.37%
lnBSEYD 3	42	32	76.19%		9.73E-11	3.53%	1.30%	100.00%	85.78%	57.11%	85.78%	100.00%	91.06%	11.67%	17.77%	6.65%	12.90%	25.26%	8.06%	25.26%	100.00%
lnBSEYD 4	20	13	65.00%		7.08E-11	3.31%	1.26%	95.42%	77.96%	51.45%	77.96%	91.42%	100.00%	10.63%	16.08%	6.14%	11.73%	22.76%	7.40%	22.76%	91.42%
lnBSEYD 5	39	30	76.92%		2.38E-06	70.31%	51.58%	31.97%	31.97%	47.37%	39.30%	26.10%	22.82%	100.00%	87.49%	84.98%	97.12%	76.19%	89.88%	88.20%	26.10%
lnBSEYD 6	21	14	66.67%		1.57E-06	58.24%	40.97%	16.66%	39.30%	56.85%	39.30%	32.42%	28.54%	87.23%	100.00%	72.33%	90.14%	88.20%	77.14%	56.56%	32.42%
lnBSEYD 7	27	17	62.96%		1.87E-08	82.30%	59.14%	52.28%	26.10%	29.02%	16.66%	12.50%	10.34%	82.51%	68.57%	100.00%	79.25%	56.56%	94.21%	76.12%	12.50%
lnBSEYD 8	26	17	65.38%		5.21E-08	63.45%	43.45%	71.37%	27.48%	43.83%	27.48%	21.53%	18.30%	96.72%	75.26%	79.72%	100.00%	85.25%	85.25%	100.00%	21.53%
lnBSEYD 9	22	15	68.18%		1.06E-06	47.63%	32.11%	95.42%	47.21%	66.73%	47.21%	39.37%	34.87%	75.26%	87.97%	60.83%	78.13%	100.00%	65.44%	65.10%	39.37%
lnBSEYD 10	22	15	68.18%		5.46E-07	78.94%	58.26%	58.26%	23.76%	37.47%	23.76%	18.79%	16.08%	89.36%	76.47%	94.78%	86.37%	65.10%	100.00%	100.00%	18.79%
lnBSEYD 11	22	15	68.18%		1.06E-06	47.63%	32.11%	32.11%	47.21%	66.73%	47.21%	39.37%	34.87%	75.26%	89.00%	60.83%	78.13%	89.07%	65.44%	100.00%	39.37%
lnBSEYD 12	21	16	76.19%		9.87E-06	13.66%	7.89%	45.07%	89.92%	68.87%	89.92%	100.00%	93.67%	26.73%	34.06%	19.44%	28.31%	41.86%	21.66%	41.86%	100.00%

p-value scale: 0% ——— >20%

Note that $p = \frac{1}{2}$ is lower than p_0 for subperiod 1, but higher than p_0 for every other data set. This means that the significance of the test statistics will increase for measures evaluated over the first subperiod, but will decrease for the other periods.

Tables 4.11 and 4.12 report likelihood statistics respectively, given the hypotheses $p = p_0$ and $p = \frac{1}{2}$ for the two subperiods using the asymptotic χ^2 distribution. The total number of signals in Columns 2 and 6 is calculated as the sum of all the entries of the indicator sequence S. P/E and logP/E ratio models produced nearly twice as many signals in Subperiod 2 than in Subperiod 1, whereas BSEYD models generated roughly the same number of signals in both subperiods. The number of signals for logB-SEYD models based on current earnings increased slightly, contrary to the logBSEYD models based on average earnings over 10 years, for which the number of signals remains constant. The Maximum Likelihood estimate $\hat{p}$ reported in Columns 3 and 7 is the probability of correctly predicting a crash that maximizes the likelihood function of the model. It is equal to the ratio of the number of correct predictions to the total number of signals.

Table 4.9 shows that all the models are statistically significant at a 99.5% level in the first subperiod. In the second subperiod, all the models are significant at a 99% or 99.5% level. In fact, the highest p-value across models is 1.44%, achieved by the BSEYD10 implementation.

Tables 4.13 and 4.14 report empirical statistics, respectively, for subperiods 1 and 2 using an empirical distribution generated by $K = 10,000$ Monte Carlo simulations. The test statistics in Columns 7 and 9 respectively are equal to $-2\ln\Lambda = -2\ln\frac{L(p=p_0|X)}{L(p=\hat{p}|X)}$ and $-2\ln\Lambda = -2\ln\frac{L(p=\frac{1}{2}|X)}{L(p=\hat{p}|X)}$. The level of significance indicated is based on the empirical distribution. Conducting the statistical eta of significance using the empirical distribution further increases the difference between Subperiods 1 and 2.

The results in Table 4.13 confirm the initial observation made under the asymptotic χ^2 distribution: all the measures are statistically significant at a 99.5% level regardless of the null hypothesis. In the second subperiod, the results in Table 4.14 show that the accuracy of all the measures is significantly different from p_0 at or around a 99% level. In fact, the highest p-values are 1.33% for logBSEYD4 and 1.31% for BSEYD2. Furthermore, the accuracy of 14 models out of 32 is significantly greater $p = \frac{1}{2}$: BSEYD7–12 and logBSEYD5–12. With the exception of BSYED 10, these models are significant at a 99.5% level. This result is noticeably different from the observation made under the asymptotic χ^2 distribution. Indeed, the critical

Table 4.11.   Robustness: maximum likelihood estimate and likelihood ratio test for each sample: Uninformed prior.

	Sample 1				Sample 2			
	Total		Test statistics		Total		Test statistics	
Signal Model	number of signals	ML Estimate $\hat{p}$	$-2\ln\Lambda$	p-value	number of signals	ML Estimate $\hat{p}$	$-2\ln\Lambda$	p-value
PE1	10	100.00%	—	—	27	55.56%	7.5993**	0.58%
PE2	8	100.00%	—	—	28	57.14%	8.8619***	0.29%
PE3	16	100.00%	—	—	39	53.85%	9.5940***	0.20%
PE4	15	100.00%	—	—	34	58.82%	12.0986***	0.05%
lnPE1	9	100.00%	—	—	28	57.14%	8.8619***	0.29%
lnPE2	8	100.00%	—	—	28	60.71%	11.2811***	0.08%
lnPE3	15	100.00%	—	—	35	54.29%	8.9212***	0.28%
lnPE4	12	100.00%	—	—	32	59.38%	11.8163***	0.06%
BSEYD1	17	100.00%	—	—	21	57.14%	6.6464**	0.99%
BSEYD2	16	93.75%	10.4672***	0.12%	23	56.52%	6.9584**	0.83%
BSEYD3	19	94.74%	13.3534***	0.03%	21	57.14%	6.6464**	0.99%
BSEYD4	18	94.44%	12.3845***	0.04%	21	57.14%	6.6464**	0.99%
BSEYD5					24	62.50%	10.1190***	0.15%
BSEYD6					22	63.64%	9.9454***	0.16%
BSEYD7					18	66.67%	9.6971***	0.18%
BSEYD8					19	63.16%	8.3431***	0.39%
BSEYD9					23	60.87%	8.8913***	0.29%
BSEYD10					19	57.89%	5.9940*	1.44%
BSEYD11					16	75.00%	13.2951***	0.03%
BSEYD12					16	68.75%	9.7846***	0.18%

lnBSEYD1	17	94.12%	11.4222***	0.07%	30	60.00%	11.5431***	0.07%
lnBSEYD2	18	94.44%	12.3845***	0.04%	26	61.54%	11.0329***	0.09%
lnBSEYD3	20	95.00%	14.3281***	0.02%	22	59.09%	7.9710***	0.48%
lnBSEYD4	19	94.74%	13.3534***	0.03%	20	60.00%	7.6954**	0.55%
lnBSEYD5					20	65.00%	9.8012***	0.17%
lnBSEYD6					21	66.67%	11.3133***	0.08%
lnBSEYD7					27	62.96%	11.7151***	0.06%
lnBSEYD8					26	65.38%	13.0279***	0.03%
lnBSEYD9					22	68.18%	13.0563***	0.03%
lnBSEYD10					22	63.64%	10.1063***	0.15%
lnBSEYD11					22	68.18%	13.0563***	0.03%
lnBSEYD12					21	76.19%	18.427***	0.00%

Notes: † significant at the 10% level;
* significant at the 5% level;
** significant at the 1% level;
*** significant at the 0.5% level.

Table 4.12. Data robustness of the crash prediction measures (Models 1–4): Arbitrary 50% threshold.

Crash prediction measure	Robust likelihood ratio	Model	Asymptotic (χ^2)		Empirical (Monte Carlo)	
			Robust test statitstics	p-value	Robust test statitstics	p-value
P/E	0.1302	P/E2	4.0776*	4.35%	4.0776[†]	7.07%
logP/E	0.0031	logP/E1	4.6665*	3.08%	4.6665*	5.21%
BSEYD	0.0003	BSEYD2	7.6648**	0.56%	6.2597**	0.94%
logBSEYD	0.0000	logBSEYD1	9.7232***	0.18%	20.3449***	0.38%

Notes: [†] significant at the 10% level;
* significant at the 5% level;
** significant at the 1% level;
*** significant at the 0.5% level.

values for the empirical distribution are lower than the critical values under χ^2 distribution.

The four measures are remarkably robust with respect to a change in the subperiod, when tested against a random uninformed signal with predictive probability p_0. All the measures are statistically significant at a 99.5% level, while 31 of the 32 implementations are statistically significant at least at a 99% level in the second subperiod. Model BSEYD10 has the lowest significance in the second subperiod, with 98.56%.

On the other hand, we see large discrepancies between the first and the second subperiods when we compare the accuracy of our measures with an arbitrary $p = \frac{1}{2}$ benchmark corresponding to 50% accuracy. While the significance of most measures improves in the first subperiod, only four measures are statistically significant at the 90% level in the second subperiod.

The explanation to this puzzle lies in Table 4.5. A random uninformed measure would have correctly predicted a crash 58.27% of the time in the first subperiod, but only 29.98% of the time in the second subperiod. Crashes are not evenly spread over time. The first subperiod lasts for about 18 years while the second subperiod lasts for 33 years, yet 11 crashes occurred in each subperiod. As a result, an arbitrary, static benchmark such as $p = \frac{1}{2}$ is ill-adapted to test the accuracy of cash measures over multiple time periods.

Table 4.13. Robustness: Monte Carlo likelihood ratio test for sample 1.

Signal model	Total number of signals	ML Estimate $\hat{p}$	Critical value: 90%	Critical value: 95%	Critical value: 99%	Test stat. $-2\ln\Lambda(p_0)$	Empirical p-value	Test stat. $-2\ln\Lambda(\frac{1}{2})$	Empirical p-value
PE1	10	100.00%	2.1284	3.2594	6.1367	—	—	—	—
PE2	8	100.00%	3.2800	3.6512	8.6403	—	—	—	—
PE3	16	100.00%	2.7910	3.8422	6.5600	—	—	—	—
PE4	15	100.00%	3.1926	3.7856	6.1516	—	—	—	—
lnPE1	9	100.00%	2.2714	4.1094	8.7857	—	—	—	—
lnPE2	8	100.00%	3.2800	3.6512	8.6403	—	—	—	—
lnPE3	15	100.00%	3.1926	3.7856	6.1516	—	—	—	—
lnPE4	12	100.00%	3.0285	3.4830	6.7444	—	—	—	—
BSEYD1	17	100.00%	2.4826	3.6347	7.3815	—	—	—	—
BSEYD2	16	93.75%	2.7910	3.8422	6.5600	10.4672***	0.00%	14.6994***	0.00%
BSEYD3	19	94.74%	3.5291	3.6360	5.9506	13.3534***	0.09%	18.5043***	0.00%
BSEYD4	18	94.44%	3.0434	4.5427	6.8549	12.3845***	0.19%	17.2292***	0.00%
lnBSEYD1	17	94.12%	2.4826	3.6347	7.3815	11.4222***	0.00%	15.9606***	0.00%
lnBSEYD2	18	94.44%	3.0434	4.5427	6.8549	12.3845***	0.14%	17.2292***	0.02%
lnBSEYD3	20	95.00%	2.6968	4.2568	6.6965	14.3281***	0.06%	19.7853***	0.00%
lnBSEYD4	19	94.74%	2.0053	3.6360	5.9506	13.3534***	0.00%	18.5043***	0.00%

Notes: † significant at the 10% level;
* significant at the 5% level;
** significant at the 1% level;
*** significant at the 0.5% level.

Table 4.14. Robustness: Monte Carlo likelihood ratio test for sample 2.

Signal Model	Total number of signals	ML Estimate $\hat{p}$	Critical value: 90%	Critical value: 95%	Critical value: 99%	Test stat. $-2\ln\Lambda(p_0)$	Empirical p-value	Test stat. $-2\ln\Lambda(\frac{1}{2})$	Empirical p-value
PE1	27	55.56%	2.5086	3.9085	7.5993	7.5993*	1.21%	0.3340	70.51%
PE2	28	57.14%	2.3179	3.6515	7.3255	8.8619***	0.29%	0.5734	57.40%
PE3	39	53.85%	2.9641	3.2182	6.4074	9.5940***	0.09%	0.2310	75.71%
PE4	34	58.82%	2.7239	4.3200	6.3878	12.0986***	0.12%	1.0644	39.44%
lnPE1	28	57.14%	2.1627	3.7756	6.7346	8.8619**	0.54%	0.5734	56.87%
lnPE2	28	60.71%	2.1627	3.7756	5.9772	11.2811***	0.06%	1.2957	34.68%
lnPE3	35	54.29%	3.0544	3.8305	6.8540	8.9212**	0.52%	0.2575	73.62%
lnPE4	32	59.38%	3.1780	3.1780	6.3371	11.8163***	0.00%	1.1317	37.80%
BSEYD1	21	57.14%	2.3786	3.9849	6.0595	6.6464**	0.74%	0.4300	67.27%
BSEYD2	23	56.52%	3.2157	3.6701	6.9584	6.9584*	1.07%	0.3924	68.06%
BSEYD3	21	57.14%	2.8317	4.5671	6.6464	6.6464*	1.54%	0.4300	66.97%
BSEYD4	21	57.14%	2.8317	4.5671	6.6464	6.6464*	1.45%	0.4300	66.78%
BSEYD5	24	62.50%	2.5581	4.4920	7.2008	10.1190***	0.32%	1.5160	31.56%
BSEYD6	22	63.64%	3.4638	3.5721	6.0855	9.9454***	0.24%	1.6573	28.62%
BSEYD7	8	66.67%	2.8341	3.9728	7.1985	9.6971***	0.14%	9.6971***	0.00%
BSEYD8	19	63.16%	2.3043	3.8482	7.8270	8.3431**	0.56%	8.3431***	0.40%
BSEYD9	23	60.87%	2.9480	3.9346	6.5576	8.8913**	0.54%	8.8913***	0.27%
BSEYD10	19	57.89%	2.3102	4.3978	7.7190	5.9940*	2.15%	5.9940*	1.75%

BSEYD11	16	75.00%	2.9295	4.4686	6.8590	13.2951***	0.06%	13.2951***	0.11%
BSEYD12	16	68.75%	2.9295	4.4686	6.8590	9.7846***	0.60%	9.7846***	0.44%
lnBSEYD1	30	60.00%	2.8307	3.6809	6.9656	11.5431***	0.07%	1.2081	35.61%
lnBSEYD2	26	61.54%	2.9920	4.5451	7.8212	11.0329***	0.18%	1.3972	32.53%
lnBSEYD3	22	59.09%	3.2437	3.8459	5.7248	7.9710**	0.82%	0.7313	51.88%
lnBSEYD4	20	60.00%	2.4356	4.6437	7.6954	7.6954*	1.31%	0.8054	51.05%
lnBSEYD5	20	65.00%	2.7098	3.1490	7.1706	9.8012***	0.00%	9.8012***	0.20%
lnBSEYD6	21	66.67%	3.1330	4.1581	6.1486	11.3133***	0.13%	11.3133***	0.00%
lnBSEYD7	27	62.96%	2.1730	3.7521	6.9972	11.7151***	0.21%	11.7151***	0.01%
lnBSEYD8	26	65.38%	2.6395	4.0936	5.8557	13.0279***	0.03%	13.0279***	0.00%
lnBSEYD9	22	68.18%	3.4880	3.5580	5.9791	13.0563***	0.00%	13.0563***	0.00%
lnBSEYD10	22	63.64%	3.4880	3.5580	5.9791	10.1063***	0.22%	10.1063***	0.10%
lnBSEYD11	22	68.18%	3.4880	3.5580	5.9791	13.0563***	0.00%	13.0563***	0.07%
lnBSEYD12	21	76.19%	3.0558	4.2590	6.2718	18.4227***	0.00%	18.4227***	0.00%

Notes: † significant at the 10% level;
* significant at the 5% level;
** significant at the 1% level;
*** significant at the 0.5% level.

Model Parameter Robustness

The last set of results presented in this section address the robustness of the four crash measures (P/E, logP/E, BSEYD and logBSEYD) with respect to a change in parameters. We temporarily leave aside the BSEYD and logBSEYD models based on corporate yields and the question of robustness with respect to a choice of interest rate. The main reason is that the choice of interest rates affects not only the period for which data are available (1964–2014 for Treasury Notes but only 1983–2014 for Aaa corporate bonds and 1986–2014 for Aaa corporate bonds), but also the number of crashes over which we can conduct the test. The best approach to this problem is to analyze the robustness of the models to a change in the underlying dataset, as we did previously.

Column 2 in Table 4.15 reports the robust likelihood ratio $\check{\Lambda}$ for each of the measures under the null hypothesis $H_0 : p = p_0$. We calculate the robust likelihood ratio using (4.11) as the highest likelihood ratio across all implementations of the measure. Higher robust likelihood ratios are indicative of lower statistical significance. Column 3 identifies the specific model, and therefore the set of parameters, corresponding to the likelihood ratio reported in Column 2. Columns 4 and 5 refer to significance tests performed using the asymptotic χ^2 distribution. Column 4 reports the robust test statistics, computed using formula (4.12), and level of significance for the measure based on the χ^2 distribution. Column 5 gives the associated p-value. Columns 6 and 7 refer to significance tests performed with the

Table 4.15. Data robustness of the Crash prediction measures (Models 1–4): Uninformed-prior.

Crash prediction measure	Robust likelihood ratio	Model	Asymptotic (χ^2)		Empirical (Monte Carlo)	
			Robust test statitstics	p-value	Robust test statitstics	p-value
P/E	0.0052	P/E2	10.5318***	0.12%	10.5318***	0.16%
logP/E	0.0031	logP/E1	11.5744***	0.07%	11.5744***	0.08%
BSEYD	0.0003	BSEYD2	16.3034***	0.00%	16.3034***	0.99%
logBSEYD	0.0000	logBSEYD1	20.3449***	0.00%	20.3449***	0.00%

Notes: † significant at the 10% level;
* significant at the 5% level;
** significant at the 1% level;
*** significant at the 0.5% level.

Table 4.16.   Data robustness of the crash prediction measures.

Crash prediction measure	Robust likelihood ratio	Model	Asymptotic (χ^2)		Empirical (Monte Carlo)	
			Robust test statitstics	p-value	Robust test statitstics	p-value
P/E	0.1302	P/E2	4.0776*	4.35%	4.0776†	7.07%
logP/E	0.0031	logP/E1	4.6665*	3.08%	4.6665*	5.21%
BSEYD	0.0003	BSEYD2	7.6648**	0.56%	6.2597**	0.94%
logBSEYD	0.0000	logBSEYD1	9.7232***	0.18%	20.3449***	0.38%

Notes: † significant at the 10% level;
* significant at the 5% level;
** significant at the 1% level;
*** significant at the 0.5% level.

empirical distribution generated by Monte Carlo simulations. Here we aim to correct for small sample bias. Column 6 reports the robust test statistics, computed using formula (4.12), and level of significance for the measure based on the empirical distribution. Column 7 gives the associated p-value. Table 4.16 reports the corresponding numbers under the null hypothesis $H_0 : p = \frac{1}{2}$.

The BSEYD and logBSEYD are robust crash prediction measures. Their robust test statistics are still significant at a 99% and 99.5% level respectively, under the stricter null hypothesis $H_0 : p = \frac{1}{2}$. By contrast, the significance of the P/E and logP/E measures slides from 99.5% significance under the null hypothesis $H_0 : p = p_0$ to between 90% and 95% under the null hypothesis $H_0 : p = \frac{1}{2}$.

However, the robust likelihood ratio and test statistics also have an important limitation, inherent in all summary measures: Because summary measures condense all available information into a single number, they are unable to give a nuanced view of a phenomenon. Having established an objective view of robustness with the robust likelihood ratio, we now discuss some of its subjective facets.

Intuitively, a crash prediction model is robust if its accuracy, reflected in the total number of signals, the number of correct predictions and the proportion of correct predictions, does not change materially with a change in the model specification. The total number of signals, number of correct predictions and proportion of correct predictions reported in Columns 1–3 of Table 4.4 suggest that all of the models are impacted by a change in the definition of earnings. For the P/E and logP/E ratios, the total number of signals jumps from 36 or 37 for models based on current earnings to between 44 and 55 for models using average earnings. The number of correct predictions also soars from about 25 to between 31 and 37. As a result, the proportion of correct predictions remains broadly constant across models. The BSEYD model is unaffected by the change in definition of earnings. On the other hand, changing from current earnings to average earnings reduces the total number of signals for the logBSEYD model while the number of correct predictions decreases only slightly. The end result is a small increase in the proportion of correct predictions by around 3%. The test statistics reported in Tables 4.6–4.8 confirm this observation and explain the robustness of the BSEYD and logBSEYD measure.

Next, we examine the effect of a change in the definitions of the threshold. We observe that all the models seem robust to a change in the definition of the threshold: the total number of signals and the number of correct predictions reported in Table 4.4 typically do not differ by more than 2. This also helps to explain the robustness of the measure. Hence, the use of Cantelli's inequality to define the threshold does not add significant value over a standard confidence interval based on a normal distribution. An explanation could lie in the tail behavior of the model. Figure 4.9(a) shows that the empirical distribution of the BSEYD measure (based on current earnings) is not Gaussian: it is bimodal and skewed to the left. However, the tail behavior of the BSEYD measure in the last decile and especially in the last 5% is close to a Normal distribution: the R^2 of two exponential regressions of the observations in the last decile against the quantiles and the quantiles squared reach 85% (see Figure 4.9(b)).

4.5. What can we conclude?

Our findings show that all 32 implementations of the four measures predict equity market crashes better than a random uninformed signal with predictive probability p_0, under both asymptotic χ^2 distribution and simulated empirical distribution. All but one implementation are significant at the 99.5% level. The highest p-value across all 32 implementations is 1.44% for BSEYD10 under the asymptotic χ^2 distribution and 2.01%, also for BSEYD10, under the empirical distribution.

The level of significance drops when we consider whether the accuracy of the measures is significantly higher than 50%. The BSEYD measures based on corporate rates are the most affected, most likely because of their

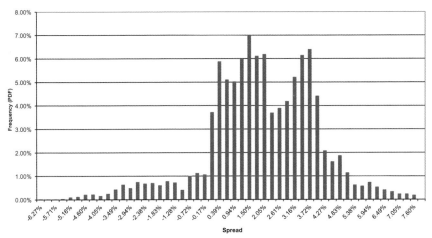

(a) The empirical distribution of the BSEYD is far from Gaussian.

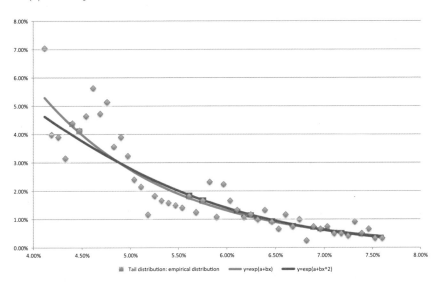

(b) But its tail behavior in the last 5% is very close to that of a
Gaussian distribution.

Fig. 4.9.   Empricial Distribution of the BSEYD measure.

smaller dataset. The significance of P/E and log P/E also falls, although
less dramatically. All eight measures are still statistically significant at the
95% level and one of them maintains 99.5% significance. By comparison,
the BSEYD and logBSEYD measures computed over the entire period are

more robust: all four logBSEYD measures and three out of four BSEYD measures are still statistically significant at the 99.5% level.

These findings support existing literatures, in particular Ziemba and Schwartz (1991) and Lleo and Ziemba (2012), which focus on short-term studies of specific market events: the BSEYD measure does predict crashes. In this chapter, we take a much longer-term perspective than previous studies, with a statistical analysis of more than 50 years of daily data. We also compare the predictive ability of BSEYD-based and P/E-based models, highlighting the crucial role played by interest rates in crash prediction. Contrary to what we expected *ex ante*, the inclusion of interest rates does not significantly increase the accuracy of the measures, but it makes the measures more robust.

The distribution of test statistics is close to the asymptotic distribution. Even with only 32–51 signals, the χ^2 distribution provides a very good approximation of the empirical distributions generated using Monte Carlo simulations. This observation is confirmed by the robustness study: the level of significance and p values of the robust test statistics under both distributions are consistent with each other.

The consistency of these findings goes a long way to explaining why the BSEYD, the logBSEYD and to a lesser extent the P/E and logP/E ratios are robust with respect to model specification under both the asymptotic χ^2 distribution and the simulated empirical distribution. The robust likelihood ratio and test statistics used to measure robustness in this study are in essence the "worst" likelihood ratio, and test statistics across all implementations of a single measure. Because all implementations have similar levels of significance, the robust statistics confirm the ranking already established by testing all the models.

This observation suggests that the effectiveness of a crash prediction model has more to do with the economic properties of the underlying measure than with the specific parameters corresponding to the model implementation. A possible explanation for the relative success of the BSEYD and logBSEYD measures is that the earnings yield may be viewed as a rough proxy for the return of equity shares and markets. As a result, these measures provide a rough approximation for the equity risk premium. In the context of crash prediction, accuracy is less important than evolution: large values for either measure indicate an abnormally low equity risk premium and suggest that a correction back to levels consistent with a historical average should occur. The exact timing of the correction is highly uncertain though.

The BSEYD and logBSEYD measures do not seem sensitive to the type of earnings used. By comparison, the test statistics of the P/E and log P/E ratios are higher for average earnings than for current earnings. This is consistent with the findings of Campbell and Shiller (1988). The interpretation of the P/E ratio as a relative measure of equity prices explains its predictive power with respect to equity crashes. Periods with abnormally high P/E ratios and prices tend to precede a correction in equity market prices. The difference in significance (and robustness) between the P/E ratio and the BSEYD or logBSEYD measures seems to imply that current levels of interest rates and their relation to equity prices add relevant information.

4.6. BSEYD and P/E

The BSEYD and P/E are useful in predicting crashes in the US, and anecdotal evidence gathered in previous chapters suggest that the BSEYD has a convincing track record in the main developed stock markets of North America, Western Europe and Japan. Naturally, the follow-up question is whether the P/E and BSEYD would work convincingly outside of these markets. In this section, we test the predictive ability of the BSEYD and P/E on the Chinese stock market. The statistical machinery that we developed above allows us to revisit the example we first encountered in Chapter 3 with more depth and breadth. The material in this section is based on Lleo and Ziemba (2016c).

4.6.1. *A brief overview of the Chinese stock market*

Mainland China has two stock exchanges, the Shanghai Stock Exchange (SSE) and the Shenzhen Stock Exchange (SZSE). The SSE is the larger of the two. With an average market capitalization of US$3.715 billion over the first half of 2016, it is the fourth largest stock market in the world.[1] The modern SSE officially came into being on November 26, 1990 and started trading on December 19, 1990. The SZSE was formally founded on December 1, 1990, and it started trading on July 3, 1991. While the largest and most established companies usually trade on the SSE, the SZSE is home to smaller and privately-owned companies.

---

[1] Source: The World federation of Exchanges, http://www.world-exchanges.org/home/index.php/statistics/monthly-reports retrieved on September 13, 2016.

The SSE Composite Index (SHCOMP) is the main Chinese stock index. It is a market capitalisation weighted index of all the A-shares and B-shares listed on the SSE. In August 2016, the SHCOMP consisted of the shares of 1,155 Chinese companies.

The SZSE Composite Index (SZCOMP) is a market capitalisation weighted index of all the A-shares and B-shares listed on the SZSE. In August 2016, 478 Chinese companies were listed on the SZSE.

With an average SSE market capitalization of US$6.656 billion over the first half of 2016, the SSE and SZSE: taken together represents the third largest stock market in the world after the New York Stock Exchange (NYSE) at US$17.970 billion, and the National Association of Securities Dealers Automated Quotation (NASDAQ) at US$6.923 billion, and before fourth place Japan Exchange Group (JPX) at US$4.625 billion and fifth place London Stock Exchange group (LSE) at US$3.598 billion.[2]

On November 17, 2014, the Chinese government launched the Shanghai–Hong Kong Stock Connect to enable investors in either market to trade shares on the other market. The Hong Kong Exchanges and Clearing is currently the eighth largest exchange in the world with an average market capitalisation of US$2.932 billion over the half of 2016.[3] This announcement was followed by the creation of a Shenzhen–Hong Kong link on August 16, 2016. These initiatives herald a closer integration between securities markets in China and further boosts the rapid development of the Chinese market.

Chinese companies may list their shares under various schemes, either domestically or abroad. Domestically, companies may issue:

- *A-shares*: common stocks denominated in Chinese Reminbi and listed on the SSE or SZSE.
- *B-shares*: special purpose shares denominated in foreign currencies but listed on the domestic stock exchange. Until 2001, only foreign investors had access to B-shares.

In addition to B-shares, foreign investors interested in the Chinese equity market may buy:

- *H-shares*: shares denominated in Hong Kong dollars and traded on the Hong Kong Stock Exchange.

---

[2]Source: *Ibid.*
[3]Source: *Ibid.*

- *L-chips, N-chips and S-chips*: shares of companies with significant operations in China, but incorporated respectively in London, New York and Singapore.
- *American Depository Receipts (ADRs)*: an ADR is a negotiable certificate issued by a US bank representing a specified number of shares in a foreign stock traded on an American exchange. As of October 2015, there were about 110 Chinese ADRs listed on American exchanges and another 200 Chinese ADRs on American over-the-counter markets.

The diversity of investment schemes available shows that although the SSE and SZSE are a large and crucial part of the Chinese equity market, they do not represent the whole market. For example, there are also *red chips* (shares of companies incorporated outside Mainland China but owned or substantially controlled by Chinese state-owned companies) and *P-chips* (shares of companies owned by private individuals and traded outside Mainland China, for example on the Hong Kong stock exchange). Our study focuses on equity market downturns on the SSE and SZSE.

Lleo and Ziemba (2016c) identify four key stylised statistical facts that distinguish the SHCOMP and SZECOMP from more mature equity markets:

(1) The return distribution is highly volatile, right skewed with very fat tails, the aggregational gaussianity, the phenomenon in which the empirical distribution of log-returns tends to normality as the time scale Δt over which the returns are calculated increases, is much weaker on the SHCOMP on SZCOMP than on the S&P500.
(2) Log returns do not exhibit a significant autocorrelation.
(3) A Gaussian Hidden Markov Chain provides a good probabilistic description of the evolution of log returns... but we need between five and six states to explain the data well.
(4) Market downturns and large market movements occur frequently.

We discuss this last stylized fact in more detail, as it lies at the heart of the discussion in this book. The return distribution of the SHCOMP has fat tails, which indicates that extreme events are more likely to occur than a Normal distribution would predict. Here, we focus on the large downward movements that occurred on the SHCOMP and SZECOMP.

Earlier studies, such as Lleo and Ziemba (2015c, 2017), defined an equity market downturn or crash as a decline of at least 10% from peak-to-trough based on the closing prices for the day, over a period of at most 1 year (252 trading days).

Table 4.17 lists the 22 downturns, defined as a decline of at least 10% in the value of the index over a year at most, that occurred between December 19, 1990 and June 30, 2016. This table was generated using the methodology outlined in Section 4.2. On average, the downturns lasted 163 days and had a 27.8% decline in the value of the SHCOMP. With 22 downturns in 25 years, the SHCOMP had as many downturns as the S&P500 had over the 50 year period from January 31, 1964 to December 31, 2014.

Table 4.18 presents the 21 downturns that occurred on the SZECOMP between April 3, 1991 and June 30, 2016. On average, the downturns lasted 122 days and had a 26.4% decline in the value of the index. While the number and magnitude of equity market corrections are comparable between both indexes, we observe that downturns tend to last noticeably longer on average on the SSE than on the SZSE.

4.6.2. *The P/E Ratio*

We start by testing the predictive ability of the P/E ratio calculated using current earnings. The advantage of this definition for the SHCOMP is that it is available over the entire period from December 12, 1990 to June 30, 2016, a total of 6243 daily observations. The same is not true for the SZECOMP earnings and therefore P/E are only available starting July 2, 2001, a total of 3,640 daily observations.

Shanghai

Table 4.19 shows that the P/E and logarithm of the P/E generated a total of 18 signals (based on normally distributed confidence intervals) and 19 signals (based on Cantelli's inequality) on the SHCOMP. The number of correct predictions across models reaches 16–17. The accuracy of the models is in the narrow range from 88.89%–89.47%. The type of confidence interval — normal distribution or Cantellis inequality — only have a minor influence on the end result.

Next, we test the accuracy of the prediction statistically. To apply the likelihood ratio test, we need to compute the uninformed prior probability p_0 that a day picked at random will precede a crash identification date by 252 days or less. We find that this probability is very high, at $p_0 = 69.57\%$.

Table 4.17. The SHCOMP Index experienced 22 crashes between December 19, 1990 and June 30, 2016.

	Crash identification date	Peak date	SHCOMP index at peak	Trough date	SHCOMP level at trough	Peak-to-trough decline (%)	Peak-to-trough duration (in days)
1	27-05-1992	25-05-1992	1421.57	17-11-1992	393.52	72.3%	176
2	23-02-1993	15-02-1993	1536.82	31-03-1993	925.91	39.8%	44
3	19-09-1994	13-09-1994	1033.47	7-02-1995	532.49	48.5%	147
4	26-08-1996	24-07-1996	887.6	12-09-1996	757.09	14.7%	50
5	6-11-1996	28-10-1996	1022.86	24-12-1996	865.58	15.4%	57
6	16-05-1997	12-05-1997	1500.4	23-09-1997	1041.97	30.6%	134
7	7-08-1998	3-06-1998	1420	17-08-1998	1070.41	24.6%	75
8	1-07-1999	29-06-1999	1739.21	27-12-1999	1345.35	22.6%	181
9	22-09-2000	21-08-2000	2108.69	25-09-2000	1875.91	11%	35
10	21-02-2001	10-01-2001	2125.62	22-02-2001	1907.26	10.3%	43
11	30-07-2001	13-06-2001	2242.42	22-01-2002	1358.69	39.4%	223
12	23-04-2003	8-07-2002	1732.93	18-11-2003	1316.56	24%	498
13	29-04-2004	6-04-2004	1777.52	13-09-2004	1260.32	29.1%	160
14	4-08-2006	11-07-2006	1745.81	7-08-2006	1547.44	11.4%	27
15	2-02-2007	24-01-2007	2975.13	5-02-2007	2612.54	12.2%	12
16	4-06-2007	29-05-2007	4334.92	5-07-2007	3615.87	16.6%	37
17	8-11-2007	16-10-2007	6092.06	4-11-2008	1706.7	72%	385
18	12-08-2009	4-08-2009	3471.44	31-08-2009	2667.75	23.2%	27
19	27-10-2010	23-11-2009	3338.66	25-01-2011	2677.43	19.8%	428
20	27-12-2012	2-03-2012	2460.69	27-06-2013	1950.01	20.8%	482
21	25-06-2014	12-09-2013	2255.6	25-06-2014	2025.5	10.2%	286
22	19-06-2015	12-06-2015	5166.35	26-08-2015	2927.29	43.3%	75

Table 4.18.   The SZECOMP Index experienced 20 crashes between March 25, 1992 and June 30, 2016.

	Crash identification date	Peak date	SZECOMP Index at peak	Trough date	SZECOMP Level at trough	Peak-to-trough decline (%)	Peak-to-trough duration (in days)
1	3-06-1992	26-05-1992	312.21	16-06-1992	233.73	25.1%	21
2	5-03-1993	22-02-1993	359.44	21-07-1993	203.91	43.3%	149
3	10-05-1996	22-05-1995	169.66	26-08-1996	152.55	10.1%	462
4	10-09-1996	4-09-1996	274.56	24-12-1996	242.01	11.9%	111
5	16-05-1997	12-05-1997	517.91	23-09-1997	312.73	39.6%	134
6	6-07-1998	3-06-1998	441.04	18-08-1998	317.1	28.1%	76
7	1-07-1999	29-06-1999	525.14	27-12-1999	395.69	24.7%	181
8	25-09-2000	21-08-2000	643.77	25-09-2000	578.76	10.1%	35
9	8-02-2001	23-11-2000	654.37	22-02-2001	568.26	13.2%	91
10	30-07-2001	13-06-2001	664.85	22-01-2002	371.79	44.1%	223
11	26-04-2004	7-04-2004	470.55	13-09-2004	315.17	33%	159
12	2-08-2006	12-07-2006	446.61	7-08-2006	380.26	14.9%	26
13	1-06-2007	29-05-2007	1292.44	5-07-2007	1015.85	21.4%	37
14	25-10-2007	9-10-2007	1551.19	28-11-2007	1219.98	21.4%	50
15	22-01-2008	15-01-2008	1576.5	4-11-2008	456.97	71%	294
16	14-08-2009	4-08-2009	1149.27	1-09-2009	900.53	21.6%	28
17	22 -12-2009	3-12-2009	1234.17	5-07-2010	921.34	25.3%	214
18	17-11-2010	10-11-2010	1389.54	25-01-2011	1136.58	18.2%	76
19	24-06-2013	30-05-2013	1043.47	25-06-2013	879.93	15.7%	26
20	28-03-2014	17-02-2014	1160.39	28-04-2014	1007.27	13.2%	70
21	19-06-2015	12-06-2015	3140.66	15-09-2015	1580.26	49.7%	95

Table 4.19. SHCOMP: Maximum likelihood estimate and likelihood ratio test for the PE and logPE.

Signal model	Total number of signals	Number of correct predictions	ML Estimate $\hat{p}$	$L(\hat{p})$	Likelihood ratio Λ	Test statistics $-2\ln\Lambda$	p-value
PE (confidence)	19	17	89.47%	1.67E-03	0.1159	4.3100*	3.79%
PE (Cantelli)	18	16	88.89%	1.88E-03	0.1486	3.8131†	5.09%
logPE (confidence)	18	16	88.89%	1.88E-03	0.1486	3.8131†	5.09%
logPE (Cantelli)	19	17	89.47%	1.67E-03	0.1159	4.31*	3.79%

Notes: † significant at the 10% level;
* significant at the 5% level;
** significant at the 1% level;
*** significant at the 0.5% level.

This finding is consistent with the stylized facts discussed in Section 2. The Likelihood ratio test indicates that both the P/E ratio and the logarithm of the P/E ratio are significant predictors of equity market downturns markets at the 90% confidence level. Moreover, the P/E ratio, computed using a standard confidence interval, and the log P/E ratio, based on Cantelli's inequality, are significant at the 95% confidence level. Thus, we cannot rule out that the P/E and log P/E have helped predict equity market downturns over the period.

We continue our analysis with a Monte Carlo test for small sample bias, presented in Table 4.20. We compute the critical values at the 90%, 95% and 99% confidence level for the empirical distribution. Because we only have a limited number of signals, the distribution is lumpy, making it difficult to obtain meaningful p-values. Still, we find that the Monte Carlo analysis is in broad agreement with our earlier conclusions about significance of the P/E ratio and its logarithm, as both measures are significant at the 90% confidence level. We conclude that small sample bias only has a very small effect on these measures and on their statistical significance.

Shenzhen

Table 4.21 shows that the P/E and logarithm of the P/E generated a total of 8–9 signals, with 7–8 correct signals. The accuracy of the models is in the narrow range from 87.50% to 88.89%. Here as well, the type of confidence

Table 4.20. SHCOMP: Monte Carlo likelihood ratio test for the PE and logPE.

Signal model	Total number of signals	ML Estimate $\hat{p}$	Critical Value 95% confidence	99% confidence	90% confidence	Test statistics $-2\ln\Lambda$	
PE (confidence)	19	89.47%	2.38	4.31	7.61	4.3100†	5.4%
PE (Cantelli)	18	88.89%	2.38	4.31	7.61	3.8131†	7.61%
logPE (confidence)	18	88.89%	2.99	3.81	6.99	3.8131†	7.84%
logPE (Cantelli)	19	89.47%	2.99	3.81	6.99	4.3100*	3.8%

Notes: †significant at the 10% level;
* significant at the 5% level;
** significant at the 1% level;
*** significant at the 0.5% level.

Table 4.21. SZECOMP: Maximum likelihood estimate and likelihood ratio test for the PE and logPE.

Signal model	Total number of signals	Number of correct predictions	ML Estimate $\hat{p}$	$L(\hat{p})$	Likelihood ratio Λ	Test statistics $-2\ln\Lambda$	p-value
PE (confidence)	9	8	88.89%	4.33E-02	0.1313	4.0607*	4.39%
PE (Cantelli)	9	8	88.89%	4.33E-02	0.1313	4.0607*	4.39%
logPE (confidence)	9	8	88.89%	4.33E-02	0.1313	4.0607*	4.39%
logPE (Cantelli)	8	7	87.5%	4.91E-02	0.1980	3.2387†	7.19%

Notes: †significant at the 10% level;
* significant at the 5% level;
** significant at the 1% level;
*** significant at the 0.5% level.

interval — normal distribution or Cantellis inequality — only have a minor influence on the end result.

The uninformed prior probability p_0 that a day picked at random will precede a crash identified date by 252 days or less is 58.49%. The likelihood ratio test indicates that both P/E ratio measures and the logarithm

Table 4.22. SZECOMP:Monte Carlo likelihood ratio test for the PE and logPE.

Signal model	Total number of signals	ML Estimate $\hat{p}$	Critical Value			Test statistics $-2\ln\Lambda(p_0)$
			90% confidence	95% confidence	99% confidence	
PE (confidence)	9	88.89%	2.31	4.06	4.92	4.0607†
PE (Cantelli)	9	88.89%	2.31	4.06	4.92	4.0607†
logPE (confidence)	9	88.89%	2.31	4.06	8.86	4.0607†
logPE (Cantelli)	8	87.50%	2.31	4.06	8.86	3.2387†

Notes: † significant at the 10% level;
* significant at the 5% level;
** significant at the 1% level;
*** significant at the 0.5% level.

of the P/E ratio calculated using a standard confidence interval are significant predictors of equity market downturns markets at the 95% confidence. The remaining measure, the logarithm of the P/E ratio calculated with Cantelli's inequality is significant at the 90% confidence level. The results of the Monte Carlo analysis, presented in Table 4.22, indicate that small sample bias only has a minor effect on the statistical significance of the measures. All the measures are still significant at the 90% confidence level.

4.6.3. The P/E ratio and the BSEYD model

Here, we test the forecasting ability of four measures:

(1) **PE0**: P/E ratio based on current earnings. This is the measure we tested in Section 4.6.2;
(2) **PE10**: PE10, which is a P/E ratio computed using average earnings over the previous 10-years;
(3) **BSEYD0**: BSEYD based on current earnings;
(4) **BSEYD10**: BSEYD using average earnings over the previous 10-years.

We also tested the logarithm of these measures: **logPE0, logPE10, logBSEYD0** and **logBSEYD10**.

Because the PE10 and BSEYD10 require 10 years of earnings data, and the Bloomberg data series for 10-year government bonds only starts on October 31, 2006, we cannot use the full range of stock market data. The analysis in this section covers the period between October 31, 2006 and September 30, 2015. Over this period, the SHCOMP experienced seven declines of more than 10%, while the SZECOMP had nine.

We omit from the discussion, results related to Cantelli's inequality because of space constraints. These results are nearly identical to the results we obtain for measures based on a standard confidence interval.

Shanghai

Table 4.23 displays the results for the eight measures, calculated with a confidence interval based on a normal distribution. First, none of the measures produced more than 5 signals. The PE10, logPE10 and BSEYD10 generated three signals each. The accuracy of the measures reaches a low of 40% for logBSEYD0 and a high of 100% for PE10 and logPE10. Only five of the eight measures are 75% accurate or better. By comparison, the uninformed prior probability that a day picked at random will precede a crash identification date by 252 days or less is $p_0 = 70.99\%$. Because of the relatively short period and small number of downturns, only PE10 and logPE10 appear significant. However, these two models only predicted three of the six crashes.

Overall, none of the models perform convincingly. The PE0 and logPE0 ratio, which we found to be significant predictors over the entire dataset

Table 4.23.   SHCOMP: Maximum likelihood estimate and likelihood ratio test for the BSEYD0, PE0, BSEYD10 and PE10 and their logarithm.

Signal model	Total number of signals	Number of correct predictions	ML Estimate $\hat{p}$	$L(\hat{p})$	Likelihood ratio Λ	Test statistics $-2\ln\Lambda$	p-value
BSEYD0	4	3	75%	1.05E-01	0.717	0.6654	41.47%
logBSEYD0	5	2	40%	3.46E-02	0.7901	0.4713	49.24%
PE0	4	3	75%	1.05E-01	0.717	0.6654	41.47%
logPE0	4	3	75%	1.05E-01	0.717	0.6654	41.47%
BSEYD10	3	2	66.67%	1.48E-01	0.9228	0.1606	68.86%
logBSEYD10	5	3	60%	3.46E-02	0.9778	0.0449	83.23%
PE10	3	3	100.00%	—	—	—	—
logPE10	3	3	100.00%	—	—	—	—

Notes: † significant at the 10% level;
* significant at the 5% level;
** significant at the 1% level;
** significant at the 0.5% level.

Table 4.24.   SHCOMP: Monte Carlo likelihood ratio test for the BSEYD0, PE0, BSEYD10 and PE10 and their logarithm.

Signal model	Total number of signals	ML Estimate $\hat{p}$	Critical Value 90% confidence	95% confidence	99% confidence	Test statistics $-2\ln\Lambda(p_0)$
BSEYD0	4	75%	4.74	4.74	6.44	0.6654
logBSEYD0	5	40%	2.62	5.92	8.05	0.4713
PE0	4	75%	4.74	4.74	6.44	0.6654
logPE0	4	75%	4.74	4.74	6.44	0.6654
BSEYD10	3	66.67%	3.55	4.83	4.83	0.1606
logBSEYD10	5	60%	2.62	5.92	8.05	0.0449
PE10	3	100.00%	3.55	4.83	4.83	—
logPE10	3	100%	3.55	4.83	4.83	—

Notes: [†] significant at the 10% level;
[*] significant at the 5% level;
[**] significant at the 1% level;
[***] significant at the 0.5% level.

in the previous section, are not significant over this restricted time period. With a 75% accuracy, they have an edge over the uniformed prior p_0. But we simply do not have enough crashes and prediction to tilt the statistical scales in their favor: the p-value remains around 40%. The results of the Monte Carlo analysis for small sample bias, presented in Table 4.24, do not give us additional information.

What's more, the BSEYD-based models do not perform as well as the P/E-based models. This is a puzzle, because the BSEYD model contains additional information that is not in the P/E, namely government bond yields. The BSEYD and logBSEYD models have been shown to perform better than the P/E ratio and PE10 on the American market and has performed well on most international markets. There are the possible explanations. The first possibility is that the sample we are studying is simply too limited. Seven crash and between three and five predictions is not enough to get reliable statistics, and leaves our conclusions vulnerable to the "law of small numbers". This is undoubtedly a main concern, which the results of our Monte Carlo analysis for small sample bias cannot dispel.

A second explanation relates to the choice of forecasting horizon. If the forecasting BSEYD-based measures generates a signal with a shorter horizon, than the forecasting horizon $H = 252$, then the measure will appear inaccurate. This is very similar to judging the quality of a camera by first blocking its depth-of-field at 6 meters, but taking a picture of a flower just centimeters away. The camera might be excellent, but the picture will appear hopelessly out-of-focus. We will be able to examine this hypothesis later, by analyzing the sensitivity of the measures to a change of horizon.

Another possible hypothesis, which we cannot test directly in the context of this study, is that the market microstructure of the SHCOMP and of the Chinese bond market makes the supply and demand for securities less sensitive to the prevailing government bond rate. If the problem is related to the definition of the interest rate, in particular if the government bond rate is not representative of the financing rate for stock traders and portfolio managers, we can expect to make similar observation on the SZECOMP. On the other hand, if the problem is linked to the microstructure of the SHCOMP, we might see BSEYD-based measures perform relatively better than P/E-based measures on the SZECOMP.

In an effort to understand this observation, we explore the sensitivity of the measures to a change in the forecasting horizon H. The results in Table 4.25 indicate that BSEYD0, PE0, logPE0, BSEYD10 and logB-SEYD10 perform best at $H = 126$, while PE10 and logPE10 reach 100% accuracy at $H = 126$. In fact, all the measures except logBSEYD0 and log-BSEYD10 are significant at the 90% confidence with the choice $H = 126$. We conclude that the measures are sensitive to the forecasting horizon, and that the standard choice $H = 252$ is suboptimal on this dataset. This conclusion comes in support of the second hypothesis we suggested to explain the relatively poor performance of the BSEYD models. It does not, however, fully explain this relative underperformance.

Shenzhen

The situation on the SZECOMP is markedly different: all the measures display a remarkable accuracy. The results in Table 4.26 show that all the measures, but one, have a 100% accuracy on the six to seven signals that they generated. The remaining measure, logBSEYD10, had six correct predictions out of seven signals, which implies a 85.71% accuracy. Although this is much higher than the uniformed prior p_0 at about 67%, the sample is too small for the difference in accuracy to be statistically significant. The Monte Carlo analysis for small bias, reported in Table 4.27 is not informative in this case, because most measures have an infinite test statistic.

Table 4.25. SHCOMP: Accuracy and statistical significance of the BSEYD and log BSEYD as a function of the forecasting horizon H. The numbers presented in this table are based on a confidence parameter $\alpha = 0.95$. With this choice, the BSEYD generated 4 signals, and the log BSEYD produced 18 signals. Row 1 presents the uninformed probability p_0 that a random guess would correctly identify an equity market downturn. Row 3 reports the number of correct signals, row 4, the proportion of correct signals as the ratio of the number of correct signals to the total number of signals for the BSEYD0. Rows 5 and 6 respectively report the test statistics and p-value. The subsequent sub tables do the same for the other models.

	63	126	189	252	63	126	189	252
Uninformed probability p_0	22.21%	33.1%	44.2%	55.31%	22.21%	33.1%	44.2%	55.31%
	BSEYD0				logBSEYD0			
Number of signals	4	4	4	4	5	5	5	5
Number of correct signals	2	3	3	3	1	2	2	2
Proportion of correct signals	50%	75%	75%	75%	20%	40%	40%	40%
Test statistics	1.4776	2.9393	1.5663	0.6654	0.0145	0.1043	0.0361	0.4713
p-value	22.41%	8.64%†	21.07%	41.47%	90.41%	74.67%	84.93%	49.24%
	PE0				logPE0			
Number of signals	4	4	4	4	4	4	4	4
Number of correct signals	1	3	3	3	2	3	3	3
Proportion of correct signals	25%	75%	75%	75%	50%	75%	75%	75%
Test statistics	0.0175	2.9393	1.5663	0.6654	1.4776	2.9393	1.5663	0.6654
p-value	89.48%	8.64%†	21.07%	41.47%	22.41%	8.64%†	21.07%	41.47%

(Continued)

Table 4.25. *(Continued)*

	63	126	189	252	63	126	189	252
	BSEYD10				logBSEYD10			
Number of signals	3	3	3	3	5	5	5	5
Number of correct signals	1	2	2	2	2	3	3	3
Proportion of correct signals	33.33%	66.67%	66.67%	66.67%	40%	60%	60%	60%
Test statistics	0.1947	1.4076	0.6132	0.1606	0.7951	1.5118	0.5019	0.0449
p-value	65.90%	23.55%	43.36%	68.86%	37.26%	21.89%	47.87%	83.23%
	PE10				logPE10			
Number of signals	3	3	3	3	3	3	3	3
Number of correct signals	2	3	3	3	2	3	3	3
Proportion of correct signals	66.67%	100%	100%	100%	66.67%	100%	100%	100%
Test statistics	2.7014	—	—	—	2.7014	—	—	—
p-value	10.03%	—	—	—	10.03%	—	—	—

Notes: † significant at the 10% level;
* significant at the 5% level;
** significant at the 1% level;
*** significant at the 0.5% level.

Table 4.26. SZECOMP: Maximum likelihood estimate and likelihood ratio test for the BSEYD0, PE0, BSEYD10 and PE10 and their logarithm.

Signal model	Total number of signals	Number of correct predictions	ML Estimate $\hat{p}$	$L(\hat{p})$	Likelihood ratio Λ	Test statistics $-2\ln\Lambda$	p-value
BSEYD0	6	6	100.00%	—	—	—	—
logBSEYD0	7	7	100.00%	—	—	—	—
PE0	6	6	100.00%	—	—	—	—
logPE0	6	6	100.00%	—	—	—	—
BSEYD10	7	6	85.71%	5.67E-02	0.5266	1.2826	25.74%
logBSEYD10	7	7	100.00%	—	—	—	—
PE10	6	6	100.00%	—	—	—	—
logPE10	5	5	100.00%	—	—	—	—

Notes: † significant at the 10% level;
* significant at the 5% level;
** significant at the 1% level;
*** significant at the 0.5% level.

Table 4.27. SZECOMP: Monte Carlo likelihood ratio test for the BSEYD0, PE0, BSEYD10 and PE10 and their logarithm.

Signal model	Total number of signals	ML Estimate $\hat{p}$	Critical Value 90% confidence	95% confidence	99% confidence	Test statistics $-2\ln\Lambda(p_0)$
BSEYD0	6	100.00%	4.81	4.81	6.48	—
logBSEYD0	5	100.00%	4.31	5.61	5.61	—
PE0	6	100.00%	4.81	4.81	6.48	—
logPE0	6	100.00%	4.81	4.81	6.48	—
BSEYD10	7	85.71%	4.31	5.61	5.61	1.2826
logBSEYD10	7	100.00%	4.31	5.61	5.61	—
PE10	6	100.00%	4.81	4.81	6.48	—
logPE10	5	100.00%	4.01	4.01	4.66	—

Notes: † significant at the 10% level;
* significant at the 5% level;
** significant at the 1% level;
*** significant at the 0.5% level.

4.6.4. *Concluding on crash predictions in China*

The Chinese stock market is certainly one of the most interesting and most complex equity markets in the world. Its size, scope, structure and the rapidity of its evolution make it unique. These characteristics inevitably affect its behavior and returns. Although the SSE and the SZSE are among the largest stock exchanges in the world, their behavior is much more volatile than that of more mature equity markets in Europe, and North America. The market is so volatile that the following straddle strategy is widely recommended by brokerage firms: buy at-the-money puts and calls. The idea is that market volatility raises the probability that either the call or the put will move deep in-the-money, making the strategy profitable (Ziemba, 2015).

Overall, this section shows clearly that crash prediction models can be applied directly to the Chinese market, and reveals potential areas for further research both on the behaviors of Chinese equity markets and on crash prediction models.

Our investigation of fundamental crash predictors reveals that the P/E and its logarithm have successfully predicted crashes on both the SHCOMP and the SZCOMP over the entire length of the study. These results are relatively robust to changes in the two key parameters of the model: the confidence level α and the forecasting horizon H.

A comparison of the BSEYD, PE and (nominal) PE10 and their logarithm over a shorter 9-year period, is less conclusive. Measures based on the BSEYD do not perform as well as measures based on the P/E and in particular, the PE10. This is a puzzle because the BSEYD contains more information than the P/E and has been more successful in other markets since 1988. However, all measures perform surprisingly well on the SZECOMP. Two possible explanations for this situation are that (i) the sample is small, so any correct or incorrect prediction has a large impact on the accuracy of the measure and its statistical test, and (ii) the market microstructure of the SHCOMP and SZECOMP differ because the SSE and SZSEs were created for two different types of companies: public companies in Shanghai and privately-owned companies in Shenzhen. Exploring this hypothesis is a possible question for future research.

Chapter 5

Other Prediction Models for the Big Crashes Averaging −25%

In this chapter, we discuss and modify to predict better Warren Buffett's value of the stock market to value of the economy prediction model as well as the Sotheby's stock price prediction model that correctly called three large stock market crashes.

5.1. Warren Buffett's ratio of the market value of all publicly traded stocks to the current level of the GNP

In an article co-authored with Carol Loomis (Buffett and Loomis, 2001), Warren Buffet discussed the "market value of all publicly traded securities as a percentage of the country's business — that is, as a percentage of GNP:"

> The ratio has certain limitations in telling you what you need to know. Still, it is probably the best single measure of where valuations stand at any given moment. And as you can see, nearly two years ago the ratio rose to an unprecedented level. That should have been a very strong warning signal.

In this article, Buffett and Loomis (2001) follow-up on an earlier interview (Buffett and Loomis, 1999), discussing the Dot.Com bubble and stock (over) valuation.

The idea behind the market value to gross national product ratio (MV/GNP) is to gauge the total market value of companies against the value of the goods and services that these companies produce. The market value of all publicly traded US securities reflects the capacity of US firms to generate revenue, and translate these revenues into stable earnings. The US GNP represents the market value of all the products and services produced by US citizens and companies regardless of where they are produced. By contrast, the US GDP is the market value of all the products and services

133

produced in the US, regardless of who produced it. To illustrate, the production of Apple in China would be part of the US GNP but not GDP, while the cars produced in the United States by Toyota would count in the US GDP but not GNP. This argument justifies the use of the GNP in the ratio.

Buffett and Loomis (2001) also suggested the following heuristic decision rule:

> If the percentage relationship falls to the 70% or 80% area, buying stocks is likely to work very well for you. If the ratio approaches 200% — as it did in 1999 and a part of 2000 — you are playing with fire.

Figure 5.1 shows the ratio of the Wilshire 5000 Full Cap Price Index, a proxy for the total market value of US stocks, to the US GNP. The ratio reached its peak at 142% in March 2000. The figure also indicates the 80% and 120% levels, which are often used by practitioners. The ratio has only risen above 120% on two instances over the past 45 years: during the Dot.Com bubble and since the end of 2014. Market commenters and investment managers have taken this pattern as evidence that the stock market is heading for a sharp decline.

Fig. 5.1.   Wilshire 5000-to-GNP ratio (1970Q4–2016Q1).

To investigate these claims, we use quarterly, seasonally-adjusted, final GNP data from the fourth quarter of 1970 up to the first quarter of 2016, for a total of 181 quarters. We use the Wilshire 5000 Full Cap Price Index as a proxy for the market value of all publicly traded securities. Using financial market and macroeconomic data series in the same measure creates a problem of synchronicity. Financial market data, such as Wilshire 5000, are directly observable and readily available. Macroeconomic data series, such as the GDP or GNP, are released with a lag and subject to revisions. Hence, we cannot determine the exact value of the MV/GNP ratio using only information available on June 30th. With this caveat in mind, it is still best to use both the June 30th market value of the Wilshire 5000 and the final release of Q2 GNP for the purpose of testing the accuracy of the MV/GNP ratio as a predictor of market downturn. The reason is that both dataset include the most accurate measurement of market capitalization and economic activity. Intuitively, if the measure does not perform well with full information, then we cannot expect it to perform well with partial information.

5.1.1. *Turning the MV/GNP ratio into a crash prediction measure*

Next, we turn the MV/GNP Ratio into a crash prediction model. The process is similar to what we have done with the P/E ratio in the previous chapter. It starts with defining the three usual components of a crash signal:

(1) the choice of measure $M(t)$;
(2) the definition of threshold $K(t)$; and
(3) the specification of a time interval H between the occurrence of the signal and that of the equity market downturn.

The Measure $M(t)$

The MV/GNP ratio, with the Wilshire 5000 Full Cap Price Index as a proxy for the market value of all publicly traded securities, is the main measure under consideration. In addition, we consider the logarithm of the MV/GNP (logMV/GNP) ratio.

The logarithm has several advantages. First, it converts products into sums and ratios into subtractions. Second, the logarithm rescales large values into smaller ones. Third, the logarithm of the market value and the logarithm of the GNP have an economic interpretation, respectively as the log return on the market value of all publicly traded securities, and as the log growth of the GNP. This means that we can interpret logMV/GNP as the difference in log return between a financial and a productive investment. Clearly, financial returns cannot outpace yields on productive investments for extensive periods of time.

In both cases, we compute the measure based on end-of period values. Our study is concerned with large deviations. Taking average values limits the amplitude and number of signals.

The Threshold K

Buffett and Loomis (2001) do not indicate a firm threshold on the upside. We use a threshold of 120% in our study. This level is often used by practitioners, probably because of its apparent symmetry with Buffett's 70%–80% downside rule.

We also test the MV/GNP measure using the usual confidence interval and Cantelli's inequality. Because we have quarterly data, the horizon for the rolling statistics is $h = 8$ quarters, or two years of data. The crash prediction literature generally suggests using one year of monthly or daily data, corresponding respectively to $h = 12$ and $h = 252$. At a quarterly frequency, one year only offers four observations to compute the rolling mean and standard deviation. Using two years of data makes for more meaningful calculations while ensuring that large and sudden equity market movements do not get "averaged out".

We pick the usual $\alpha = 95\%$ for the standard confidence interval and $\beta = 25\%$ for Cantelli's inequality.

5.1.2. *The horizon H*

The last parameter we need to specify is the horizon H. We set the horizon to $H = 8$ quarters, prior to the local peak that preceded the equity market downturn. This approach differs slightly from Lleo and Ziemba (2017) who set the horizon with respect to the crash identification date. The choice reflects a tradeoff. Using the peak date as a reference point gives us a greater control over the time horizon because we do not need to take the time between the peak and the crash identification into consideration. However, the peak date is only a by-product of the crash identification date. As such it is not a key determinant of the model. Overall, both choices are equivalent and yield similar results.

To summarise, we are testing the accuracy of six different models:

- MV/GNP with a fixed threshold at a 120% level;
- MV/GNP with a threshold computed using a standard 95% one-tail confidence interval based on a Normal distribution;
- MV/GNP with a threshold computed using Cantelli's inequality;
- logMV/GNP with a fixed threshold at a 120% level;
- logMV/GNP with a threshold computed using a standard 95% one-tail confidence interval based on a Normal distribution;
- logMV/GNP with a threshold computed using Cantelli's inequality;

5.1.3. *Results*

Table 5.1 presents the total number of signals, number of correct and incorrect predictions, and proportion of correct and incorrect predictions for

Table 5.1.   Proportion of correct and incorrect predictions for each signal model.

Model (1)	Total number of signals (2)	Number of correct predictions (3)	Proportion of correct predictions (%) (4)	Number of incorrect predictions (5)	Proportion of incorrect predictions (%) (6)
MV/GNP (fixed threshold)	2	2	100.00%	0	0.00%
MV/GNP (confidence interval)	11	8	72.73%	3	27.27%
MV/GNP (Cantelli)	11	8	72.73%	3	27.27%
logMV/GNP (fixed threshold)	2	2	100.00%	0	0.00%
logMV/GNP (confidence interval)	10	8	80.00%	2	20.00%
logMV/GNP (Cantelli)	10	8	80.00%	2	20.00%

each model. The two models based on a fixed threshold at 120% generated only two signals. The MV/GNP models based on confidence interval and Cantelli's inequality produced 11 signals each, while the logMV/GNP models based on confidence interval and Cantelli's inequality generated 10 signals each. These numbers are markedly lower than the total number of equity market downturns recorded over the period. The GNP is only released quarterly, limiting the frequency of calculation and reducing the number of signals. The accuracy of the model, defined as the proportion of correct predictions, ranges from 70% for MV/GNP based on confidence interval and Cantelli's inequality to 100% for the MV/GNP and logMV/GNP models with a fixed threshold. The accuracy of the logMV/GNP based on confidence interval and Cantelli's inequality is in between at 80%.

The probability p_0 is the probability to identify an equity market downturn within 4 quarters of a randomly selected period. To compute p_0 empirically, we tally the number of quarters that are at most 4 quarters before a peak and divide by the total number of quarters in the sample. For the entire period 1970 Q4 to 2016 Q3, we find that $p_0 = 39.08\%$. We can confirm this number heuristically. Given that 20 distinct crashes occurred, then at most $4 \times 20 = 80$ quarters in our sample fall within 4 quarters prior to a peak. Because there are 181 quarters in the dataset, the heuristic probability is $\frac{80}{179} = 44.69\%$, a bit higher than the empirical probability. The difference between the heuristic and empirical probability is due to the fact that in reality equity market corrections are not spread evenly through the period. In fact, corrections might occur in quick succession, as was the case in the late 1990s when three crashes occurred within less than two years.

Table 5.2 presents the maximum likelihood estimates, likelihood ratio and test statistics for each of the six models. With an accuracy of only 100%, the MV/GNP and logMV/GNP with fixed thresholds have a 100% track record, but out of two predictions only. The MV/GNP models using a confidence interval or Cantelli inequality are significant at a 5% level while their logarithmic version, logMV/GNP, are significant at a 1% level. Overall, all the models demonstrate an ability to predict equity market downturns.

Table 5.3 reports the maximum likelihood estimate, empirical critical value at a 90%, 95% and 99% confidence, as well as the test statistics and p-value for each model. The results confirm the analysis developed in the previous paragraph: all models based on time-varying thresholds are significant at a 5% level. This analysis reveals that overall, the likelihood

Table 5.2. Maximum likelihood estimate and likelihood ratio test: uninformed prior.

Model	Total number of signals	Number of correct predictions	ML Estimate $\hat{p}$	$L(\hat{p})$	Likelihood ratio Λ	Test statistics $-2\ln\Lambda$	p-value
MV/GNP (fixed threshold)	2	2	100.00%	—	—	—	—
MV/GNP (confidence interval)	11	8	72.73%	1.59E-03	0.0830	4.9755**	2.57%
MV/GNP (Cantelli)	11	8	72.73%	1.59E-03	0.0830	4.9755**	2.57%
logMV/GNP (fixed threshold)	2	2	100.00%	—	—	—	—
logMV/GNP (confidence interval)	10	8	80.00%	6.71E-03	0.0301	7.0072***	0.81%
logMV/GNP (Cantelli)	10	8	80.00%	6.71E-03	0.0301	7.0072***	0.81%

Notes: * significant at the 10% level;
** significant at the 5% level;
*** significant at the 1% level.

Table 5.3.   Monte Carlo likelihood ratio test.

Signal Model	Total number of signals	ML Estimate $\hat{p}$	Critical Value: 90% confidence	Critical Value: 95% confidence	Critical Value: 99% confidence	Test statistics $-2\ln\Lambda(p_0)$	Empirical p-value
MV/GNP (fixed threshold)	2	100.00%	3.7119	3.7119	3.7119	—	—
MV/GNP (confidence interval)	11	72.73%	2.5960	4.9755	5.2161	4.9755*	5.87%
MV/GNP (Cantelli)	11	72.73%	2.5960	4.9755	5.2161	4.9755*	5.87%
logMV/GNP (fixed threshold)	2	100.00%	3.7119	3.7119	3.7119	—	—
logMV/GNP (confidence interval)	10	80.00%	1.7536	4.4102	6.8522	6.8522**	1.58%
logMV/GNP (Cantelli)	10	80.00%	1.7536	4.4102	6.8522	6.8522**	1.58%

Notes: * significant at the 10% level;
** significant at the 5% level;
*** significant at the 1% level.

ratio test based on the asymptotic χ^2 distribution has proved remarkably accurate.

Lleo and Ziemba (2015b) showed that Warren Buffett's market value of all publicly traded securities as a percentage of GNP (MV/GNP), and its parent the logarithm of the market value of all publicly traded securities as a percentage of GNP (lnMV/GNP), can be a statistically significant predictors of future market downturns. However, for these measures to have predictive value, we need to transform into a signal using time-varying confidence-based thresholds similar to what is done with the BSEYD, rather than the fixed thresholds suggested by Warren Buffett.

5.1.4. *Concluding on Warren Buffett's ratio of the market value of all publicly traded stocks to the current level of the GNP*

Our analysis shows that Warren Buffett's market value of all publicly traded securities as a percentage of GNP (MV/GNP), and its parent the logarithm of the market value of all publicly traded securities as a percentage of GNP (lnMV/GNP), can be a statistically significant predictors of future market downturns. However, for these measures to have statistically significant predictive value, time-varying confidence-based thresholds rather than fixed thresholds must be used.

This conclusion dispels a common myth about the MV/GNP ratio: that absolute level matters. This myth has led market commentators and investment practitioners to suggest that the level of the MV/GNP is the harbinger of an impeding market meltdown. After all, they argue, the MV/GNP has only been higher than its current level once: in the wake of the Dot.Com bubble. Our findings indicate that this claim cannot be substantiated. Using an arbitrary threshold fixed at 120%, the MV/GDP would have signaled at most 2 out of the 20 equity market corrections that occurred between 1970 Q4 and 2015 Q1. This is not to say that the absolute level of the ratio is altogether irrelevant. However, in itself, the level does not provide sufficient evidence to forecast most equity market downturns.

A major and very practical limitation of the MV/GNP ratio is its reliance on the GNP, which is only released quarterly and subject to revisions. This reliance prevents more timely measurements which are crucial to identify and anticipate possible market downturns. The recent launch of the Atlanta Fed's GDPNow responds to a rising interest in more frequent data releases. Until a 'GNPNow' is available, our work suggests that we can use GDPNow as a proxy without a significant loss of accuracy.

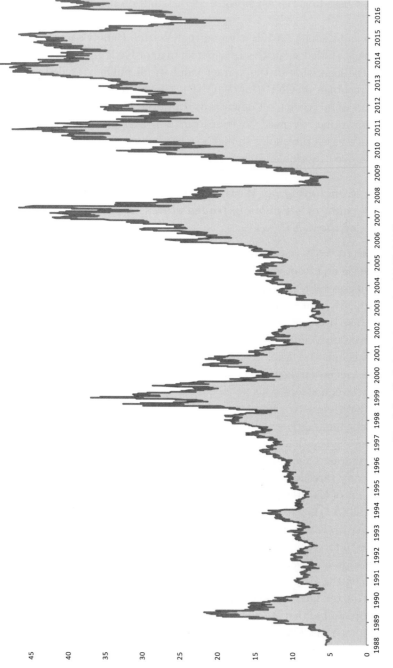

Fig. 5.2. Sotheby's share price (1988–2016).

5.2. Sotheby's stock price

The Sotheby's stock price has proved an accurate predictor of bubbles and crashes, forecasting the Japan (1989), US technology (2000) and the Global Financial Crisis in 2008. Sotheby's is a high end auction house. The idea is that Sotheby's wealthy clients will tend to sell some of the items that they have accumulated in the recent boom years near the peak. Sotheby's auction volume and stock performance soars right at the top only to collapse once the market implodes.

Figure 5.2 shows the evolution of Sotheby's stock price since April 1988. The peaks reached in August 1989, April 1999 and September 2007 are clearly visible. Figure 5.3 compares the evolution of Sotheby's stock price with that of the S&P500. In 1989, 1999, 2007 and 2011, Sotheby's stock price peaked before or the S&P entered into a correction or bear market. Figure 5.4 provides another view point by displaying Sotheby's stock price in two different ways: its nominal price (in nominal US$) with a price deflated by the S&P500. In essence, this deflated price gives the value of the Sotheby's stock relative to the current value of the S&P500. This last

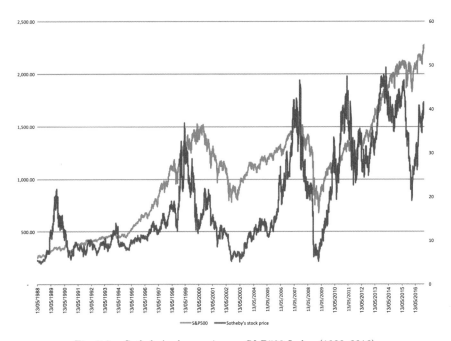

Fig. 5.3.   Sotheby's share price vs. S&P500 Index (1988–2016).

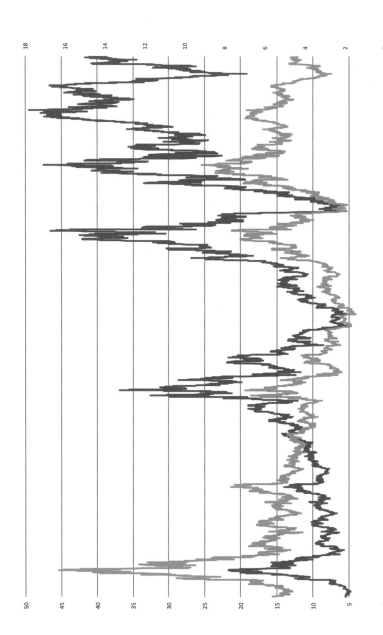

Fig. 5.4. Sotheby's share price: nominal price vs. price deflated by the S&P500 Index (1988–2016).

figure shows that the peaks reached by Sotheby's stock price were large, not only in absolute terms but also relative to the S&P500 index.

In January 2017, Sotheby's stock price was around $40 after gaining 100% since its January 2016 low. To signal a bubble, the stock price would need to be above $60. The figure below shows three large crashes called by the Sotheby's crash model.

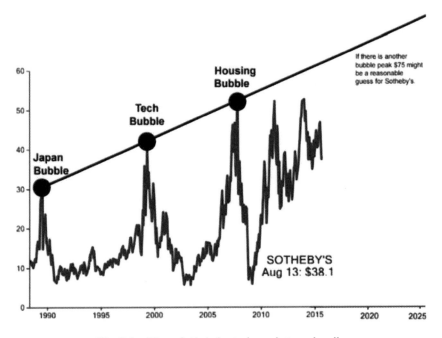

Fig. 5.5.   Three Sotheby's stock market crash calls.

Source: Floatingpath.

Chapter 6

Effect of Fed Meetings and Small-Cap Dominance

In this chapter we discuss the generally positive effects on the US stock market of FED meetings and small cap stocks.

Sixty-fourty pension fund fixed mix and presidential party effects are studied along with the effects on the stock market when congress is in session.

Five strategies are presented and two simple presidential party strategies have over long periods produced higher returns than small or large cap stocks and about twenty times more final wealth than the highly recommended 60-40 stock-bond mix.

6.1. The importance of the Fed meetings

Former Federal Chairman Alan Greenspan wrote in his 2007 memoir:

> People would stop me on the street and thank me for their 401(k); I'd be cordial in response, though I admit I occasionally felt tempted to say, 'Madam, I had nothing to do with your 401(k).' It's a very uncomfortable feeling to be complimented for something you didn't do.

This is naive — his policies created a stock market bubble which burst and then created a bubble in real estate which also crashed.

A study by Lucca and Moench (2011, 2015) of the New York Fed shows the influence of the Fed Open Market meetings since they were publicized and announced in 1994 through mid 2011.[1] Since then, the S&P500 has risen from 450 to 1300. More than 80% of the equity premium on US stocks was earned over the 24 hours preceding scheduled Federal Open Market

---

[1]This Chapter relies on Housel (2012), Dzahabrov and Ziemba updated the data to 2015 here.

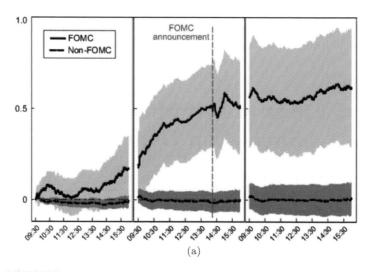

Fig. 6.1. S&P500 returns around Fed meetings, 1994–2011. (a) S&P500 returns and their variation during Fed meetings. (b) S&P500 returns with and without Fed meetings.

Source: Motley Fool.

Committee (FOMC) meetings and virtually all in the 3-day window around these meetings.

The S&P500 returns shown in Figure 6.1(a) are uncertain with a positive bias but of considerable variation. So the Fed effect does seem to work but there is risk in it in a particular meeting. Given the confidence intervals, one sees the returns are not straight up. Also, some tests Constantine Dzhabarov ran for Ziemba indicate that the effect is less pronounced in recent data ending September 30, 2012.

Matt Koppenheffer of the Motley Fool used market data going back to 1994. He randomly removed 136 days (eight per year for 17 years, or one for every FOMC meeting). He ran the simulation several hundred times, removing different sets of random days, see Figure 6.1(b). The difference was trivial. Nothing came within a third of the skew caused by removing the days shortly before FOMC meetings. Over the long haul, stocks are driven by fundamentals, in the short term they are impacted by headlines including waiting for the FOMC announcements which add to volatility.

To study this further, we updated this research to July 2015 using the S&P500 mini futures as well as the Russell2000 mini futures plus we investigated the 5-day period adding one day before and one day after the 3-day Fed meeting. The results are shown in Figures 6.2 and 6.3.

Looking at the whole period which contains the various FOMC meetings, the gain in points per S&P500 mini futures contract from September 1997 to July 2015 peaked at slightly above 700 (that is, $35,000 per contract, a huge gain) in September 2007 and was lower, about $425 at the end of the Lucca and Moench (2011, 2015) study. The drop coincided with the S&P500 drop from a peak of 1522.50 on July 14, 2007 (see Lleo and Ziemba, 2012 for the June 14, 2007 signal exiting the S&P500 based on the BSEYD model being in the danger zone). The March 9, 2009 low was 676.53. Since then, there have been gains back to the peak level. The Russell2000 small-cap index had a similar pattern but with a much lower low and a much lower total gain which peaked at 215 in June 2015 versus a local high of 205 in September 2003. According to Hensel and Ziemba (1995, 2000) and Ziemba (2012), small stocks are supposed to outperform large caps with Democratic presidents and handily beat a 60–40 stock–bond mix. In fact, during Obama's two terms, small caps did outperform but not during these Fed meeting periods. Small cap is still beating the S&P500 which is still beating 60–40 (see Fig. 6.4).

The Fed announcement and statement is at 1 pm eastern time on day 4. Days 3 and 4 prior to the announcement have had high gains but neither closed in July 2015 at the peak. Days 2, 3, 4 and 5 all had gains that were similar in total up to July 2015. Day 1 had losses that have accelerated since September 2012. The Fed anomaly is a powerful one which I watch carefully.

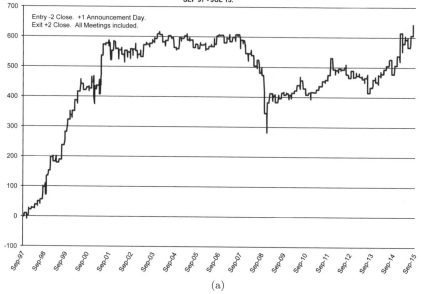

(a)

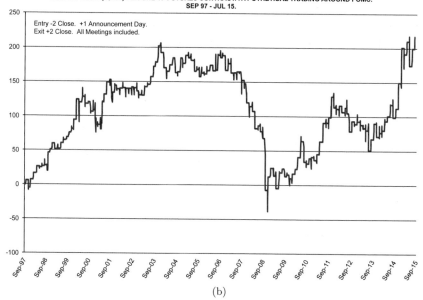

(b)

Fig. 6.2. Cumulative returns during Fed meetings, 1994–2015. (a) S&P500 (b) Russell2000.

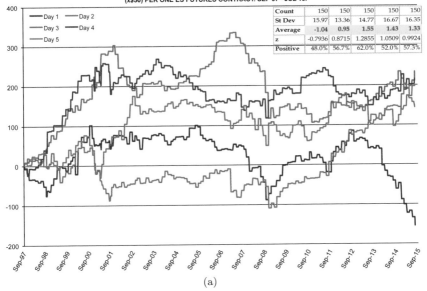

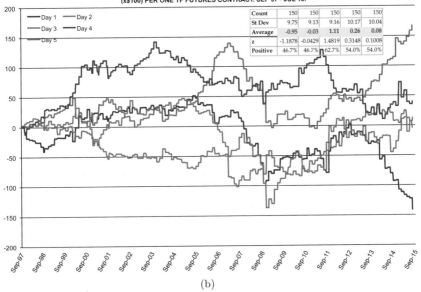

Fig. 6.3. Cumulative 5-day returns during Fed meetings, 1994–2015. (a) S&P500 (b) Russell2000.

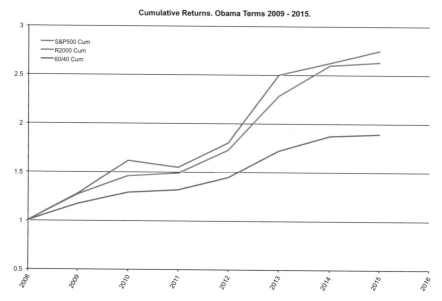

Fig. 6.4.   Small-stock Russell2000, large-cap S&P500 and a 60–40 S&P500-bond mix.

The large cap minus small cap advantage in this period is another trading opportunity. We see that the effect during the Fed meetings is mainly in the large cap stocks with the small cap stocks hardly moving.

6.2.   60–40 pension fund mixes and presidential party effects

Pension funds frequently suggest a 60–40 stock–bond mix.[2] This tends to lower risk as during stock market declines bonds tend to rise and when both stocks and bonds rise, the correlation is sufficiently low to diversify. However, US investment returns have been presidential party dependent; and returns in the last two years of all administrations have exceeded those in the first two years. This chapter studies election cycles, the effect of presidential party affiliations in the White House and the wisdom of the 60–40 stock–bond and other long-term investment rules from 1937 and 1942. I begin with the early literature. The strategies of small cap stocks with Democrats and intermediate bonds or large cap stocks with Republicans

---

[2]This section summarizes results in Ziemba (2013).

yield final wealth about six times the large cap index, 50% more than small caps and more than 20 times the 60–40 mix that is frequently recommended because of its diversification effects since 1942. The 60–40 mix does have lower standard deviation risk than the other strategies but the cost is much lower mean and total return. These results are very similar to the earlier results of Hensel and Ziemba (1995, 2000) and include out-of-sample results for the two Clinton, two Bush and one Obama terms. For comparison, the earlier to 1997 results as well as the full data set results to 2011 are shown.

Herbst and Slinkman (1984), using data from 1926 to 1977, found a 48-month political/economic cycle during which returns were higher than average; this cycle peaked in November of presidential election years. Riley and Luksetich (1980) and Hobbs and Riley (1984) showed that, from 1900 to 1980, positive short-term effects followed Republican victories and negative returns followed Democratic wins. Huang (1985), using data from 1832 to 1979 and for various subperiods, found higher stock returns in the last 2 years of political terms than in the first two. This finding is consistent with the hypothesis that political re-election campaigns create policies that stimulate the economy and are positive for stock returns. These studies concerned large cap stocks.

Stoval (1992) and Hensel and Ziemba (1995, 2000) documented the Presidential Election Cycle effect, which exhibited that stock markets generally had low returns during the first 2 years after a US Presidential election and high returns during the last 2 years. Other subsequent studies have documented the economically and statistically significant difference in equity returns during the first and second half of presidential terms for Republican and Democratic administrations. Some studies use more detailed models. Wong and McAleer (2008) examine the cyclical effect that presidential elections have on equity markets using a spectral analysis technique and an exponential GARCH Intervention model to correct for time-dependence and heteroskedasticity. They consider the period from January 1965 to December 2003 using weekly data with dummy variables to designate the year of the term and the President's party.

Wong and McAleer find a cyclical trend that mirrors the 4-year election cycle with a modified cycle of between 40 and 53 months. They find that stock prices generally fall until a low-point during the second year of a Presidency and then rise during the remainder, peaking in the third or fourth year. During the 2009–2012 Obama Democratic administration, the low was in March 2009 in his first year and the market has doubled since then to the end of April 2012. Wong and McAleer also find this Presidential Election Cycle effect to be notably more significant under Republican administrations, leading them to posit that the Republican Party may engage in policy manipulation in order to benefit during elections relatively more than their Democratic counterparts. For instance, the second-year and third-year effect estimates are not significant for Democratic administrations.

6.2.1. *Election cycles*

Wong and McAleer explain the Presidential Election Cycle as follows. During the first year of a Presidency, voters are on average optimistic, and Presidents are likely to put their most divergent and expensive new policies in place, because they have the mandate of the voters and re-election time is furthest away. These early measures are relatively disadvantageous to business profits and stock prices because they usually involve higher taxes and spending and possibly new regulations. Then, during the second-year of a term, Presidents begin to alter their policies to ones that are less drastic and more voter-friendly.

The Presidential Election Cycle effect persists when looked at by President and by party. For instance, the only two Presidents who did not exhibit the cycle effect were Ronald Reagan and Bill Clinton during their second terms, during which they would not have re-election incentives like first-term Presidents. Empirical results also find that Republicans who were subsequently re-elected had a positive effect during the second-year of their term instead of the negative effect expected by the Presidential Election Cycle hypothesis. This suggests these Republicans may have used government policies to their favor to win re-election and should be useful for incumbent Presidents to consider in their electoral strategy. This last conclusion, however, does not follow from the conflicting observation that bull markets have tended to coincide with sub-periods under Democratic administrations. Wong and McAleer conclude that this anomaly was present during most of the last 40 years and is likely still present in the market.

Hensel and Ziemba (1995, 2000) investigated several questions concerning US stock, bond and cash returns from 1928 to 1997, such as: Do small and large capitalization stock returns differ between Democratic and Republican administrations? Do corporate bond, intermediate and long-term government bonds and Treasury bill returns differ between the two administrations? Do the returns of various assets in the second half of each

4-year administration differ from those in the first half? Were Clinton's administrations analogous to past Democratic administrations? I also discuss here the terms of George W. Bush and Barack Obama to update to the end of 2010.

Their results demonstrate a significant small cap effect during Democratic presidencies. Small cap stocks (the bottom 20% by capitalization) had higher returns during Democratic than Republican administrations. There has also been a small cap minus large cap S&P advantage outside the month of January for the Democrats. The higher returns with Democrats for small cap stocks are the result of gains rather than losses in the April–December period. The turn-of-the-year small firm effect, in which small cap stock returns significantly exceed those for large cap stocks in January, under both Republican and Democratic administrations, occurred during these 70 years. This advantage was slightly higher for Democrats, but the difference is not significant. Large cap stocks had statistically identical returns under both administrations. For both Democratic and Republican administrations, small and large cap stock returns were significantly higher during the last 2 years of the presidential term than during the first 2 years. Moreover, bond and cash returns were significantly higher during Republican compared with Democratic administrations. The results also confirm and extend previous findings that equity returns have been higher in the second half compared with the first half of presidential terms. This finding is documented for small and large cap stocks during both Democratic and Republican administrations. Finally, two simple investment strategies based on these findings yielded superior portfolio performance compared with common alternatives during the sample period. The results cast doubt on the long run wisdom of the common 60–40 stock–bond strategy since all 100% equity strategies investigated had much higher wealth at the end of the sample period. Indeed the 1942–1997 returns were 24 times higher with the strategy small caps with Democrats and large caps with Republicans than the 60–40 mix and the updated 1998–2010 returns shown in Table 6.7 show similar outperformance in an update to the end of 2010.

Table 6.1 shows that both small and large cap stocks had lower mean returns in the 13 months following an election. Figure 6.6 shows the specific months following the election for large (S&P500) and small cap (bottom 20%) stocks.

The 1928–1997 period encompassed 18 presidential elections with an update to 2010 with three more elections. The end of 1997 included the

Table 6.1.   Annual average equity returns minus annualized monthly averages for presidential election months and the subsequent 13 months, 1928–1997, 1998–2010 and 1928–2010*.

Return Period	1928–1997		1998–2010		1928–2010	
	Large	Small	Large	Small	Large	Small
Election + next 13 Months	8.12	6.51	4.08	12.20	7.54	7.33
Annual average	10.12	12.02	5.19	8.22	9.34	11.42
Annual difference	−2.00	−5.51	−1.11	4.00	−1.79	−4.09

Note: *Monthly means were annualized by multiplying by 12.
Source: Updated from Hensel and Ziemba (2000).

first year of Clinton's second term. There were 33 years of Republican and 37 years of Democratic administrations during this period. The update to the end of 2010 covers the last three years of Clinton's second term plus two George W Bush terms plus the first two years of Barack Obama's administration, namely 1998–2010, a period where small cap stocks outperformed large cap stocks. Tables 6.2 and 6.3 list and compare the first year, first 2 years, last 2 years and the whole term mean returns under Democratic and Republican administrations from January 1929 to December 1997 and for January 1937 to December 1997, a period that excludes one term for each party during the 1929 crash, subsequent depression and recovery period plus the update to 2010. Each term is considered separately, so two-term presidents have double entries. The *t*-values shown in Table 6.2 test the hypothesis that, during the 1928–1997 period, returns did not differ between Democratic and Republican administrations.

From 1929 to 1997, the mean returns for small stocks were statistically higher during the Democratic presidential terms than during the Republican terms. The data confirm the advantage of small cap over large cap stocks under Democratic administrations. Small cap stocks returned, on average, 20.15% a year under Democrats compared with 1.94% under Republicans for the 1929–1997 period. This difference, 18.21%, was highly significant. The first year return differences for this period were even higher, averaging 33.51%.

The right-hand panel of Table 6.2 presents the return results after eliminating the 1929 crash, the Depression and the subsequent period of stock price volatility. Removing these 8 years (1929–1936) from the study eliminates one Democratic and one Republican administration from the data. The small stock advantage under Democrats was still large (an average

Table 6.2. Average annual returns for the first and second years and the 4 years of Democratic and Republican presidencies* to 1997.

| | Jan 1937 to Dec 1997 | | Jan 1929 to Dec 1997 | |
	S&P500 TR	U.S. Small Stk TR	S&P500 TR	U.S. Small Stk TR
Democrat				
Avg 1st Yr	6.58	11.32	10.24	19.06
Avg 1st 2Yrs	6.14	11.85	8.09	15.90
Avg Last 2Yrs	16.13	24.11	17.40	24.65
Avg. Term	10.81	16.71	12.62	20.15
Std.Dev. Term	16.35	27.76	18.26	30.69
# Years	36.00	36.00	37.00	37.00
Republican				
Avg 1st Yr	1.87	−6.22	0.54	−14.45
Avg 1st 2Yrs	6.98	1.39	3.77	−6.29
Avg Last 2Yrs	15.03	16.95	9.06	10.18
Avg. Term	11.00	9.17	6.42	1.94
Std.Dev. Term	15.12	19.89	21.17	27.81
# Years	28.0	28.0	32.0	32.0
Diff 1st Yr	4.72	17.54	9.71	33.51
Diff 1st 2Yrs	−0.84	10.46	4.32	22.19
Diff Last 2Yrs	1.10	7.16	8.33	14.47
Diff Term	−0.19	7.55	6.20	18.21
1st year t-values (Ho:Diff=0)	0.67	1.39	1.15	**2.58**
First 2-years t-values (Ho:Diff=0)	−0.14	1.13	0.69	**2.39**
Last 2-years t-values (Ho:Diff=0)	0.20	0.69	1.20	1.41
Term t-values (Ho:Diff=0)	−0.05	1.04	1.29	**2.57**

Source: Hensel and Ziemba (2000).
Note: *In this and subsequent tables, statistically significant differences at the 5% level (2-tail) are shown in bold.

of 7.55% per 4 year term) but was no longer statistically significant. The large cap (S&P500) returns during Democratic rule were statistically indistinguishable from the returns under Republican administrations. Table 6.3 updates to 2010.

For Democratic and Republican administrations, the mean small and large cap stock returns were much higher in the last 2 years compared with the first 2 years of presidential terms for both of the time periods

Table 6.3. Average annual returns for the first year and 4 years of Democratic and Republican presidencies*; update to 2010

	Jan 1937 to Dec 2010		Jan 1929 to Dec 2010		Jan 1998 to Dec 2010	
	S&P500	Small Cap	S&P500	Small Cap	S&P500	Small Cap
Democrat						
Avg 1st yr	8.79	13.08	11.86	19.87	26.46	27.19
Avg 1st 2 yrs	8.74	12.65	10.19	16.07	23.49	17.16
Avg last 2 yrs	14.10	21.11	15.32	21.83	5.97	9.12
Avg Term	11.56	16.35	13.08	17.75	16.48	13.94
Std Dev Term	16.21	26.79	17.95	29.71	15.19	15.46
# years	38	38	42	42	5	5
Republican						
Avg 1st yr	0.68	−4.05	−0.19	−11.18	−3.49	3.52
Avg 1st 2 yrs	4.69	1.35	2.48	−4.92	−3.32	1.23
Avg last 2 yrs	12.14	14.86	7.78	9.70	2.02	7.56
Avg Term	8.41	8.11	5.01	2.43	−0.65	4.39
Std Dev Term	16.96	21.21	21.24	27.28	21.51	24.90
Avg 1st yr	36	36	40	40	8	8
# years	36	36	40	40	8	8

Source: Updated from Hensel and Ziemba (2000).

presented in Table 6.2. For example, small cap stocks returned 24.65% during the last 2 years compared with 15.90% during the first 2 years for Democrats and 10.18% compared with −6.29% for Republicans from 1929 to 1992. Returns on large cap stocks increased to 17.40 from 8.09% for Democrats and to 9.06% from 3.77% for Republicans for the same period. This result is consistent with the hypothesis that incumbents embark on favorable economic policies in the last two years of their administrations to increase their re-election chances and that the financial markets view these policies favorably.

The advantage of small stocks over large stocks under Democratic administrations was not a manifestation of the January small stock effect. Instead, Tables 6.4 and 6.5 and Figure 6.5 show the relative advantage of small over large cap stocks under Democrats compared with that under Republicans was attributable to having fewer small stock losses, as well as higher mean small stock returns, in the April–December period. Under Democrats, the mean returns were positive in each of these months, except October, and the small minus large differential was positive during 10 of the 12 months; under Republicans, the small minus large differential was negative during 9 of the 12 months.

Table 6.4.   Average monthly small- and large-cap stock returns during Democratic and Republican presidencies, January 1929–December 1997.

	Democratic Administrations			Republican Administrations		
	S&P500 Total Return	US Small Cap Total Return	Small Cap minus Large Cap	S&P500 Total Return	US Small Cap Total Return	Small Cap minus Large Cap
January	1.72	6.45	4.72	1.65	5.93	4.28
February	−0.38	0.74	1.11	1.59	2.78	1.19
March	−0.58	−0.91	−0.34	0.96	1.21	0.25
April	2.25	2.58	0.33	−0.24	−1.82	−1.57
May	1.07	1.40	0.33	−0.50	−1.52	−1.02
June	1.57	1.71	0.14	0.78	−0.40	−1.18
July	1.95	2.81	0.86	1.69	1.11	−0.58
August	1.17	1.65	0.47	1.73	1.25	−0.47
September	0.40	0.78	0.38	−2.87	−3.31	−0.45
October	0.42	−0.24	−0.67	−0.40	−2.66	−2.26
November	1.44	1.61	0.17	0.44	−0.53	−0.97
December	1.56	1.58	0.02	1.59	−0.09	−1.68

Source: Hensel and Ziemba (2000).

The small cap advantage also occurred in the months following Democrat Clinton's first election. From November 1992 to December 1993, the small cap index rose 36.9% versus 14.9% for the S&P500. This domination continued until the second election. Small caps returned 1.58% per month versus 1.31% per month for the S&P500 from November 1992 to October 1996. However, large cap S&P500 returns began exceeding small cap returns in 1994 and this continued through 1997. The January 1994–December 1996 returns were small cap 1.36% per month versus 1.50% per month for the S&P500. From November 1996 to December 1997, small caps returned 1.81% per month and the S&P500 2.44% per month. There was a phenomenal growth in S&P500 index funds and much foreign investment in large cap stocks during this period. While small caps had very large returns, those of the S&P500 were even higher.

How does inflation vary with political regimes? The results for the 1929–1997 period, using the Ibbotson inflation index, indicate that inflation was significantly higher under Democrats, but this difference was contained in the 1929–1936 period. Excluding this early period, inflation was slightly higher, on average, under Democrats but not statistically different from inflation under Republican. Inflation rates differed across the years of the presidential terms. For example, for the 1937–1997 period, in the first year

Table 6.5.   Average monthly small- and large-cap stock returns during
Democratic and Republican presidencies, January 1929–December 2010.

	Democratic			Republican		
	S&P500	Small Cap	Small - S&P	S&P500	Small Cap	Small - S&P
Jan 1929 to Dec 1997						
January	1.24	5.29	4.05	0.73	5.82	5.10
February	−0.46	0.85	1.31	−1.53	−0.68	0.85
March	0.29	−0.42	−0.71	0.18	2.74	2.56
April	2.29	2.86	0.56	3.23	1.21	−2.02
May	0.74	0.89	0.15	1.93	2.78	0.84
June	1.55	1.68	0.13	−2.61	−0.35	2.26
July	1.93	2.53	0.60	−0.63	−3.32	−2.68
August	0.80	0.98	0.18	1.62	2.52	0.90
September	0.62	1.24	0.62	−6.44	−7.23	−0.79
October	0.75	−0.28	−1.03	0.54	−1.30	−1.83
November	1.41	1.60	0.18	2.91	3.05	0.13
December	1.87	2.39	0.52	2.36	2.17	−0.20
Jan 1998 to Dec 2010						
January	−2.33	−3.33	−1.00	−2.97	5.39	8.36
February	−1.08	1.63	2.71	−13.99	−14.51	−0.52
March	6.75	3.23	−3.51	−2.95	8.85	11.80
April	2.62	4.92	2.30	17.12	13.35	−3.77
May	−1.71	−2.87	−1.16	11.66	19.96	8.30
June	1.42	1.43	0.02	−16.15	−0.15	16.00
July	1.78	0.49	−1.29	−9.93	−21.03	−11.10
August	−1.93	−4.00	−2.07	1.16	7.58	6.42
September	2.21	4.63	2.41	−20.71	−22.91	−2.20
October	3.21	−0.53	−3.75	4.28	4.16	−0.12
November	1.22	1.51	0.29	12.81	17.35	4.54
December	4.17	8.42	4.25	5.46	11.20	5.74

of the presidential term, inflation under the Democrats was significantly
lower than it was under the Republicans. An analysis of the first and second 2 years of administrations during this same period indicated that inflation was higher under Democrats but the difference was not statistically
significant.

6.2.2.   *US bond returns after presidential elections*

The bond data are also from Ibbotson Associates and consist of monthly,
continuously compounded total returns for long term corporate bonds,

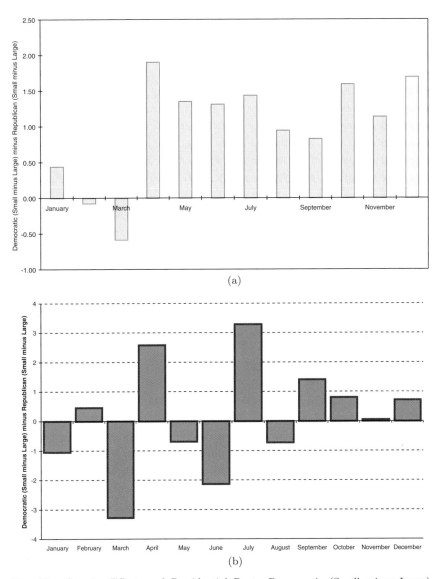

Fig. 6.5.   Cap-size Effects and Presidential Party, Democratic (Small minus Large) minus Republican (Small minus Large). (a) 1929–1997. (b) 1929-2010.

long-term (20-year) government bonds, intermediate (5-year) government
bonds, and cash (90-day T-bills).

Figure 6.6(a) illustrates average return differences for bonds during election months and the subsequent 13 months (1929–1997) minus each months
1928–1997 average return. Figure 6.6(b) updates this to 2010. Corporate,
long-term government, and intermediate government bond returns were all
higher than the monthly average in the year following an election only in
May, October, and November in the 1928–1997 period. Both government
bonds also exceeded the average in some other months. The update only
has three elections and the monthly pattern is different than it was in
the past.

As Table 6.6 indicates, the performance of fixed income investments
differed significantly between Democratic and Republican administrations.
All fixed income and cash returns were significantly higher during Republican than during Democratic administrations during the two study periods.
The high significance of the cash difference stems from the low standard
deviation over terms. The performance of fixed income investments differed
very little between the first 2 years and the last 2 years of presidential terms.

The distribution of Democratic and Republican administrations during
the 1929–1997 period played a part in the significance of the fixed income
and cash returns. As Table 6.6 indicates, the cash returns for the first
four Democratic administrations in this period (1933–1948) were very low
(0.20%, 0.08%, 0.25% and 0.50% annually). This result largely explains
why the term cash-return differences are so significant (*t*-statistic = −12.31
for 1929–1997). Democratic administrations were in power for three of the
four terms during the 1941–1956 period, when government bonds had low
returns. Bond returns in the 1961–1968 period (both Democratic terms)
and 1977–1980 period (Democratic) were also low.

6.2.3.   *Political effects: When Congress is in session*

Ferguson and Witte (2006) find a strong correlation between Congressional
activity and stock market returns such that returns are higher and volatility
lower when Congress is in session. They use four data sets, including the
Dow Jones Industrial Average since 1897, the S&P500 index since 1957,
and the CRSP value-weighted index and CRSP equal-weighted index since
1962. They compare mean daily stock returns and annualized returns when
the US Congress is in and out of session. Depending on the index tested,
statistically significant differences in average daily returns range from 4–11

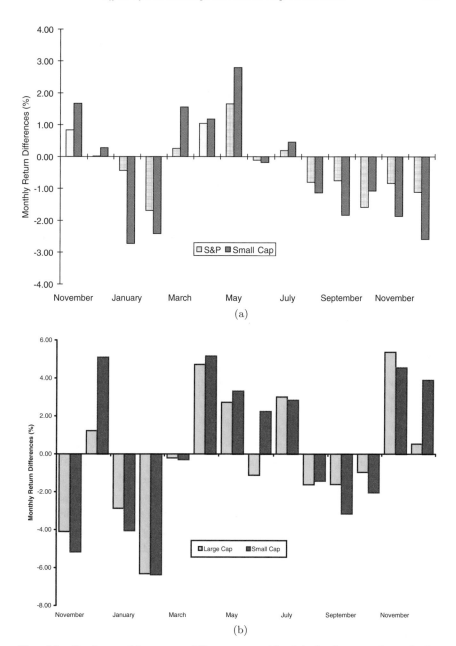

Fig. 6.6. Stock monthly return differences: presidential election months and the subsequent 13 months minus monthly averages. (a) 1928–1997. (b) 1998–2010.

Source: Hensel and Ziemba (2000)

Table 6.6.   Annualized average monthly return.

Term	President	Party	Bonds	Cash	Bonds–Cash
1929–1932	Hoover	Republican	4.61	2.26	2.35
1932–1936	Roosevelt	Democratic	5.05	0.20	4.85
1937–1940	Roosevelt	Democratic	3.73	0.08	3.65
1941–1944	Roosevelt	Democratic	1.74	0.25	1.49
1945–1948	Roosevelt/Truman	Democratic	1.48	0.50	0.98
1949–1952	Truman	Democratic	1.24	1.35	−0.11
1953–1956	Eisenhower	Republican	1.19	1.66	−0.47
1957–1960	Eisenhower	Republican	4.24	2.54	1.70
1961–1964	Kennedy/Johnson	Democratic	3.21	2.84	0.37
1965–1968	Johnson	Democratic	2.76	4.43	−1.67
1969–1972	Nixon	Republican	7.06	5.19	1.87
1973–1976	Nixon/Ford	Republican	7.42	6.25	1.17
1977–1980	Carter	Democratic	3.17	8.11	−4.94
1981–1984	Reagan	Republican	13.71	10.39	3.32
1985–1988	Reagan	Republican	10.35	6.22	4.13
1989–1992	Bush	Republican	10.77	6.11	4.66
1993–1996	Clinton	Democratic	5.74	4.30	1.44
1997–2000	Clinton	Democratic	5.77	5.07	0.69
2001–2004	Bush	Republican	3.69	1.84	1.85
2005–2008	Bush	Republican	4.00	3.40	0.61
2009–2010	Obama	Democratic	2.06	0.14	1.92

Source: Updated from Hensel and Ziemba (2000).
Note: From 1998–2010 we used the 3-month T-bill secondary market rate discount basis
for cash and market yield and US Treasury securities at 5-year constant maturity, quoted
on investment basis for bonds.

basis points per day. Annualized stock returns are 3.3–6.5% higher when
Congress is out of session, and between 65% and 90% of capital gains have
occurred when Congress is not in session (which is notably greater than the
proportionate number of days Congress is not in session).

Ferguson and Witte also test these results in several ways. First, they
analyze if the Congressional Effect is just a proxy for other known calendar
effects, such as the Day-of-the-Week Effect, January Effect, and Pre-Holiday
Effect. They conclude that, after controlling for these anomalies, there is
still a Congressional Effect of 3–6 basis points per day, which means that
no more than half of the Congressional Effect is captured by controlling for
other known anomalies. The study also tests for robustness and finds there
is a low probability that these results are the effect of a spurious statistical
relationship.

Next, they test if public opinion toward Congress accounts for the Congressional Effect by using public polling data as a proxy for general investors

attitudes toward Congress. They use 162 polls from 1939 to 2004, though 112 of these were conducted after 1989. They find that an active Congress does not itself lead to poor stock returns but rather that the public opinion of that active Congress accounts for the depressed returns. They also find that each index exhibits volatility that is significantly lower when Congress is not in session and that this is also driven by public opinion.

Then Ferguson and Witte test the implications of this predictive capability on optimal investor asset allocation using the models of Kandel and Stambaugh (1996) and Britten-Jones (1999); they find that trading on the Congressional Effect would allow investors to better allocate between equities and cash and to achieve a higher Sharpe ratio.

Ferguson and Witte consider three alternatives as possible explanations of the Congressional Effect, concluding that their findings may be explained by viewing public opinion of Congress as a proxy for investors moods, regulatory uncertainty, or rent-seeking. The mood-based hypothesis follows other studies in behavioral finance that suggest depressed investors are relatively risk averse, which in this case would imply that negative public opinion of Congress was depressing investors and dampening returns. The regulatory uncertainty hypothesis follows from the implication that there is more uncertainty in the market when Congress is in session, such that risks and therefore returns are higher. The rent-seeking hypothesis is based on Rajan and Zingales (2003) and suggests that concentrated economic interests limit the efficiency of markets such that they are less efficient and biased toward powerful financial players when Congress is in session.

6.2.4. *Some simple presidential investment strategies*

Two presidential party-based investment strategies suggest themselves. The first is equity only and invests in small caps with Democrats and large caps with Republicans; the second, a simple alternating stock–bond investment strategy, invests in small cap stocks during Democratic administrations and intermediate government bonds during Republican administrations. The test period was January 1937 through December 1997 with an update from 1998 to 2010.

The common 60–40 (large cap/bonds) portfolio investment strategy provides a benchmark for comparison with the two strategies. Transaction costs were not included, but they would have a minor effect on the results because the higher return presidential strategies trade at most every 4 years. These

Table 6.7.   Value of $1 initial investment in 1997 and 2010.

Date	Large Cap (S&P)	Small Cap	Presidential (SC/Int)	Presidential (SC/LC)	60–40 Benchmark
Jan 1937–Dec 1997	346.1	453.2	527.9	963.2	140.5
Jan 1942–Dec 1997	639.0	2044.1	2380.9	4343.8	180.9
Jan 1937–Dec 2010	565.2	959.5	1310.6	1407.9	242.4
Jan 1942–Dec 2010	1043.5	4327.6	5910.8	6349.5	312.1

Source: Updated from Hensel and Ziemba (2000).

investment strategies all lost money until the early 1940s, see Table 6.7 which shows the cumulative wealth.

The two presidential investment strategies performed well over the sample period. The strategy of investing in small cap stocks during Democratic administrations and large cap stocks during Republican administrations produced greater cumulative wealth than other investment strategies. The alternating stock–bond strategy of investing in small cap stocks under Democrats and intermediate bonds under Republicans produced the second highest cumulative wealth. Both of these presidential party-based strategies had higher standard deviations than large cap stocks alone during the 1937–1997 period. Clinton's first administration had returns for small and large cap stocks, bonds and cash consistent with the past. However, in the first 14 months of his second administration large cap stocks produced higher returns than small cap stocks.

In the update in Table 6.7 we see that, for the 1942–2010 period, small cap stocks (Russell2000 from 1998) produced about four times the gains of large cap S&P500 stocks (4327.6 versus 1043.5). But the small cap with Democrats and large cap with Republicans was even higher at 6349.5, a bit above the 5910.8 of small caps with Democrats and intermediate bonds with Republicans. Meanwhile, the 60–40 portfolio was at 312.1 less than $\frac{1}{20}$th as much!.

Table 6.8 displays the mean returns and standard deviations for the various subperiods for the various strategies. The 60–40 portfolio does have lower standard deviation but this risk-reduction is swamped by the much lower mean and total returns.

6.2.5.   *Final remarks*

An important finding of this study was the much higher small-stock returns during Democratic administrations as compared with Republican

Table 6.8. Average returns and standard deviations for different investment strategies for different investment horizons.

Dates	# years	Large Cap.		Small Cap.		Strategies Pres (SC–Int).		Pres (SC/LC).		60–40	
		Mean	St.Dev	Mean	St.Dev	Mean	St.Dev	Mean	St.Dev	Mean	St.Dev
Jan 1937–Dec 1997	61	10.9	15.8	13.3	24.5	12.6	20.7	14.1	22.8	8.6	10
Jan 1938–Dec 1997	60	11.8	15.5	14.9	23.7	14.3	19.8	15.8	22	9.2	9.8
Jan 1948–Dec 1997	50	12.3	14	13.9	19.2	13.1	12.7	14.9	16.5	9.7	9
Jan 1958–Dec 1997	40	11.6	14.2	14.7	20.2	14.6	13	15.6	17	9.7	9.3
Jan 1968–Dec 1997	30	11.4	15.1	12.7	21.5	14.3	12.4	14.3	17.5	10.1	9.9
Jan 1978–Dec 1997	20	15.4	14.7	16.3	19.5	15.9	13.8	17.2	17.9	12.9	9.9
Jan 1988–Dec 1997	10	16.6	11.9	15.2	14.9	13.7	9.9	16.2	13.2	13.2	8.2
Jan 1993–Dec 1997	5	18.4	10.6	17.7	13.3	17.7	13.3	17.7	13.3	13.5	7.4
Jan 1995–Dec 1997	3	27.1	11.2	22.1	15.1	22.1	15.1	22.1	15.1	19.7	7.6
Jan 1993–Dec 1993	1	9.5	6.1	19	9.4	19	9.4	19	9.4	10	4.3
Jan 1993–Dec 1994	2	5.4	8.5	11.1	9.8	11.1	9.8	11.1	9.8	4.3	6.5
Jan 1995–Dec 1996	2	26.3	8.4	22.9	14.2	22.9	14.2	22.9	14.2	19.3	5.9
Jan 1997–Dec 1997	1	28.8	15.8	20.5	17.6	20.5	17.6	20.5	17.6	20.5	10.5
Jan 1937–Dec 2010	74	8.9	16	12	23.5	11.9	20.1	12.5	22	7.9	11.7
Jan 1938–Dec 2010	73	9.6	15.7	13.3	22.8	13.2	19.3	13.9	21.2	8.4	11.6
Jan 1948–Dec 2010	63	9.7	14.6	12.3	18.7	12.1	13.7	12.8	16.5	8.7	11.5
Jan 1958–Dec 2010	43	10.7	14.9	15.5	19.5	16.1	14.1	16	16.9	10.4	12
Jan 1968–Dec 2010	33	10.2	15.6	14	20.3	16.3	14	14.9	17.3	11	12.7
Jan 1978–Dec 2010	23	13.2	15.5	17.7	18.5	18.5	15.1	17.7	17.4	13.9	13.4
Jan 1988–Dec 2010	13	12.4	15	17.8	16	18.9	14.5	17.3	15.4	14.9	14.3
Jan 2003–Dec 2010	8	7.7	15.2	12.4	20.5	9.7	13.3	9.3	17.4	5.9	9.1
Jan 2008–Dec 2010	3	−0.3	16.7	6.2	21.9	8.3	15.7	4.9	19.7	4.7	10

Source: Updated from Hensel and Ziemba (2000).

administrations. This finding is consistent with the hypothesis that Democrats devise economic policies that favor small companies and consequently, their stock prices. The 33.51% point difference between small stock performance in Democratic and Republican administrations in the first year in office and the 18.21% difference for the full four-year term from 1929 to 2010 are very large. Also the update from 1998 to 2010 has similar results.

This political party effect is different from the well-known January small firm effect which has been present for Republicans as well as Democrats. There is also a substantial small stock/large stock differential outside of January during Democratic rule (see Table 6.5). Large stock returns were statistically indistinguishable between Democrats and Republicans, but bond and cash returns were significantly higher during Republican than during Democratic administrations. This also confirms and updates Huang's finding that large cap stocks have had higher returns in the last 2 years of presidential terms; this finding applies regardless of political party and for both small and large cap stocks.

A study of the differences in economic policies that lead to the divergence of investment results according to which political party is in office would be interesting. Clearly, candidates seeking re-election are likely to favor economic policies that are particularly attractive to the public; and those policies are consistent with higher stock prices. Cash returns did not differ significantly between the first and second 2-year periods of Democratic and Republican presidential terms.

Chapter 7

Using Zweig's Monetary and Momentum Models in the Modern Era

In this chapter we discuss the stock market prediction models of legendary advisor and investor Marty Zweig. They use momentum and monetary FED movements and build on Jessie Livermore's ideas. The predictions still perform well some years after Zweig's 2013 death. We discuss how Zweig called the 1987 stock market crash and its recovery as well as his Zweig Forecast that was the top rated advisory service for a 15 year period.

7.1. Background

Marty Zweig was a regular panelist on Wall Street Week with Louis Rukeyser.[1] He was a technical trader and researcher and was one of the original data/anomaly researchers in an era of simpler stock market analysis. He tested and invented concepts like the put–call ratio. He had a PhD from Michigan State. He was a follower of legendary investor Jesse Livermore. His newsletter *The Zweig Forecast* ran for 26 years and during its last 15 years it was rated the best in risk-adjusted performance according to the *Hulbert Financial Digest*. In 1997, he stopped the newsletter and went into mutual funds and money management. It was so successful that he was able to purchase a 16 room penthouse with 23 foot ceilings and 17th century fixtures atop the Pierre Hotel on 5th Avenue in New York worth $70 million in 2004. Following his death, Zweig's widow sold the apartment, which had a $47,000 monthly maintenance fee, for $125 million.

Ziemba recalls his appearance on Wall Street Week the Friday before the 1987 stock market crash on Monday October 19, 1987. His face white

---

[1] This chapter is jointly written by John Swetye of Hypernormal Enterprises of Darien, Connecticut and William T Ziemba. It also appeared in *Wilmott*, January 2017.

as a sheet, he said "I don't know how much the market will fall on Monday but it will be a lot" and it did. He was given credit for calling the crash. Ziemba's colleague Blair Hull is given some credit for stopping the crash with clever buying to boost prices. Zweig summarized his models and results in his books Zweig (1986, 1987).

Zweig died on February 18, 2013 so he did not have the chance to revise his theories in light of 2017 modern markets with very low interest rates and considerable programmed and high frequency trading. Ziemba's colleague John Swetye has been using Zweig's ideas in this recent era and this chapter is meant to describe the ideas and see how well they currently work.

7.2. Zweig's model

Zweig describes the development of monetary and momentum models that are used to make buy and sell decisions.[2] The monetary model is based on indicators consisting of the Prime Rate, the Discount Rate, Reserve Requirements, and Installment Debt. Each indicator is given a numerical score. The scores are combined to yield a "composite reading on monetary conditions". Zweig developed a set of rules to use with the monetary model to make buy and sell decisions.

Zweig's momentum model is based on price and volume of NYSE listings as well as the price of the Value Line Index. Each indicator is given a score. The combined scores of the various indicators give a reading on the momentum of the market. A set of rules are used to make buy and sell decisions.

The composite scores of the two models are then combined to form what he calls the "Super Model". His simple system suggests being 100% invested or 100% in cash, but he says it could be used in any number of more complex ways. For example, being 75% invested and 25% in cash when the model shows a slightly lower than peak reading.

7.2.1. *Prime rate indicator*

The first monetary indicator is based on the movement of the Prime Rate. Zweig uses 8% as an arbitrary dividing line for the Prime Rate. He wrote that small decreases in the Prime Rate when it is below 8% are enough to give a bullish signal, but somewhat larger increases are required for a bullish signal if the decrease comes from above 8%. Conversely, small

---

[2]Our discussion follows the book's closely with much in Zweig's own words. We have edited as necessary.

increases when the rate is above 8% are enough to give a bearish signal, but below 8% somewhat larger increases are needed to give a bearish signal. He wrote that his studies showed that the trend in the Prime Rate is more significant than the level itself.

For the 29 years preceding 1993, Zweig wrote that there were an average of 10.7 Prime Rate changes per year. There were no changes in the Prime Rate from January 2009 to November 2015 — nearly 7 years. The Fed raised the Prime Rate from zero to a quarter point on December 16, 2016. Buy Signal:

(1) Any initial cut in the prime rate if the prime's peak was less than 8%.
(2) If the peak is 8% or higher, a buy signal comes on either the second of two cuts or on a full 1% cut.

A buy signal is worth 2 points. Sell Signal:

(1) Any initial hike in the rate if the prime's low is 8% or greater.
(2) If the prime's low is less than 8%, a sell signal comes on the second of two hikes or a full 1% hike.

A sell signal resets the indicator to zero points. This factor only has two values, 2 or 0.

7.2.2. *Fed indicator*

The discount rate and reserve requirements are graded separately and then combined. It is important to know that the bank reserve requirements have been effectively abolished since the 1990s. The discount rate is the only factor now used in the Fed Indicator.

Negative Points:
An increase in either the discount rate or reserve requirements is bearish. A hike in either one receives minus one point for that component. Every 6 months, if there are no changes the indicator becomes stale and one point is added back on to the indicator until it reaches zero. It remains at zero until there are positive or negative changes in the rate.

Positive Points:
Zweig wrote: "Moves by the Fed toward easing have a greater positive impact on stock prices than the negative effect created by tightening moves." So an initial cut in either the discount rate or reserve requirements wipes out all negative points that may have accumulated, but it also

adds two positive points. An initial cut is the first one following a rise in that component. Or a cut is initial if it marks the first change in that instrument in at least two years. As the initial change grows stale, one point is lost after every 6 months of no changes.

If a second cut were made in the discount rate it would add one more point for a total of three points. That point becomes stale after 6 months and would drop out. Each consecutive cut is treated the same way.

Calculating the Fed Indicator:
Add together the points of the discount rate indicator and reserve requirement indicator.

- Extremely Bullish = +2 or more points
- Neutral = 0 or 1 point
- Moderately Bearish = −1 or −2 points
- Extremely Bearish = −3 or more points

There is no Moderately Bullish rating.

7.2.3. *Installment debt indicator*

Zweig personally used a complicated consumer installment debt factor, but says that a simple one does very well at calling market moves. He used the non-seasonally adjusted number. Expansion of installment debt is bearish.

Find the consumer installment debt for this month. Divide it by the same factor from the same month a year ago and then subtract 1.000. This gives you the non-seasonally adjusted change in installment debt.

Buy Signal:
A buy signal is given when the year-to-year change in installment debt has been falling and drops to under 9%.

Sell Signal:
A sell signal is given when the year-to-year change in installment debt has been rising and hits 9% or more.

7.2.4. *Monetary model*

The Monetary Model is a market timing tool that combines the four factors mentioned earlier in the chapter: Prime Rate; Discount Rate; Reserve Requirement; and Installment Debt. To make the model ratings, the various indicators points must first be graded. To grade them, start by adding together the Discount Rate Indicator Points and the Reserve Requirement Points. Fed Indicator Gradings:

Indicator points	Rating	Model points
+2 or more points	Extremely Bullish	4
0 or +1 points	Neutral	2
−1 or −2 points	Moderately Bearish	1
−3 or fewer points	Extremely Bearish	0

7.2.5. *Installment debt gradings*

Buy Signal = 2 Model Points
Sell Signal = 0 Model Points

Buy and Sell Signals from The Monetary Model:
The Monetary Model is the addition of all model points. The maximum score is 8 and the minimum is 0. There is no way to get to 7 points because the Fed Indicator can never be 3, it can only be 0, 1, 2 and 4. The other two indicators are either 0 or 2.

When the Monetary Model reaches 6 points, it triggers a buy signal. That buy signal remains in effect until the model falls to 2 points, which then is a sell signal. The sell remains in effect until 6 is reached again which triggers a buy.

7.2.6. *4% model: the 4% model is a momentum indicator*

The 4% model gives continuous bearish or bullish signals. To calculate the model, the Value Line Index is used.[3] The S&P500 and other indicators do not work as well because they are less volatile. Find the most recent Value

---

[3]The Value Line is a small-cap index of about 1650 stocks equally weighted. Ziemba (2012) used the Value Line in the 14 turn-of-the-year trades for 1982/83-1995/96. Subsequently, the past 7 years are with the Russell2000, a value-weighted small-cap index. The first 20 of these 21 trades produced profits, see Ziemba (2012). In 2015–2016, there was a loss. This was a period following the first Fed interest rate increase in 7 years, with a threat that did not materialize, of many more rate hikes. Those hikes are finally planned for 2017.

Line Index peak or low. A buy signal is given when the VL Index rises 4% from a recent low. A sell signal is given when the VL Index falls 4% from a recent high.

A buy signal counts 2 model points. A sell signal resets the model to 0 points.

The points from the 4% Model are added to the Monetary Model to create the Super Model which can range from 0 to 10. If the sum of the points of the Super Model is 6 or greater, then a buy signal is given. If the sum of the points is 3 or less, a sell signal is given.

Zweig observed that from 1966 to 1993, the Super Model gave 13 buy signals and 14 sell signals. $10,000 invested only during the buy signal periods would have become $176,270 in a total of 199 months (16.5 years) for an 18.9% annualized return.

Trading 12 of the 13 buy signals produced a profit. One buy signal produced a loss of 1.6%.

7.2.7.   *Other momentum indicators*

Another strong Zweig buy signal is when there is a 2:1 ratio of up-stocks to down-stocks over a 10-day period.

If the ratio of advancing stocks to declining stocks over a 10 day period is 2:1 or greater, it is a very strong bullish indicator. It is a rare signal that happened 11 times from 1953 to 1993. It happened over the 10-day period from July 10, 2009 to July 23, 2009. There were signs as early as December 8, 2008 that a bull market was on the horizon when the indicator reached 1.73:1. On January 6, 2009, the indicator reached 1.96:1.

The market has been very strong since then. He wrote that on average the market rises 7.5% per quarter after this indicator occurs and 10% or more in virtually every case. The 10-day average hit 1.97:1 on February 18, 2014 but the last time it actually exceeded 2:1 was on 3 consecutive days in July 2009 which preceded a strong bull market. On October 15, 2015, the ratio was 1.70:1. That, in my opinion, is a bullish indicator because it is still relatively rare.

If the ratio of the advancing stock volume to the declining stock volume is 9:1 or greater that is a rare and bullish signal that occurs about twice per year. The ratio was 15.92:1 on October 5, 2015. Zweig says that if there is one more day in the next 3 weeks where the ratio is 9:1 or greater without an intervening 9:1 down day it is even more bullish. He calls it a "double 9 to 1".

A 9:1 down ratio is moderately bearish, but not to the degree that a 9:1 up ratio is very bullish. One sees a lot of Kahneman and Tversky behavioral finance in this.

7.3. Bull markets

There is an astute passage in Zweig's book where he writes about the beginnings of a bull market.

> "I have found that strength does indeed tend to lead to great strength. Every single bull market that I've seen has started with a tremendous rally." He continues, "For a raging bull market, you need falling interest rates, probably an economic recession (that helps the Fed to loosen up and rates to fall), lots of cash on the sidelines, good values in market namely, low price/earnings ratios and a great deal of pessimism because, as we'll see later, pessimism means there's an abundance of cash. If all these conditions converge, the market should rally very, very strongly, and the first rally of the bull market should be the best one."

The S&P500 closed on October 29, 2007 at 1540.98, and due to worsening economic conditions, by October 29, 2008 it had fallen to 930.09. By March 9, 2009, it had reached bottom and closed at 676.53.

Despite the gloom, and even though the bottom would not be reached for 3 more months, green shoots had started to appear as early as December of 2008 when the advance/decline ratio reached 1.73:1.

The advance/decline ratio hit 1.96:1 on January 6, 2009 which was very close to Zweig's bull market signal of 2:1.

A week after the March 9, 2009 bottom, the S&P500 had rallied by about 17% — 120 points.

The advance/decline ratio hit 2.17:1 on July 23, 2009 and remained above 2:1 for three straight days and was "bookended" by 1.91+ days. The S&P500 had already risen to 976 about 44% from its low. All the ingredients were in place for the kind of tremendous rally that Zweig predicted. The S&P500 would more than double over the next several years.

7.4. Example

Two of the Zweig model indicators since mid-April, 2015 — right before "Sell in May" — the Zweig 4% Model and the Ratio of Declining Volume to Rising Volume Indicator:[4]

- Prior to May 1, the Zweig Super Model had been indicating that an investor should be long stocks. The Value Line Index (VL) hit a cyclical high of 519.05 on April 10, 2015. A sell signal would occur after a 4% drop from the most recent high. The VL would need to fall to 498.29 in order for a sell signal to be triggered.

- VL reached 519.88 on April 24. This was a new high. The trigger for a sell signal was increased so that the VL would have to fall 4% to 499.08 to trigger a sell.

- The VL remained in the range of 519.88 to about 506 through Friday, July 3. Note that a new high had not been significantly breached since the April 10 cyclical high of 519.05.

- Monday, July 6, a sell signal was triggered when the VL closed at 497.73 — more than 4% below a recent peak. The next buy signal would be triggered if the VL closed at 517.64 — 4% above the recent low of 497.73.

- The VL kept falling and reached 443.06 on Monday, August 24 — more than 10% below the level of the previous sell signal and nearly 15% below its recent peak. The VL would need to rise 4% to 460.78 in order to show a buy signal.

- A sell indicator was triggered on August 24 when the ratio of down-volume to up-volume on the NYSE was greater than 9:1. This sell indicator is not as powerful as the 4% model, but adds value.

- The next day, on Tuesday, August 25, the VL fell to at 439.18 — more than 15.5% below its recent peak. The next buy signal would be at 456.75.

- Two days later on August 27, the VL reached 462.28 — more than a 4% rise. This 4% rise triggered a buy signal. The next sell signal would be at 443.79.

- Then on Tuesday, September 1, a sell indictor was triggered when declining volume outpaced buying volume by more than 9:1. In 7 trading days, there were two sell indicators triggered and one buy signal. This whipsaw WWW type action made it difficult to know which way the market was headed. Since the 4% model is a stronger signal than the declining to advancing ratio it seemed better to stay long stocks.

- The VL kept falling and a double sell indicator was triggered on Friday, September 25. The declining stock to advancing stock ratio was greater

---

[4]For on update on Sell in May and Go Away, see Dzhabrov and Ziemba (2016).

than 9:1 and the VL feel more than 4% below a recent high to 444.77. The next buy signal would be at 462.56.

- On Monday, September 28, another sell signal was received, but it was just a continuation of Friday's action. The declining stocks outnumbered advancing stocks by more than 9:1. The VL fell to a new low of 432.32 — nearly 17% below the spring peak. The buy signal was reset to a new level of 449.61. The VL fell to 431.31 the next day and the buy signal was reset to 448.56.

- It didn't take long for a rally to occur. On Monday, October 5th a very strong Zweig buy indicator appeared when the ratio of advancing stocks to declining stocks was 15:1. (The ratio of advancing stocks to declining stocks indicator is more predictive than the ratio of declining stocks to advancing stocks.) A buy signal based on the 4% model was also triggered when the VL closed at 456.59 — a 5.6% rally.

- After the October 5th advance/decline volume buy signal of 15:1, the weekly closing price of the S&P500 closed higher than the previous weekly close for 5 weeks running.

- Zweig's indicator of a 2:1 Ratio of Up-Stocks to Down-Stocks over a 10-day period was nearly triggered when the ratio hit 1.81:1 on Monday, October 12. This was further proof that the buyers dominated the market. The ratio remained strong the rest of the week with ratios of 1.74, 1.72, and 1.61 on Tuesday, Thursday, and Friday, October 13, 15, and 16.

- The October rally continued and the VL subsequently reached new cyclical highs on 5 occasions. The peak occurred on November 3, 2015 at 475.8 — a more than 10% rally from 9:1 sell signal received on September 28. The sell signal was reset to 456.77.

- The VL fell to 455.27 on Thursday, November 12 and a sell signal was triggered. The buy signal was reset to 473.48. 2 points were deducted from the Super Model giving it a score of 6. A Super Model score of 6 or above is bullish.

- The VL fell again the next day to 451.13 and the buy signal was reset to 469.18.

- Monday, November 16 was the start of a small rally and by Tuesday, December 1 the VL reached 470.63 and a buy signal was triggered. The sell signal was reset to 451.80.

- Zweig warned that the 4% model can sometimes have a whipsaw effect, but in the long run the model helps the investor stay in sync with the trend of the market. The investor who follows the Super Model will experience less of a whipsaw effect.

- The rally was short-lived. The VL closed at 450.94 on Thursday, December 10. The buy signal was reset to 468.98.
- There was another big down day on Friday as the VL fell to 441.21. The buy signal was reset to 458.86.
- There was a second Zweig sell signal on Friday. The ratio of down volume to up volume was 9:1.
- The VL continued to fall the following week and by Friday, December 18 a new low of $436.84 was reached. The buy signal was reset to VL 454.31.
- There was a slight rally as the end of 2015 got nearer to 453.65 on December 29, but that just narrowly missed the buy target.
- The VL fell to 411.12 on January 11, 2016 after 8 straight trading days of losses and the buy signal was reset to 427.56.
- The VL fell to 400.58 two days later and a Zweig sell signal was triggered when the NYSE declining volume to advancing volume ratio exceeded 9:1.
- The VL ended the week at 398.23 the first time it was below 400 since April 2013. The buy signal was reset to 414.16.
- The VL fell to a new cyclical low of 392.58 on January 20. The buy signal was reset to 408.28.
- The VL began to climb the following day and advancing volume exceeded declining volume most days over the next week and a half.
- A buy signal was given when the ratio of advancing volume to declining volume reached almost 11:1 on January 26. This was followed by another advance/decline ratio of a little over 11:1 on January 29 and the VL closed out the week at 413.98 and a buy signal given by the 4% Model. The new sell signal was reset to 397.42.
- The VL reached a peak in the spring of 2015 when it hit 519.88, about 20% higher than the January 29, 2016 closing price.

The story of this period is to be compared to the VIX related story in Chapter 8.

7.4.1. *Where does the model sit as we go to press?*

Zweig's Monetary Model stands at 4 points and his 4% Model has 2 points. The sum of the two models creates a Super Model worth 6 points, which is a buy signal.

2	Prime Rate Indicator
0	Fed Indicator
2	Installment Debt Indicator
4	Total Points for the Monetary Model
2	Total Points for the 4% Momentum Model
6	Total Points for the Super Model

Buy at 6 or more points

Sell at 3 or fewer points

7.4.2. *Update*

Update for the period of January 16, 2016 to October 14, 2016 along with a 6 month prediction:

- The VL fell by 5.3% to 392.24 on February 8, 2006. This triggered a 4% Model sell signal. The new 4% Model buy signal was reset to 399.17. About a week later, on February 17, the VLCI rose by 5.2% and a buy signal was triggered. The sell signal was reset to 393.34. The up volume to down volume ratio indicator was almost hit on February 17 when it reached 8.46:1. The market remained strong the following week and the advancing stocks to declining stocks indicator was almost triggered in the same week when it reached 1.90:1. It stayed in the range of 1.70:1–1.90:1 over the next 2 weeks which indicated a strong upward momentum. Over the next 4 months, a series of new highs in the VL were reached. It finally topped out at 473.73 on June 8 and the sell signal was reset to 454.78.
- June 24 saw a sell-off and the VL fell to 449.48 triggering a sell signal. The buy signal was reset to 467.36.
- Four days later, on June 28, a buy signal was triggered on the Zweig 9:1 up volume/down volume indicator when the ratio reached 9.3:1. It reached 9.3:1 on June 29, also. The VL closed at 442.54 on the first of those days.
- A series of new VL highs were hit and the sell signal was reset each time. The up volume/down volume signal hit 15.6:1 on July 8 — probably a continuation of the previous week's momentum. The sell signal was increased to 448.26 as the VL closed out the week at 466.94.
- The 4% Model was triggered when the VL increased from a recent low by 4.8% to 470.75 on Monday, July 11.

- The next day, July 12, Zweig's strongest signal was given when the up stocks/down stocks ratio over a 10-day period exceeded 2:1.
- The VL saw a series of new highs throughout July and August and reached a new peak on September 7 when it closed at 489.19. The 4% Model sell signal was reset to 469.62.
- September is often a weak month for the stock market. The VL was relatively flat for the rest of the month. The 9-1 signal was nearly hit on September 21 when the up volume to down volume indicator stood at 8.15:1, but a rally did not materialize. The VL closed at 471.14 on Friday, October 14 — slightly below the peak of 489.19 on September 7.
- Zweig's research showed that after his 2:1 up stocks to down stocks ratio is triggered, the market increases on average by about 15% over the next six months. The S&P500 closed at 2152.14 on July 12 — the day the 2:1 ratio was reached. That suggests the S&P500 could reach 2475 by January 12, 2017. We went to press in May 2017 — the S&P500 has hit 2400 but not 2475, but there has been large gain.
- The S&P500 closed at 2132.98 on October 14, 2016.

7.5.　Postscript on using Zweig's methods for equity selection

Professional investor John Reese has also followed Zweig's methods focussing on stock portfolios as opposed to index movements as Swetye and I. In an October 7, 2016 post on his website www.validea.com/hl/hotlistissues/A-Look-at-the-Investment-Strategy-of-Martin-Zweig-2016-10-7.asp he wrote as follows:

> Our portfolio based on his book *Winning on Wall Street* has almost doubled the market's return since its inception in 2003.
>
> Zweig was also an avid collector of a variety of different kinds of memorabilia. *The Wall Street Journal* has reported that he owned such one-of-a-kind items as Buddy Holly's guitar, the gun from Dirty Harry, the motorcycle from Easy Rider, and Michael Jordan's jersey from his rookie season with the Chicago Bulls.

Zweig called the 1987 crash as noted above. Reese reminds us that Zweig predicted a quick recovery, reaching pre-crash levels in about a year.

> Zweig was a growth investor, and his methodology was dominated by earnings-based criteria. He looked at a stock's earnings

from a myriad of angles, wanting to ensure that he was getting stocks that had been producing strong growth over the long haul and even better growth recently — and he wanted their growth to be coming from the right sources.

Zweig's thoroughness paid off. His *Zweig Forecast* was one of the most highly regarded investment newsletters in the country, ranking number one for risk-adjusted returns during the 15 years that *Hulbert Financial Digest* monitored it. It produced an impressive 15.9% annualized return during that time. Zweig also managed several mutual funds, and was co-founder of Zweig Dimenna Partners, a multibillion-dollar New York-based firm that has been ranked in the top 15 of Barron's list of the most successful hedge funds.

Zweig may have spent his cash on some flashy, fun items, but the strategy he used to compile that cash was a disciplined, methodical approach. His earnings examination of a firm spanned several categories, and I've incorporated them into the Zweig-inspired model I base on his book, *Winning on Wall Street.* They include:

Trend of Earnings: Earnings should be higher in the current quarter than they were a year ago in the same quarter.

Earnings Persistence: Earnings per share should have increased in each year of the past five-year period; EPS should also have grown in each of the past four quarters (versus the respective year-ago quarters).

Long-Term Growth: EPS should be growing by at least 15% over the long-term; a growth rate over 30% is exceptional.

Earnings Acceleration: EPS growth for the current quarter (versus the same quarter last year) should be greater than the average growth for the previous three quarters (versus the respective three quarters from a year ago). EPS growth in the current quarter also should be greater than the long-term growth rate. These criteria made sure that Zweig wasn't getting in late on a stock that had great long-term growth numbers, but which was coming to the end of its growth run.

While Zweig's EPS focus certainly put him on the "growth" side of the growth/value spectrum, his approach was by no means a growth-at-all-costs strategy. Like all of the gurus I follow, he included a key value-based component in his method. He made sure that a stock's price–earnings (P/E) ratio was no greater than three times the market average, and no greater than 43, regardless of what the market average was. (He also didn't like stocks with P/Es less than 5, because they could be indicative of an outright dog that investors were wisely avoiding.)

In addition, Zweig wanted to know that a firm's earnings growth was sustainable over the long haul. And that meant that the growth was coming primarily from sales — not cost-cutting or other non-sales measures. My Zweig model requires a firm's revenue growth to be at least 85% of EPS growth. If a stock fails that test but its revenues are growing by at least 30% a year, it passes, however, since that is still a very strong revenue growth rate.

Like earnings growth, Zweig believed sales growth should be increasing. My model thus requires that a stock's sales growth for the most recent quarter (versus the year-ago quarter) to be greater than the previous quarter's sales growth rate (versus the year-ago quarter).

Finally, Zweig also wanted to make sure a firm's growth wasn't driven by unsustainable amounts of leverage (a key observation, given all that's happened in recent years). Realizing that different industries require different debt loads, he looked for stocks whose debt/equity ratios were lower than their industry average.

He relied on technical factors to adjust how much of his portfolio he put into stocks, and the indicators he used are quite relevant given today's environment. Some included the Federal Reserve's discount rate; installment debt levels; and the prime rate. His mottos included "Don't fight the Fed" (meaning investors should be more bullish when interest rates were low or falling) and "Don't fight the tape" (which related to his practice of getting more bullish or bearish based on market trends).

Those rules are tough for an individual investor to put into practice; Zweig used what he called a "Super Model" that meshed all of his indicators into a system that determined how bullish or bearish he was. But over the years, I've found that using only the quantitative, fundamental-based criteria Zweig outlined in his book can produce very strong results. My Zweig-inspired 10-stock portfolio has been a very strong performer since its July 2003 inception, returning 315.1%, while the S&P500 has gained 199.2%. Here are the portfolio's current holdings:

CUSTOMERS BANCORP INC (CUBI)
WALKER & DUNLOP, INC. (WD)
AMTRUST FINANCIAL SERVICES INC (AFSI)
ENTERPRISE FINANCIAL SERVICES CORP (EFSC)
HAIN CELESTIAL GROUP INC (HAIN)
LGI HOMES INC (LGIH)

FRANKLIN FINANCIAL NETWORK INC (FSB)
SERVISFIRST BANCSHARES, INC. (SFBS)
BANCO MACRO SA (ADR) (BMA)
UNITEDHEALTH GROUP INC (UNH)

Zweig's strategy is a growth approach. It examines earnings growth from various angles making sure that it is "strong, improving, and sustainable".

Chapter 8

Analysis and Possible Prediction of Declines in the −5% to −15% Range

In this chapter we discuss small stock market declines in the −5 to 15% area that are not predictable but might be expected at some unknown future time. We found that simple VIX versus S&P 500 graphs were helpful in analyzing and trading during crises such as the January–February 2016 decline following the first FED rate increase in seven years in December 2015. A major fear was not the rate increase itself but rather the fear of many more rate increases that never occurred. There were also concerns about Chinese growth and policy uncertainty and some concerns not very founded about growth in the United States. The discussion then covers the Brexit, the Trump election, the French election and the Trump-Comey bad scenario crisis.

8.1. Predictable crashes versus those that are surprises

I focus on four large crash prediction measures[1]: The first is my bond–stock earnings yield differential (BSEYD) which compares the long bond interest rate with the reciprocal of the trailing price–earnings (P/E) ratio (P/E ratio) which is an earnings yield. The second measure is my T-option, a measure of market confidence sentiment related to puts versus calls prices. The third is Warren Buffett's value of the economy to the value of stock market. The fourth is Sotheby's behavioral finance measure based on the enthusiasm for Sotheby's stock. Here, I discuss eleven declines that none of these measures predicted but we can deal with, namely:

(1) Attacks in the US, September 11, 2001,
(2) May to June, 2006,

---

[1]This chapter was written by Ziemba. An earlier version of this material was in *Wilmott*, November, 2016.

(3) February 27 to April 6, 2007,

(4) European debt crisis, August 2011,

(5) October 20 to November 10, 2014,

(6) August 18 to September 18, 2015,

(7) January 1 to February 12, 2016,

(8) Brexit vote, June 23 to June 28, 2016,

(9) Trump election worries. October 24 to November 10, 2016,

(10) The French election,

(11) The Trump-Comey firing and Russian hacking situation.

In some case, these crashes could be anticipated like (8) the Brexit and (9) the Trump election crashes, or have a fall that feeds on itself such as October 20–November 10, 2014.

The BSEYD is able to predict many, if not most, of the big crashes as we saw in Chapters 2–4. Those are over 10% and average 25%. But there are a lot of mini declines that occur in the 5–15% range. Some are explainable or predictable and some are not. Examples include the 1991 attack on 9–11 on New York's World Trade Center. Then the market was limit down in futures, some −6%, then with trading suspended for a week, it fell −14% in total. Besides these bad scenarios, there can be declines that simple feed on themselves. In October 2014, there was constant talk in the business news "we have not had a −10% correction is a long time". So selling started with no other news. It never quite got to a −10% in closing prices, but was −9.86% on the close of the market at the bottom. The market turned when −10% was hit in the middle of a trading session and it was straight up from there for a huge retracement.

That was a **V**-shaped decline that's relatively easy to deal with. In my trading, I sometimes shift from largely C trades, that is short puts deep out of the money with a large amount of capital behind each position to an **A** trade where you short futures to delta neutralize the long positions in the short puts. Then when it rallies, you eliminate the short futures which are not losing money. A full **A** trade buys long calls, so if that's the move, one does not get hurt on the rally by the short futures. Alternatively, I might have an **X**–**Y** trade where **X** is a ridge of short puts with a 10–90% advantage in expected value and −**Y** is a short futures and short futures call hedge. Then the options time decay is the advantage. VIX and risk control must be watched carefully.

The August 2015 worldwide massive decline began on August 18 and had similar elements with many individual stocks including Apple Computer, indices such as the Russell2000 small cap index, and countries, actually in 20% plus decline bear markets. The spot VIX was 28.03 (up 46.45% on Friday August 21) with the future VIX lower, up 8.89 versus 19.14 on Thursday August 20. It was 13 on Tuesday August 18.

On Wednesday (August 19), options on the September 1700 S&P500 puts, which were 30 cents, closed at 1.15 on Thursday, then $8.20 on Friday, then 27.50 before they fell to $8.30 on Wednesday. They are 3.40 on Thursday. I bought some back at $3 and others at $1.80. Later on September 8, I closed the position at $0.95 so the trade made a profit. I also bought some 1650 September puts for $2 that I sold on Wednesday for $8. These closed at $2.40 on Thursday. The VIX peaked at 40 in the spot, but the futures VIX was much lower, below 30. Historically, after a 40+ VIX, the next 12 months has very large gains, see Ziegler and Ziemba (2015). All the puts were trading at huge premiums. The DJIA was more than 10% below its May high. So again *sell in May and go away* was working.

On Thursday August 20, the DJIA fell 358 (2.06%). On Friday August 21, it fell 530.94 (−3.1%) to 16,459.75. Meanwhile, the S&P500 was down some 7% from its recent peak and it then fell 64.84 points on Friday, August 21, an option expiry day. It seems clear that some type of flash crash — or computerized selling, was going on. The Nasdaq fell 3.5% (−171.45) to 4706.04 on Friday. The VIX rose more than 10% on each of Wednesday, Thursday, Friday and Monday. The VIX rose 118%, the largest weekly gain since 1990. On Monday August 24, the VIX actually rose an additional 90% with the DJIA down 1000 points at one stage, similar to the flash crash bottom. There were an enormous number of forced buying of short puts because of margin calls. For example, 1850 puts sold for $3–5 rose to $28 or $30 and were bought in for many customers including me in an Ameritrade account. In Investorline of the Bank of Montreal which uses very strict rules to limit positions, a small number of mine were bought in for $14.80 and $13 in two accounts on August 30. I had bottom fished and bought some AAPL stock a few days earlier which increased the margin and was partially responsible for the buy in. These losses ate up some months of previous gains, but occur from time to time with put selling, if one is not hedged or fully capitalized and does not anticipate the decline, which was hard to do here.

On Tuesday, there was a big rally of about 35 S&P500 points only to lose it on the last hour to close −25(3.9%) on the S&P500. But an encouraging sign was a drop of 5 points in the VIX to the 35 area. For example, the September 1700 puts fell from 27.50 to 20 despite the S&P500 falling. Then on Wednesday the market stabilized and was up about 35, then dropped to +12 and then there was a massive rally with the S&P500 up 72.9. Thursday was much the same with a big rally of 45+ S&P points then to fall to almost even and then it rallied to close up 50 points. It was quite a roller coaster.

What was the trigger or twig that got this multiple-day decline with Thursday, Friday and Monday being the big down days?

It seems to be nothing really new but a final recognition of a bunch of current worries. There had been a long period of low volatility with cheap money fueling the market rise with an accommodating Fed. Then once the market started falling, it fell on itself and accelerated on Thursday through Tuesday and finally seemed to bottom out. Chinese markets fell into a 20% plus bear market and this suggested that global growth was slowing and then that drove the US market lower.

Is this a tempest in a teapot that will pass or an end to the 6 year bull market?

One observer said it has been 75 years since such a percent drop occurred. The drop in closing prices was about 11% from an August 17 high to a low on the 25th. Many such as young people with three times S&P long ETFs got blown out.

This decline instead of being **V** shaped was a sequence of **W**s, WWWW, up, down, up, down with fast violent moves in both directions. That made the market very difficult to trade. In my case, I basically moved most positions to December at high volatility premiums way away from the money. So selling high volatility rather than the low volatility before the crisis hopefully will work out well.

So the drop in the week was 118 S&P points (-5.65%). The drop to the bottom on Monday was 334.83.

We will see how this plays out. Then, finally in the options expiry week, September 14–18, the market began to stabilize and gently rise. Monday, September 14 had a loss of -8 S&P500 points. Then on Tuesday, September 15, the day before the 2-day September Fed meeting, the S&P500 rose 25.70 points to 1979.75 in the September futures. These Fed announcement-induced rallies are as expected given the past data. Finally, there was the Fed announcement effect, see Ziemba and Ziemba (2013) and Ziemba (2017). As usual in the Fed week, the market rallied in options expiry weeks, Also, in options expiry weeks, the market usually rallies, so there were the two effects, see Ziemba (2012). The odds favored no rate rise because of the troubles in the US and especially abroad.

Following the announcement of no change, largely due to the overseas economic downtown, especially China, the market made various up and down moves in a violent reversing fashion. It then became weak in the period during Fed chair Janet Yellen's speech after the announcement. The market closed down −5 in the S&P500. Subsequently, during the night before the Friday morning settlement, it fell. Then on Friday September 18, the stock market fell sharply, down 1.61% or −32.12 S&P500 points. Monday, September 21 has a 0.45% gain, then Tuesday had another 1.23% drop in the S&P500. The rest of that week was slightly down with Wednesday, Thursday and Friday falling from 1942.74 on Tuesday's close to 1931.34, some −11.4 S&P500 points. Then on Monday, September 28, it was rumored that Saudi Arabia and Norway were selling equities to make up for oil revenues not received due to the low oil prices and needed to cover expenses. That led to a −2.57% S&P500 decline. The market then stabilized during the turn of the month of October with rallies on September 29, 30 and October 1, 2 and 3. This took the S&P500 from 1881.77 to 1987.05, gain of over 100 points. In this period, the VIX decreased from 27.63 to 19.54. Mohamed el Erian and others predicted continuing high volatility, See Table 8.1.

We are soon coming to the best part of the year, namely the end of the sell in May and go away period. This is by my definition, the −5 day of November which is the 25th of October. There is a lot of conflicting opinions and analyses. Also there is record short positions in the market comparable to 2008. For example Blair Hull's new ETF product, 6 month model, is predicting −10% for the next 6 months. I was asked to comment on this model and gave some suggestions, some of which were used. The model then suggested −20% allocation and later −30%. Finally, after many days of gains, it is at zero. It is difficult for these models to be accurate all the time and this model has been successful in the past. My current positioning in my futures fund is cautiously optimistic using high VIX option sales of deep out of the money options, hedged with short futures so that the delta is close to zero. As of October 12 we have had nine consecutive days of falling VIX.

This graph in Figure 8.1 shows the VIX during the period August to October 12 and you can see that the multiple **W** type crisis ended at the turn of the month of October with the VIX declining in the last nine days.

The worries are as follows:

- Earnings have been dropping, so the stock market is adjusting to the new pricing.

Table 8.1.   The DJIA, the S&P500 and the VIX moved as follows during the crisis.

Date	DJIA	% Change	500	% Change	VIX	% Change
14-Aug	17,477.40		2091.54		12.83	
17-Aug	17,545.18	0.39%	2102.44	0.52%	13.02	1.48%
18-Aug	17,511.34	−0.19%	2096.92	−0.26%	13.79	5.91%
19-Aug	17,348.73	−0.93%	2079.61	−0.83%	15.25	10.59%
20-Aug	16,990.69	−2.06%	2035.73	−2.11%	19.14	25.51%
21-Aug	16,459.75	−3.12%	1970.89	−3.19%	28.03	46.45%
24-Aug	15,871.35	−3.57%	1893.21	−3.94%	40.74	45.34%
25-Aug	15,666.44	−1.29%	1867.61	−1.35%	36.02	−11.59%
26-Aug	16,285.51	3.95%	1940.51	3.90%	30.32	−15.82%
27-Aug	16,654.77	2.27%	1987.66	2.43%	26.10	−13.92%
28-Aug	16,643.01	−0.07%	1988.87	0.06%	26.05	−0.19%
31-Aug	16,528.03	−0.69%	1972.18	−0.84%	28.43	9.14%
1-Sep	16,058.35	−2.84%	1913.85	−2.96%	31.40	10.45%
2-Sep	16,351.38	1.82%	1948.86	1.83%	26.09	−16.91%
3-Sep	16,374.76	0.14%	1951.13	0.12%	25.61	−1.84%
4-Sep	16,102.38	−1.66%	1921.22	−1.53%	27.80	8.55%
8-Sep	16,492.68	2.42%	1969.41	2.51%	24.90	−10.43%
9-Sep	16,253.57	−1.45%	1942.04	−1.39%	26.23	5.34%
10-Sep	16,330.40	0.47%	1952.29	0.53%	24.37	−7.09%
11-Sep	16,433.09	0.63%	1961.05	0.45%	23.20	−4.80%
14-Sep	16,370.96	−0.38%	1953.03	−0.41%	24.25	4.53%
15-Sep	16,599.85	1.40%	1978.09	1.28%	22.54	−7.05%
16-Sep	16,739.95	0.84%	1995.31	0.87%	21.35	−5.28%
17-Sep	16,674.74	−0.39%	1990.20	−0.26%	21.14	−0.98%
18-Sep	16,384.58	−1.74%	1958.08	−1.61%	22.28	5.39%
21-Sep	16,510.19	0.77%	1966.97	0.45%	20.14	−9.61%
22-Sep	16,330.47	−1.09%	1942.74	−1.23%	22.44	11.42%
23-Sep	16,279.89	−0.31%	1938.76	−0.20%	22.13	−1.38%
24-Sep	16,201.32	−0.48%	1932.24	−0.34%	23.47	6.06%
25-Sep	16,314.67	0.70%	1931.34	−0.05%	23.62	0.64%
28-Sep	16,001.89	−1.92%	1881.77	−2.57%	27.63	16.98%
29-Sep	16,049.13	0.30%	1884.09	0.12%	26.83	−2.90%
30-Sep	16,284.70	1.47%	1920.03	1.91%	24.50	−8.68%
1-Oct	16,272.01	−0.08%	1923.82	0.20%	22.55	−7.96%
2-Oct	16,472.37	1.23%	1951.36	1.43%	20.94	−7.14%
5-Oct	16,776.43	1.85%	1987.05	1.83%	19.54	−6.69%

- Oil: Oil has been dropping for months. It is now at the $40 level, it is so low that many companies and countries are in serious financial trouble.
- China: The stock market and currency are in decline and global growth may be declining, hence it impacts the US stock market. China's Caixin purchasing managers index fell again this week. The RMB was devalued in early August by the largest amount since 1994. Neighboring countries

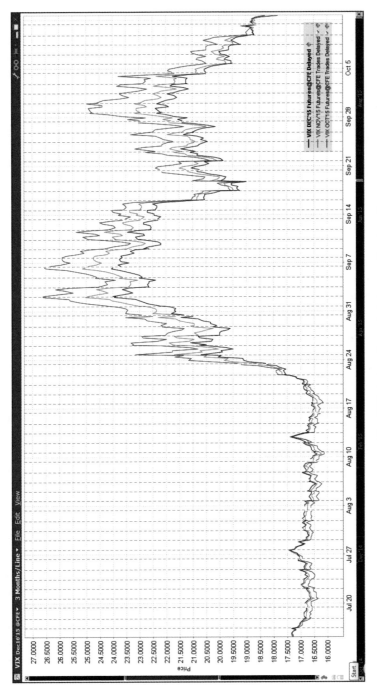

Fig. 8.1.   The VIX during the period August–October 12.

currencies are greatly affected. Kazakhstan floated its currency and it fell 25%. To maintain the RMB, China is selling dollars but its not enough.

China did nothing until a rate cut on Tuesday and some buying on Thursday. Also, they forbade negative comments on stocks and halted many from trading.

- Commodities: China was stockpiling many commodities and is now dumping them to raise cash which affects stock markets and currencies.
- Fed: Worries regarding the start of interest rate rises and their paths up. They continue to say "the data will tell us what to do". Interest rates have not increased in 9 years. There is much worry about when they will raise rates and the pace up.
- August: There seems to often be seasonal troubles in August. Historically September and October have been the weakest months. But August now seems to anticipate the September drops.
- A 6-year bull run fed by easy money putting $10 trillion into stock markets.
- Other markets (from 2015 intraday highs): Japan -7.2%, Germany -17%, Hong Kong -21%.

In my trading, I use various corrective actions, here are two of them:

(1) If net long: One can short futures, but then you must adjust the positions to get out of these positions as the rally unfolds. This, in my terminology, is what I call an A trade. The A trade has three or four elements. Doing them all simultaneously is complicated but they can be approximated. One shorts a ridge of puts, call the sum of the premiums P. At the same time buy a ridge of calls of value C. Then short futures so the short puts are delta neutralized. If $T = P - C$ is over 100, there have been no quarterly losses since 1985 when you rule out BSEYD crash danger signals. Then it is a good play as T is a measure of how good the play is. But if T is less than zero then it is a short term crash signal. There have been six cases with T less than zero from 1985 to 2015. The sum of the S&P500 changes in the next quarter was -41.7%. The last such signal was in 2003. If you think that the market is very very weak then you can delta neutralize the long calls as well to get a **B** trade. The fourth element is to short very deep out of the money calls. There is no risk here as you are long other calls closer to the money and they have expected return as low as 1.7 cents per dollar invested.

(2) Alternatively, you can move positions to make your portfolio a safer one with similar premium to be made, but later in time.

If net short: one can do similar things but in reverse for (1) or (2).

There have been additional small corrections including several 6–9% declines from July to September 2004 and March to June 2005. In an April 9, 2007 Barron's article, Michael Santoli notes that there has been one such pullback each year since 2004. In each case, a recovery quickly followed each decline and each retreat has been shallower than the preceding one and a faster recovery of the loss. Buying on the declines has been rewarded as bidders try to beat the crowd and speed up the recovery. Buying on these dips has worked so far, as has selling put options during the greatly expanded volatility which returned to low levels after the decline. The 2007 decline followed this pattern. As of April 6, 2007, the futures market returned to pre-decline levels with the VIX at 13.23.

8.2.   Some background on crash measures

Historically, the bond–stock crash measure has been successful in predicting 10%+ market corrections, including the declines in October 1987 (US and Japan), the 1990 Japan, the 2000 US and the 2002 US. In Japan from 1948–1988, there were twenty 10%+ declines even though the market went up 221 times in yen (and 550 times in US dollars). The bond–stock measure had a 12/12 record in predicting crashes in that period, that is, whenever the measure was in the danger zone, there was a fall of 10%+ within one year from the time the measure went into the danger zone. This is a very good forecasting record, but eight declines in Japan during these 40 years were not predicted by this measure.

8.3.   Declines and crashes not predicted by the measures

Although the measures have a good record, there are some key episodes which it did not predict. Studying these declines and their triggers helps us to assess shocks. The September 11, 2001 attacks and the stock market decline of 14% in the S&P500 that followed after a one week market closure was largely a random, that is unforeseen event. But the size of the decline was exacerbated due to the then weak stock market and US economy which had a recession starting in spring 2001. The stock market was weak because although prices had fallen, earnings had fallen more. The bond–stock model which had been in the danger zone in April 1999, predicting the April 2000 decline, then returned to the danger zone in the fall of 2001 predicting the 22% fall in the S&P500 in 2002. The T-measure for 3Q2002 at −142.8 predicted the 12% fall in the S&P500 that quarter.

The S&P500 fell 37% from 1460.25 at the end of December 1999 to 885.76 on 31 October 2002.

In May to June, 2006 the S&P500 fell 7% and markets in some emerging economies fell 20% or more. Worries that valuations of some emerging market stocks were too high enlarged their losses. For example, the closed end emerging market fund RNE (Russian New Europe) was at a very high 37%+ premium on May 10 to net asset value — an amount way above historical values. The trigger for the decline was a rumor that the Bank of Japan would raise interest rates. These higher interest rates did not materialize but the fear that they would spark a rally in the yen led some yen carry trade players to unwind their short yen, long higher yielding non-Japanese asset positions, especially emerging market currencies. In turn this led to sales of various stocks and indices including the S&P500 and the decline was largest (elements of mean reversion) in those areas that had gained the most, namely the emerging markets. The VIX volatility index, rose from around 10% before the crisis to the 22% level before dropping back to 10% after the sell-off.

The third decline was February 27 to April 6, 2007 with the early April S&P500 well above its February 27 and March 13 lows of 1399.04 and 1377.95, respectively. For months, there was talk of the current period being the longest time without a 2% decline in one day or a large monthly decline. The stock market had low volatility since the 2006 decline.

An example of these sentiments was made by Bob Stovall, a 50-year Wall Street veteran, in a talk on November 15, 2006 to investment students at Stetson University. Stovall argued that given the current real economic growth in 2006, it would be very difficult for stocks in the S&P500 to continue to increase in price. Without economic growth, companies would have trouble meeting earnings expectations. He said that the average bull market in US history lasts approximately 56 months. At that time, the US was approaching the 50th month of the bull market. He concluded that a shift toward steady cash flow stocks with dividends was preferable to large capital gains stocks.

The paper of Lleo and Ziemba (2012) discussed in Chapter 3, which discusses the bond–stock earnings yield predictions of three market crashes in the 2006–2009 period, namely China, Iceland and the US, had a clear sell signal on June 14, 2007 and a huge decline occurred.

It is known that bull markets start with low PE ratios and end with high PE ratios, see page 52. Lleo and Ziemba (2016) as discussed in chapter 4 compare the BSEYD and Shiller's high PE model with more than 50 years of US data. Both add value but BSEYD dominates.

On Tuesday, February 27, 2007, the S&P500 fell 50.33 points or 3.47% to 1399.04. On that drop, the VIX volatility index rose from 11.15 to 18.31%, a jump of 64.22%. Several concurrent triggers have been mentioned for the fall, which were exacerbated by the confused reaction of market participants to these events. The first was a 9% fall in the Shanghai and Shenzhen stock markets, itself triggered by rumors that the Chinese government was going to raise the bank's reserve requirement and make regulatory changes to slow speculative activity in the soaring Chinese equity markets. The Chinese market drop triggered substantial sell-offs in Asia (where most equity markets were near peaks) and Europe as well as in the US. While *I* believe that China is one of the most interesting financial markets to study now, I also feel that this drop is **not** the underlying cause of the S&P persistent weakness. The Shanghai index was up more than 100% in 2006 and way up in early 2007 so the 9% fall is a minor blip in the long-run growth trend, and likely motivated by profit-taking and a concern about over-valuation. Furthermore, it is not an indication of slowing of the Chinese economy which is expected to grow around 9–10% in 2007. Chinese markets tend to be quite volatile. Several weeks before the February 27 decline, the Shanghai exchange fell 11% in one week in early February, a decline which received little attention in international markets because it was spread over a week. These two declines were the greatest since February 1997, when news of Deng Xiaoping's ill health triggered a sell-off. Thus, the Chinese decline may have determined the timing of the global equity decline, and return of increasing volatility and risk aversion but is not the underlying cause. Indeed in early April 2007 the Chinese market indices rose to new highs well above the February 25 interim high.

I expect that just like Japan, whose Nikkei stock average rose 221 times in yen and 550 times in US dollars from 1948 to 1988, but with 20 declines of 10%+, China will likely have higher gains in dollars than RMB, be over-priced like Japan, propelled up by fast growth and low interest rates and high liquidity and still experience many corrections.[2] The BSEYD crash signal was in December 2006. But the *market* did not understand this. Rather, many market actors tend to react as a herd to such events, seeking to minimize their losses, but the more recent response appears to be buy on dips.

---

[2]See Ziemba and Schwartz (1991, 1992) and Stone and Ziemba (1993) regarding Japan and Lleo and Ziemba (2012) regarding the crash in 2008 of the Shanghai index. These papers are covered in Chapter 3 for the China 2008, Iceland and the US crashes. Discussion of Japan is in Chapter 9.

Other news also contributed to the fall in the S&P500 and worldwide markets on that Tuesday included a statement by former Fed Chair Alan Greenspan that a recession in the US was a possibility although it was not probable as well as some weak economic numbers.

Greenspan later said the probability of a recession was 25%. At the time, bond prices were actually estimating a higher probability. I assume, that even though it might be wise for a former Fed Chair to let the current Fed Chair do the talking, audiences like the one in Hong Kong, require that Greenspan say something interesting to earn his $150,000 speaking fee.

The decline was exacerbated by a large unwinding of yen carry trades who sold stock and created a short covering rally in the yen that moved the USD/JPY exchange rate from 127 to 116 on the yen dollar rate from March 30, 2006 to March 30, 2007. However, it appears that those who foresaw the end of the yen carry trade spoke too soon. Although the Bank of Japan recently doubled interest rates (in February 2007), the benchmark rate of 0.5% remains far below other interest rates — encouraging Japanese retail and institutional investors to continue to seek higher returns abroad, and foreign investors to use the weak yen as a financing currency — even if Morgan Stanley recently argued that yen-denominated loans to retail investors remain very small.

Accentuating the tension were political as well as economic risks. Many commentators such as Lawrence Summers (former Treasury Secretary and Harvard President and DE Shaw hedge fund consultant) have argued that the market was not pricing in the worldwide risks in most assets including the S&P500. However, both of my large crash 10%+ measures were not in the danger zone. The decline in February 27 to early April, and possibly beyond, had not reached a 10% fall and the VIX which reached 19% was bouncing around the 13–16% range most of the time.

8.3.1.   *The mini crash, January 1 to February 12, 2016*

The Fed finally raised short-term interest rates by $\frac{1}{4}$% at their December meeting. The $\frac{1}{4}$% is arguably trivial but it sent a message that there is more to come. Indeed, the Fed Chair, Janet Yellen, suggested that they might raise rates gradually but have up to four raises in 2016 and more later. This might eventually in 2–3 years yield a short interest in the 3.5% area. All this spooked the emerging markets especially. Starting on the first trading of 2016, the US stock market fell and in the first five days of January the S&P500 fell 113.47 S&P500 points or −5.57%. This was the largest fall in the first five days of January in the past 50+ years, from 2035.50 at the close of December 31, 2015 to 1922.03 on January 8, 2016. Meanwhile the VIX rose from 18.21 to 27.01. These are very negative signals, see Ziemba (2012). In addition, full January 2016 was down 4.68%, closing at 1940.24 with the VIX at 20.20, another negative signal.

The market bottomed on February 12, 2016 at 1864.78, down 170.72 or −8.39% in 2016 year to date, with the VIX at 30.90 intraday high, closing at 28.14. From there, the market began to rally with the VIX starting to fall, it signaled the end of the crisis. The market reached 2049.58 with the VIX falling to 14.02 on March 18.

The S&P500 and the VIX in 2016 evolved as follows in Figure 8.2.

8.3.2. *Brexit vote, June 23 to June 28, 2016*

British Prime Minister David Cameron made a huge mistake. To win election in 2015 and appease a wing of his party, he promised a vote, he thought he could win, on remaining in the European Union. Former London mayor Boris Johnson and cabinet member Michael Gove among others campaigned for Brexit promising control over immigration and more money for the National Health Service among other issues. One of the cornerstones of

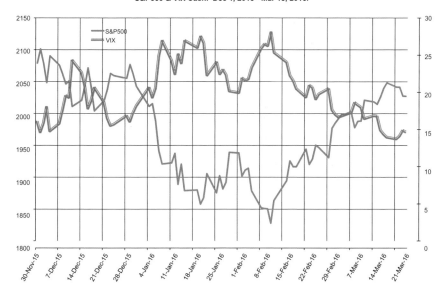

Fig. 8.2.

the EU is free movement of people. This has made it more difficult for even highly educated people from non-EU countries, like me, to get visas. I found getting a UK visa to teach a course more work than actually teaching the course. The UK polls had the vote close, but the London bookmakers had it about 70–30 for remain.

During the day of the vote June 23, 2016, the preliminary polls had it looking like remain was winning and the S&P500 rose sharply from 2076.75 to 2105.75 with the VIX falling to 17.25 from 21.17. The market players assumed remain would win and the S&P was flying upward during the night. I was following this while in France. I covered most of my short puts which had fallen in value and hedged the portfolio with S&P futures short setting buy back limits on them assuming that there would be trouble at some stage. In the morning I saw that as the vote came in, Brexit was winning and there was a huge reversal. My short futures got bought back at a small gain. Had I not had limits, I could have made more because the VIX went up almost 50% to 25.76 and the S&P500 fell to 2018.5, a drop of 87.25 points or nearly 5%. The short puts that I had went up in value with the higher VIX, but I did not have too many of them. The next day, June 27, the S&P fell further to 1985, but the VIX dropped to 23.85. Thus the crisis was over and a big rally ensued. The market assumed that the Fed would not raise rates and the low interest rates would favor stocks.

The S&P500 and VIX graphs were as follows in Figure 8.3.

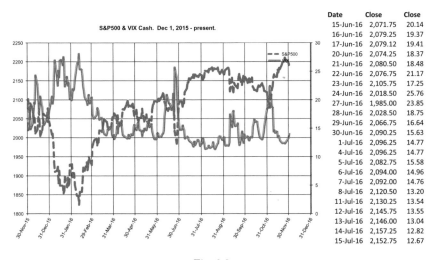

Date	Close	Close
15-Jun-16	2,071.75	20.14
16-Jun-16	2,079.25	19.37
17-Jun-16	2,079.12	19.41
20-Jun-16	2,074.25	18.37
21-Jun-16	2,080.50	18.48
22-Jun-16	2,076.75	21.17
23-Jun-16	2,105.75	17.25
24-Jun-16	2,018.50	25.76
27-Jun-16	1,985.00	23.85
28-Jun-16	2,028.50	18.75
29-Jun-16	2,066.75	16.64
30-Jun-16	2,090.25	15.63
1-Jul-16	2,096.25	14.77
4-Jul-16	2,096.25	14.77
5-Jul-16	2,082.75	15.58
6-Jul-16	2,094.00	14.96
7-Jul-16	2,092.00	14.76
8-Jul-16	2,120.50	13.20
11-Jul-16	2,130.25	13.54
12-Jul-16	2,145.75	13.55
13-Jul-16	2,146.00	13.04
14-Jul-16	2,157.25	12.82
15-Jul-16	2,152.75	12.67

Fig. 8.3.

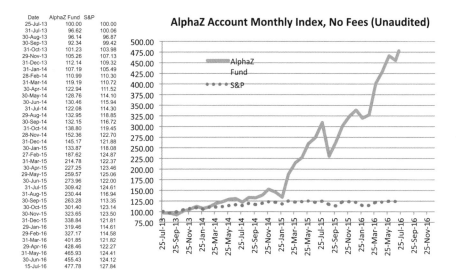

Date	AlphaZ Fund	S&P
25-Jul-13	100.00	100.00
31-Jul-13	96.62	100.06
30-Aug-13	96.14	96.87
30-Sep-13	92.34	99.42
31-Oct-13	101.23	103.98
29-Nov-13	105.26	107.13
31-Dec-13	112.14	109.32
31-Jan-14	107.19	105.49
28-Feb-14	110.99	110.30
31-Mar-14	119.19	110.72
30-Apr-14	122.94	111.52
30-May-14	128.76	114.10
30-Jun-14	130.46	115.94
31-Jul-14	122.08	114.30
29-Aug-14	132.95	118.85
30-Sep-14	132.15	116.72
31-Oct-14	138.80	119.45
28-Nov-14	152.36	122.70
31-Dec-14	145.17	121.88
30-Jan-15	133.87	118.08
27-Feb-15	187.62	124.87
31-Mar-15	214.78	122.37
30-Apr-15	227.25	123.46
29-May-15	259.57	125.06
30-Jun-15	273.96	122.00
31-Jul-15	309.42	124.61
31-Aug-15	230.44	116.94
30-Sep-15	263.28	113.35
30-Oct-15	301.40	123.14
30-Nov-15	323.65	123.50
31-Dec-15	338.84	121.81
29-Jan-16	319.46	114.61
29-Feb-16	327.17	114.58
31-Mar-16	401.85	121.82
29-Apr-16	428.46	122.27
31-May-16	465.93	124.41
30-Jun-16	455.43	124.12
15-Jul-16	477.78	127.84

Fig. 8.4.

My futures fund went back to its old high as shown here in Figure 8.4.

8.3.3. The trump election risk, October 24 to November 10, 2016

Throughout the presidential election campaign Donald Trump used a strategy that tested the boundaries of acceptability: he insulted opponents and called them derogatory names. He argued that only he could save the country. He appealed to the uneducated and poor white while insulting many groups of color. But he developed a following that did not care about his actions and thought he could help them.

He made markets jittery by threatening to tear up alliances and trade deals. He kept a focus on Clintons's emails though nothing indictable was found and he has court cases pending threats to Clinton and a sexually explicit tape that infuriated women.

About a week before the election, the FBI director said there were more emails to be checked and Trump rallied in the polls. Then, near the election day, the FBI director said there was nothing indictable in them but Clinton didn't recover and many had already casted their votes in the interim. Whenever it looked like Trump was winning the market got nervous and fell.

As the vote came in, the markets first rallied when it looked like Clinton would win and then fell, especially worldwide as it became clear Trump would win. The Dow Jones was down 800 points. Noted investor Carl Ichan bought $1 billion of S&P500 stock and futures near the bottom. I bought more as

S&P500 & VIX Cash. Dec 1, 2015 - present.

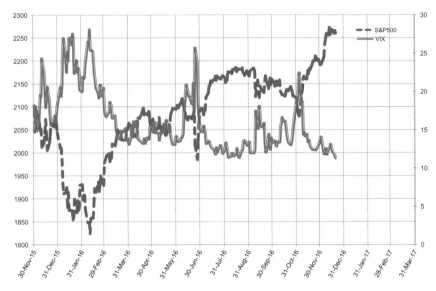

Fig. 8.5.

well. Then the market rallied when Trump gave a very conciliatory acceptance speech praising Clinton. The VIX then fell and the S&P rallied sharply as shown in Figure 8.5. These movements are on the VIX-S&P500 graphs.

Trump won the electoral college and thus the presidency while Clinton won the popular vote by over 2.5 million votes with 4 million who voted for Obama not voting. Thus making for a very divided country.

The market does not like uncertainty and they are uncertain about Trump's policies — some are potentially good like infrastructure and bringing jobs back to the US. The claim is that for the wealthy, the tax will be the same with fewer deductions but this is not realistic given his cabinet choices.

But he wants both to reduce taxes on corporations and the wealthy while pursuing jobs and building programs which would vastly increase the deficit.

He seems to want to run his empire with the help of his children from the Oval Office. Conflicts of interest and nepotism are wide spread. We will see the result.

Small caps outperformed large cap stocks in the post election rally. For 15 consecutive days, the Russell2000 gained and beat the S&P500 which also rallied. This led me to two types of trades:

(1) Long March Russell2000 short Russell2000 calls for a covered call position with the calls on the steep part of the decay curve in January. This is for a basically rising market partially hedged.

(2) Long Russell2000 short S&P500 spreads to capture the effect of small
caps outperforming large caps. This is normally what I do for the January turn-of-the-year effect which occurs in December. This trade was
successful 20 out of 20 times until the December 2015–January 2016
period which was in chaos because of the first quarter point increase by
the Federal Open Market Committee (FOMC). The real fear then was
a large number of rate increases which never materialized. My presidential effect research with Chris Hensel is that during Democratic
regimes, the small caps greatly outperform the large caps during the
year not only at the turn of the year. So far, the Trump transition to the
presidency seems to suggest policies that are more like the Democratic
policies that favor the small caps over the large caps.

7 Russell 2000–8 S&P500 Cash Spread ×$100. Dec 1, 2015–Dec 23,
2016. This is seen in Figure 8.6.

My futures fund did well, making 5% on the night of the Trump victory.
We can see from the VIX-S&P500 graph, once the VIX turned, the S&P500
turned and I was able to keep my cool in the crisis and did not panic, so my

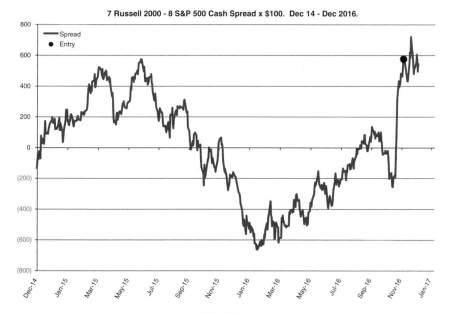

Fig. 8.6.

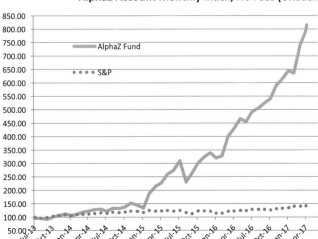

Fig. 8.7.   Alpha Z Futures Fund

futures fund went to another new high in early December 2016 and ended the month at a new high as shown in Figure 8.7.

Throughout December, the market rallied through the options expiry and the Fed FOMC decision to raise short-term interest rates by $\frac{1}{4}\%$. The Fed Chair Janet Yellen announced that they plan to increase interest rates three more times in 2017. This departure from an expected two raises caused a little selloff and then the market resumed its rise. The small cap stocks did not continue to outperform in December with the large cap S&P500 outpacing it. We will see if the traditional turn-of-the-year period has the Russell2000/S&P500 spread gaining, this is seen in Figure 8.8.

8.3.4.   *The French Election*

The election, which drew worldwide attention, was in two rounds: Sunday April 23 and Sunday May 7, 2017. Incumbent president François Hollande of the Socialist Party (PS), though eligible to run for a second term, decided, on December 1, 2016, not to seek reelection, a decision motivated by voter approval ratings. With several candidates calling for a referendum on France's future in the European Union, and following an increase in populist sentiments across several elections, the race was important across Europe and thus global markets.

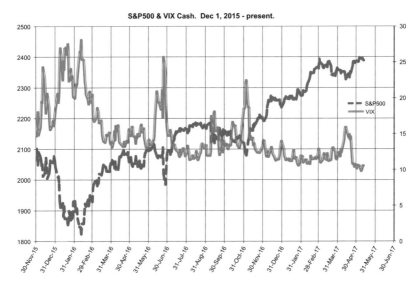

Fig. 8.8.

In the first run off there were five major candidates among the ten that were running. One, Melenchon, on the very far left who wanted to Frexit the European Union. One on the far right, master debater lawyer Marine Le Pen, also wanted a Frexit and advocated more restrictions. Le Pen had ousted her father Jean-Marie Le Pen, the founder of the nationalist and anti-immigrant National Front (FN) party. Both Melenchon and Le Pen, if elected, could have caused a great financial crisis given the increased risk of moving toward a new currency back to the old French franc, isolationist policies on immigration likely triggering a stock market steep fall in France, widening of French credit spreads and potentially enough EU instability, to cause US markets to fall as well. Just winning the election would not have automatically triggered an exit. The legislature would have needed to allow a vote and then the population would have had to vote yes. Several steps to final transition, but nonetheless risk.

There were two centrist candidates. François Fillon of the right-leaning establishment Republican Party (LR) won his party nomination but had the Penelopegate scandal where he employed family members (his wife) in possibly fictious positions. Finally there was Emmanuel Macron of the new En Marche (EM) party. Though a new party, created less than a year before the elections, Macron had a background having served in previous governments. Fillon and Le Pen led first round opinion polls in November 2016 and mid January 2017. Polls tightened by late January and after the scandal, Macron passed Fillon and was second in the polls behind Le Pen. At the same time, Hamon won the socialist primary and became fourth in the polls. Because of his debating skills, Jean-Luc Mélenchon of the La France Insournise Party overtook Hamon and was just slightly behind Fillon.

Ahead of elections polls had Macron in first place. The first round winners were Macron and Le Pen. When the other centrist candidate Fillon endorsed Macron, I knew that the risk of breakup of the EU was over. Macron would win in the final round because other centrists would join Macron as well and the stock market would fly. My four futures accounts made over half a million that night, the best I ever remember.

In the vote, Macron got 20,743,128 (66.1%) to Le Pen's 10,638,475 (33.9%). Le Pen only won two small areas in the North of France and conceded defeat. Macron took his presidential office on May 14, 2017 for his five year term and named Edouard Philippe Prime Minister. Macron at 39, a former economy minister, was the youngest candidate in the race.

8.3.5. *The opening segment of the Trump bad scenario and the two Trumps*

For months, I and countless others around the world have expected a Trump induced disaster. But this bad scenario did not happen. The reason seems to be from a trading perspective there are two Trumps. Trump #1 lies, insults countless people, fires people at will and behaves like a banana republic dictator. He makes bold statements about punitive actions against specific countries but when he actually meets and talks with the leaders of these countries he flip-flops to the opposite position. Three example of this are Premier Justin Trudeau regarding sanctions against Canadian trade; China as a currency manipulator; and Saudi Arabia. Trump #2 is very good at reading a speech prepared by his staff. This Trump has lots of good ideas to stimulate the economy with a few rather silly ideas such as reviving the coal industry and getting unskilled poor workers into high paying modern jobs. Both Trumps do not do their homework very well and shoot from the hip, making wide claims that his supporters eat up like filet mignon. Trump #1 scares the stock market. Trump #2 is very bullish for the stock market.

His economic team from Wall Street consisting of Treasury Secretary Steven Mnuchin, Gary Cohen, chair of the economic council, and Secretary of Commerce Wilbur Ross, are attempting to carry out his agenda. The administration has had lots of bumps such as the failed health bill to replace the popular Obamacare, but the proposed sharp drop in personal and corporate income taxes is expected to yield massive return of foreign low taxed income to the US. Apple Computer is a typical company with about $250 billion overseas, should that return to the US there would likely be large dividends and other goodies. This will help the Federal budget and deficit by collecting tax on this at a low rate.

For quite a while there has been a media story about Russian influence in US politics. Mostly it is hacking of computers. First there was interference in the Democratic campaign of Hilary Clinton against her and the party. FBI director James Comey hurt Clinton badly at crucial times just prior to the November 8, 2016 election. There have been at least three major Trump associates who have been persons of interest in Russiagate. First there was National Security Advisor Michael Flynn who was working for foreign governments such as Russia and Turkey without the proper authority. He was put in the position where Trump had to fire him yet Trump stood loyally behind him. Trump #1 insulted the media and called the accusation false, but Trump #2 did enough to hang on.

Here is a list of people who have been fired by Trump:

1. Arnold Schwarzeneger was fired from his role replacing Trump on the TV show the Apprentice;
2. Sally Yates; acting Attorney General
3. Mike Flynn; National Security Advisor;
4. Preet Vharara; US Attorney for the Southern District of NY
5. Angella Reid; White House Chief Usher
6. James Comey, FBI director;

Some who may be fired:

1. Sean Spicer, who has been the butt of many jokes since becoming Trump's White House Press Secretary, most notably on Saturday Night Live. After James Comey was fired, Spicer apparently hid in the bushes in the White House grounds apparently to avoid the press and the president.
2. Kelly Anne Conway, senior advisor, whose alternative facts fiasco was a humiliating episode for Trump, she also referred to the Bowling Green massacre a terrorist incident which never occurred.
3. Steve Bannon, Chief Executive Officer
4. Reince Preibus, Chief of Staff

Various parties who were fired will be testifying on aspects of the case. Whether or not Trump survives and is not impeached is unclear at this point, however, the Republican guru Ronald Reagan had similar issues and avoided trouble.

The bad scenario finally came on Monday May 14, 2017, when Trump fired Comey amid rumors that Comey had asked for more resources to investigate Russian hacking and possible Trump campaign involvement.

Trump greatly insulted Comey and was in a media frenzy against him. It looked like Trump's firing put him in big trouble or so the market thought. The VIX volatility index was at a record low in the 9's. Fearing Trump trouble in this low volatility, which I believed could not be sustained for a long period, I bought September 10 strike VIX calls that allowed for about 120 days to expiry. On Monday, the VIX rose to the 15 area, up nearly 50% and the S&P500, which had hardly moved for a long period, fell by a full 40 points, see Figure 8.9. I am used to these bad scenarios so positioned myself so I would not lose much and gain on the possible rebound, which I expected. The week of May 15–19 was options expiry and the rally did occur with the VIX dropping and my AlphaZ fund and other accounts went to new highs, Figure 8.10. This saga will continue and you can watch it in the press. This book closed this analysis on May 19, 2017.

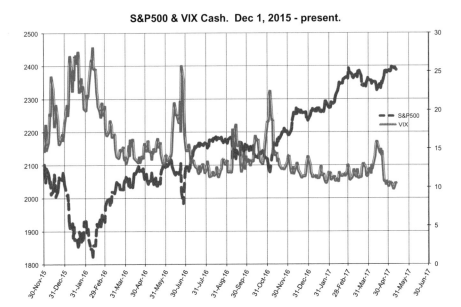

Fig. 8.9.

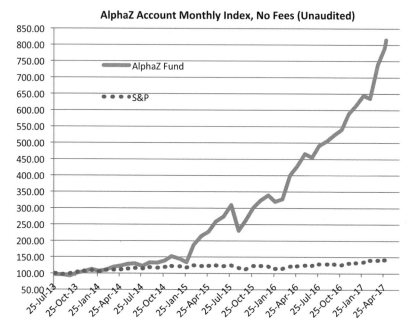

Fig. 8.10.

Chapter 9

A Stopping Rule Model for Exiting Bubble-like Markets with Applications

We present applications of a stochastic changepoint detection model in the context of bubble-like financial markets. The aim is to detect a direction change in a sequence of stock market or other asset index values as soon as it happens. A detection rule thus models an exit strategy in a possible market crash. We describe theoretical results in Sections 9.2 and apply them to several bubbles including markets in the US, China, Japan and Iceland in Sections 9.3–9.5.

9.1. Introduction

In this chapter, we study bubble-like markets, which are ones that are going up just because they are going up and often result eventually in a crash. We study strategies to optimally exit such markets.[1]

Trading bubbles is difficult and even the best traders sometimes lose a lot of money by shorting too soon. The finance and economics literature has little on timing bubbles. There is, however, some interest by inefficient market researchers, see for example, Stiglitz (1990) and Evanoff et al. (2012). In this chapter, we present a model that seems to work well, timing when to exit a long position. The basic idea is that there is a fast rate of growth in prices, then a peak and then a fast decline. The model tries to exit near the peak in prices. The mathematics of the model is sketched in Section 9.2 and is an application of the *changepoint detection* theory for random processes. For readers interested in how the model works, Appendix B should

---

[1]This chapter relies heavily on our three papers concerning this model, namely, Shiryaev, Zhitlukhin and Ziemba (2014, 2015) and Zhitlukhin and Ziemba (2016).

be helpful, but it is not important to read it to understand the results of the model which are in tables and figures showing entries and exits.

Changepoint detection methods have been successfully applied in production quality control, radiolocation, information security, and have shown their usefulness. Their history goes back to the pioneering works of Shewhart of 1920s, and the first results by Page, Roberts, Shiryaev and others of 1950–1960s. Surveys of the history and the recent developments in this field can be found in e.g. the introduction to the book by Poor and Hadjiliadis (2009).

In the financial context, a changepoint may represent a moment when the market starts to decline. It can be identified with a moment of time when the trend of the sequence of the market's index value becomes negative. The objective of the model is to detect this change after it occurs and to close a long position maximizing the gain.

We emphasize that the changepoint model does not *predict* a decline of price, but considers the problem to detect it *after* it has started, taking into account that temporal declines may be caused by the volatility of the price rather than a real change of the trend. In particular, such a decline need not necessarily be caused by a crash of a bubble, but can be due to e.g. a structural change in an economy or bad news for a company. Thus we do not need the price process to be a bubble in terms of one definition or another.

This chapter contains applications of the changepoint model to various stock market situations where there was a crash, with the view to test how the model can find exit points in markets that appeared to be bubbles. We apply the method to the three crashes in the US markets in 1929, 1987 and 2008, to the crash in the Iceland market in 2008, and to the crash in the Chinese market in 2015 plus Apple Computer stock in 2012, the NASDAQ in 2000 and the circa 1990 Japanese stock and land markets.

In part, the choice of the data was motivated by the fact that these various crashes had somewhat different characteristics, if judged by the pattern of underlying market indices or stock prices. The 1929 and 1987 crashes were similar in the behavior before the crash, showing a steady growth and then a sharp decline; the recovery patterns were much different though: it took about 2 years for the S&P500 to reach the value its pre-crash peak in 1987, while the Dow Jones Industrial of Average (DJIA) needed almost 25 years to recover only in 1954 (there were of course different macroeconomic environments, but our model is unaware of those because it uses only historical time series of index values). The crash of 2008 was characterized by a slow growth preceding the crash, and then a slow decline. In contrast, the Chinese market in 2014–2015 showed the fastest growth and the decline was comparable to the 1929 and 1929 US crashes. The Japanese stock and land markets crashed and ushered in a 20+ year depression-like atmosphere in the country. Even now in 2016, the Nikkei stock average is well below its 1989 value. We refer to Consigli *et al.* (2009), Lleo and Ziemba (2012, 2016a,b) and the references already cited, all of which discuss crashes in various markets and possible methods of how to predict them.

9.2.   A brief overview of the mathematics of the model

Broadly speaking, a *changepoint* is a random time when a random sequence (or a random process) changes the structure of its probability distribution. The basic example is a sequence of independent random variables with one value of the mean before a changepoint and another value of the mean after the changepoint, with all other parameters being the same before and after. The general theory of changepoint detection, of course, is not limited to detection of changes in means only; but the model we will use is of this basic type. This model is derived from one of the pioneering papers, Shiryaev (1963), but adapted to our investigation of bubble-like markets. The reader is referred to specialized literature for the state of the art changepoint detection methods; e.g. the monograph Tartakovsky *et al.* (2014) provides a detailed exposition of the theory.

The problem of detecting a changepoint consists in that an observer does not know when a change occurs and she can make a conclusion about it based only on the observed random sequence. We will consider *online* changepoint detection problems, which are characterized by the fact that new observations in a random sequence arrive one by one, and a decision about a possible change of the probability distribution should be made based on the data available up to the current moment of time. The goal is to recognize the change as soon as possible after it happens, but not earlier. (*Offline* changepoint problems, on the other hand, assume the whole realization of a random sequence is available.)

In the context of bubble-like markets, a changepoint is a moment when the price trend reverses and the observer wants to detect the reversion soon after it happens. The quantitative side of the problem is to distinguish between temporal declines in prices caused by volatility and a real structural change.

We will model bubble-like prices of stock or index values by a random sequence S_t, where time t runs through $t = 0, 1, \ldots, T$; the moment $t = 0$ is the start of observations, $t = T$ is the terminal moment specifying the time horizon of the model. The sequence of prices S is assumed to follow a geometric random walk with mean μ_1 and volatility σ_1 before a changepoint, and mean μ_2 and volatility σ_2 after a changepoint. Both pairs (μ_1, σ_1) and (μ_2, σ_2) are assumed to be known or can be estimated (see the remark below how to estimate them). It is assumed there is no more than one changepoint between $t = 0$ and $t = T$, occurring at some time $t = \theta$. Thus, the sequence S can be described by its log-returns X_t as follows:

$$X_t := \log \frac{S_t}{S_{t-1}} = \begin{cases} \mu_1 + \sigma_1 \xi_t, & t < \theta, \\ \mu_2 + \sigma_2 \xi_t, & t \geq \theta, \end{cases} \quad \text{for } t = 1, 2, \ldots, T,$$

where ξ_t are independent standard normal random variables.

We will work in the Bayesian setting, assuming that θ is a random variable taking values in the set $\{1, 2, \ldots, T+1\}$ with known prior probabilities $p_t = P(\theta = t)$. It is assumed θ is independent of the sequence ξ_t. The value p_1 is the probability that from the beginning of observation the sequence S follows parameters (μ_2, σ_2) (e.g. the bubble burst before the beginning of observation), and p_{T+1} is the probability that S_t follows (μ_1, σ_1) until the end of the time horizon of the model (e.g. the bubble continues at least until T).

Under an appropriate criterion of the optimality of a detection rule (see Appendix B, which contains all the mathematical details) we show that the optimal detection rule can be expressed through the *Shiryaev–Roberts statistic* ψ_t, which is a sequence constructed recursively as follows:

$$\psi_0 = 0, \ \psi_t = (p_t + \psi_{t-1}) \cdot \frac{\sigma^1}{\sigma^2} \exp\left(\frac{(X_t - \mu_1)^2}{2\sigma_1^2} - \frac{(X_t - \mu_2)^2}{2\sigma_2^2} \right),$$

$$t = 1, \ldots, T.$$

The main theorem that we prove in Appendix B states that it is optimal to declare a changepoint when the value of ψ_t exceeds a certain time-dependent threshold $b(t)$:

$$\text{the first time } t \text{ when } \psi_t \geq b(t).$$

The threshold $b(t)$ depends on the parameters of the problem, such as μ, σ, p_t, etc., and it is shown in the Appendix how one can compute it.

The parameters $\mu_1, \mu_2, \sigma_1, \sigma_2$ are required to be estimated. This is not a restrictive assumption for μ_1, σ_1 since they can be estimated from past data.

On the other hand, μ_2 and σ_2 cannot be estimated before a changepoint. So their values should be chosen in advance, and it might be a difficult problem to predict appropriate values for them. We will not study this question, however, all our applications that even a simple choice $\mu_2 = -\mu_1$, $\sigma_2 = \sigma_1$ gives acceptable results in many cases.

The same applies to the prior distribution of θ. In all the cases where we apply the model it is simply assumed to be uniform over $t = 1, \dots, T$ with a reasonable choice of probability 0.25 that there is no changepoint before T. We tried several other choices, which however does not give much difference, see our papers mentioned in the introduction to this chapter for details.

9.3.   Stock market crashes in the US

9.3.1.   *The great crash in 1929*

The substantial economic advance of the later half of the 1920s led to the significant growth of the US stock market. That growth was further increased by a speculative bubble, which attracted more people to the stock market in a hope that the prices would continue to increase. The market measured by the DJIA index peaked on September 3, 1929 but then declined by 10% by the end of the month. There was a short stabilization during the first half of October, which was followed by the crash on Black Thursday, October 24 and Black Tuesday, October 29, when the market was down almost 40% from its peak.

We applied the changepoint model to the values of the DJIA index with several choices of the parameters: five starting dates throughout 1928–1929, five combinations of the post-changepoint parameters (depending on the values of the pre-changepoint parameters estimated from the data), and two possible terminal dates corresponding to the time horizon T in the model (see the mathematical description). The parameters of drift and volatility μ_1, σ_1 of the model were estimated from 1 year of past data before each entry point; based on them, the post-changepoint parameters were chosen as shown in Table 9.1. In all the combinations of parameters, we took the changepoint probability to be 75% that a change in the drift happens in the given time horizon.

The results are presented in Table 9.1 and Fig. 9.1. The table shows the exit dates corresponding to the different choices of parameters and the percent ratio of the price on the exit date and the peak value (in brackets).

Stock Market Crashes

Table 9.1.   The DJIA 1929 crash exit points.

Entry	Exit date (% of max. value)				
	$\mu_2 = -\mu$ $\sigma_1 = \sigma_2$	$\mu_2 = -2\mu$ $\sigma_1 = \sigma_2$	$\mu_2 = -2\mu$ $\sigma_1 = 2\sigma_2$	$\mu_2 = -3\mu$ $\sigma_1 = \sigma_2$	$\mu_2 = -3\mu$ $\sigma_1 = 3\sigma_2$
	T = end of 1929				
1927-07-01	29-10-21 (84)	29-10-03 (87)	27-10-10 (50)	29-05-27 (77)	27-10-10 (50)
1928-01-01	29-10-03 (87)	29-05-27 (77)	28-06-11 (54)	28-12-10 (69)	28-06-12 (53)
1928-07-01	29-10-03 (87)	29-09-27 (90)	28-12-06 (73)	29-05-27 (77)	28-12-06 (73)
1929-01-01	29-10-03 (87)	29-09-27 (90)	29-02-11 (81)	29-05-27 (77)	29-03-25 (78)
1929-07-01	29-10-01 (90)	29-09-27 (90)	29-08-12 (92)	29-09-27 (90)	29-08-12 (92)
	T = end of 1930				
1927-07-01	29-10-28 (68)	29-10-23 (80)	27-10-10 (50)	29-10-04 (85)	27-10-10 (50)
1928-01-01	29-10-21 (84)	29-10-03 (87)	28-06-11 (54)	29-10-03 (87)	28-06-13 (55)
1928-07-01	29-10-23 (80)	29-10-21 (84)	28-12-06 (73)	29-10-03 (87)	28-12-07 (71)
1929-01-01	29-10-23 (80)	29-10-04 (85)	29-04-01 (79)	29-10-03 (87)	29-05-22 (79)
1929-07-01	29-10-23 (80)	29-10-23 (80)	29-10-07 (91)	29-10-23 (80)	29-10-07 (91)

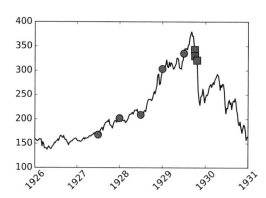

Fig. 9.1.   The DJIA index in 1926–1930 and the exit points for $\mu_2 = -\mu_1$, $\sigma_2 = \sigma_1$.

The shaded cells mark the dates after the peak on September 3 and before the Black Monday.

   Although the model had some false detections before the crash (caused by short-time declines), and acted too late for particular choices of the parameters after the crash, in most of the cases it was able to provide an exit point well before the local market trough. It follows that with respect to the post-crash volatility, the choice $\sigma_1 = \sigma_2$ gave results better than the other choices. With respect to the drift μ, the choices $\mu_2 = -\mu_1$ and

$\mu_2 = -2\mu_1$ are preferable to $\mu_2 = -3\mu_1$, as the latter detected false exit points in May 1929. The exit points for the parameters $\mu_2 = -\mu_1$, $\sigma_2 = \sigma_1$ are shown by the red marks on the graph in Fig. 9.1.

9.3.2. *The 1987 crash of S&P500*

On Monday October 19, 1987 the S&P500 futures fell 29% and the S&P500 cash index fell 22%. It was the greatest one-day decline ever in US history. Portfolio insurance which sold futures when they were falling was part of the cause. The BSEYD model based on high interest rates relative to stock earnings discussed in Chapters 2–4 did predict the crash. So did the T-model based on high call prices relative to put prices discussed in Chapter 5. The pre-crash and the crash price patterns resemble those of the 1929 crash. However, while the 1987 crash was very severe in a short term, it did not lead to a depression as in 1929 or even a recession. The market bounced back, and in about 2 years the S&P500 reached its pre-crash values.

The results of the application of the changepoint model to the crash are in Table 9.2 and Fig. 9.2. We use the same notation and estimate the parameters in the same way as in the previous section. The shaded cells in the table shows the exit points after the market peak on August 25 and before the Black Monday October 19.

Table 9.2.   Exit points for S&P500 during the crash of 1987.

	Exit date (% of max. value)				
Entry	$\mu_2 = -\mu$ $\sigma_1 = \sigma_2$	$\mu_2 = -2\mu$ $\sigma_1 = \sigma_2$	$\mu_2 = -2\mu$ $\sigma_1 = 2\sigma_2$	$\mu_2 = -3\mu$ $\sigma_1 = \sigma_2$	$\mu_2 = -3\mu$ $\sigma_1 = 3\sigma_2$
	T = end of 1987				
1985-07-01	87-10-15 (89)	87-10-12 (92)	86-07-08 (72)	86-09-12 (68)	86-07-07 (72)
1986-01-01	87-10-12 (92)	86-09-12 (68)	86-01-08 (62)	86-09-11 (70)	86-01-08 (62)
1986-07-01	87-10-14 (91)	87-09-21 (92)	86-07-15 (69)	86-09-12 (68)	86-09-11 (70)
1987-01-01	87-10-14 (91)	87-09-21 (92)	87-04-14 (83)	87-09-08 (93)	87-04-15 (84)
1987-07-01	87-10-12 (92)	87-09-21 (92)	87-10-14 (91)	87-09-08 (93)	87-10-14 (91)
	T = end of 1988				
1985-07-01	87-10-16 (84)	87-10-16 (84)	86-07-15 (69)	87-10-15 (89)	86-07-15 (69)
1986-01-01	87-10-15 (89)	87-10-15 (89)	86-04-08 (69)	86-09-12 (68)	86-01-08 (62)
1986-07-01	87-10-16 (84)	87-10-15 (89)	86-07-15 (69)	87-10-15 (89)	86-09-11 (70)
1987-01-01	87-10-19 (67)	87-10-16 (84)	87-04-15 (84)	87-10-16 (84)	87-10-15 (89)
1987-07-01	87-10-19 (67)	87-10-16 (84)	87-10-15 (89)	87-10-16 (84)	87-10-16 (84)

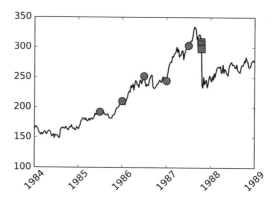

Fig. 9.2.   The S&P500 index in 1984–1988 and the exit points for $\mu_2 = -\mu_1$, $\sigma_2 = \sigma_1$.

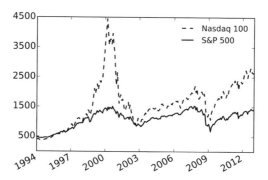

Fig. 9.3.   The Internet crash in the US in 2000–2002.

Again, the choice of $\sigma_1 = \sigma_2$ seems to work the best of the settings considered, while both the choices of $\mu_2 = -\mu_1$ and $\mu_2 = -2\mu_1$ still provide good results (however, the latter reacted exactly on the day of the crash under the assumption that the time horizon of the model is chosen as the end of 1988), and $\mu_2 = -3\mu_1$ works well in that case too.

9.3.3.   *The internet bubble crash during 2000–2002*

Alan Greenspan, the chairman of the US Federal Reserve System (Fed), began in 1994 a low interest rate policy that reduced short-term rates continuously over a multiyear period. This led to an increase in the S&P500 stock index from 470.42 in January 1995 to 1469.25 at the end of 1999, as shown in Fig. 9.3. The price earnings (P/E) ratios were high and Shiller used these to predict the crash starting in 1996, see Campbell and Shiller (1998) and Shiller (1996, 2000, 2009). It is known that stock price rises usually start with low P/E ratios and end with high P/E ratios, see Bertocchi, Schwartz and Ziemba (2010). But predicting when the market will crash using just P/E ratios is problematic.

However, as discussed in Chapters 2–4, it has been found in many markets over many years the BSEYD model predicts crashes better than just high P/E ratios, see Ziemba and Schwartz (1991), Ziemba (2003) and Lleo and Ziemba (2012) and our summary in Chapters 2–4. The model signaled a crash in the S&P500 in April 1999. It was in the danger zone all of 1999 starting in April and it got deeper in the danger zone as the year progressed, see Table 9.2. The signal did work but the real decline was not until September 2000 with a temporary fall from the March 24, 2000 high of 1552.87 and a recovery into the September 1, 2000 peak of 1530.09. By October 10, 2002 S&P500 fell to 768.63 having two temporary recoveries from the local lows of 1091.99 on April 4, 2001 and 944.75 on September 21, 2001. There were other signals:

> History shows that a period of shrinking breadth is usually followed by a sharp decline in stock values of the small group of leaders. Then broader market takes a more modest tumble. Paul Bagnell in late November 1999 in the *Globe and Mail*.

Ziemba (2003, Chapter 2) describes this episode in stock market history. There was considerable mean-reversion in the eventual crash in 2000, the September 11, 2001 attack and in the subsequent 2002 decline of 22%. This decline was similar to previous crashes.

The concentration of stock market gains into very few stocks with momentum and size being the key variables predicting performance was increasing before 1997 in Europe and North America. Table 2.6 in Ziemba (2003) shows that in 1998, the largest cap stocks had the highest return in North America and Europe but small cap stocks outperformed in Asia and Japan. The situation was similar from 1995 to 1999 with 1998 and 1999 the most exaggerated.

Fully 41% of the stocks in the S&P500 did not fall or actually rose during this period and an additional 19% declined by 10% or less annualized. These were small cap stocks with market values of $10 billion of less. The fall in the S&P500 was mainly in three areas: information technology, telecommunications and large cap stocks. Information technology stocks in the S&P500 fell 64% and telecom stocks fell 60% from January 1 to October 31, 2002. The largest cap stocks (with market caps of $50 billion plus) lost 37%. But most other stocks either lost only a little or actually gained. Materials fell 10% but consumer discretionary gained 4.5%, consumer staples gained 21%, energy gained 12%, financial services gained 19%, health care gained 29%, industrials gained 7% and utilities gained 2%. Equally weighted, the S&P500 index lost only 3%. So there was a strong small cap effect. The stocks that gained were the very small cap stocks with market caps below $10 billion. Some 138 companies with market caps between $5–10 billion gained 4% on average and 157 companies with market caps below $5 billion gained on average 23%.

While the BSEYD model has been shown to be useful in predicting S&P500 declines, it is silent on the NASDAQ technology index of the largest 100 stocks by market capitalization, the NDX100. This index with a major Internet component had a spectacular increase during a period where many thought the Internet companies would prosper despite P/E ratios of 100 plus and many with no earnings at all (see Fig. 9.3). Valuation attempts were made to justify these high prices; see Schwartz and Moon (2000) for one such example. Predicting the top of this bubble was not easy as the Internet index (not shown) fell 17% one day and then proceeded to reach new highs. For example, the noted investor George Soros lost some $5 billion of the $12 billion in the Quantum hedge fund during this crash.

The Nasdaq 100 peaked at 4816.35 on March 24, 2000 starting from 398.26 in 1994. In the decline, it fell to 795.25 on October 8, 2002. Below we apply the changepoint model to the questions when to close a long–short positions on NDX100 for various entering dates. The results appear in Table 9.3 and Fig. 9.4. Depending upon the long position entry, the exit yielded about 65–75% of the maximum price. Here the parameters $\mu_2 = -\mu_1$, $\sigma_2 = \sigma_1$ seem to show better performance than the other choices, however, all the three values of μ_2 with $\sigma_2 = \sigma_1$ give quite close results.

9.3.4. *The 2008 crash*

The roots of the 2008 crash can be found in the mortgage market problems. US real estate prices peaked in 2005–2006 and included loans to many unqualified buyers who were only safe if the real estate prices continued

Table 9.3.   Exit points for NDX100 during the Internet crash.

	Exit date (% of max. value)				
Entry	$\mu_2 = -\mu$ $\sigma_1 = \sigma_2$	$\mu_2 = -2\mu$ $\sigma_1 = \sigma_2$	$\mu_2 = -2\mu$ $\sigma_1 = 2\sigma_2$	$\mu_2 = -3\mu$ $\sigma_1 = \sigma_2$	$\mu_2 = -3\mu$ $\sigma_1 = 3\sigma_2$
	T = end of 2000				
1997-07-01	00-05-23 (64)	00-04-14 (68)	97-10-27 (21)	00-04-12 (77)	97-10-27 (21)
1998-01-01	00-10-10 (68)	00-05-23 (64)	98-08-31 (24)	00-04-14 (68)	98-08-31 (24)
1998-07-01	00-04-14 (68)	00-04-13 (76)	98-08-31 (24)	00-04-12 (77)	98-08-31 (24)
1999-01-01	00-04-14 (68)	00-04-12 (77)	00-01-07 (75)	00-04-12 (77)	00-01-07 (75)
1999-07-01	00-04-14 (68)	00-04-12 (77)	00-01-10 (79)	00-04-12 (77)	00-01-11 (75)
	T = end of 2001				
1997-07-01	00-10-12 (64)	00-04-14 (68)	97-10-27 (21)	00-04-14 (68)	97-10-27 (21)
1998-01-01	00-11-30 (53)	00-11-20 (59)	98-08-31 (24)	00-11-10 (61)	98-08-31 (24)
1998-07-01	00-10-11 (66)	00-04-14 (68)	98-08-31 (24)	00-04-14 (68)	98-08-31 (24)
1999-01-01	00-05-23 (64)	00-04-14 (68)	00-01-07 (75)	00-04-13 (76)	00-01-10 (79)
1999-07-01	00-10-10 (68)	00-04-14 (68)	00-01-11 (75)	00-04-14 (68)	00-04-12 (77)

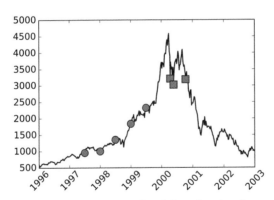

Fig. 9.4.   The Nasdaq 100 index in 1996–2002 and the exit points for $\mu_2 = -\mu_1$, $\sigma_2 = \sigma_1$.

to rise. Unlike the two crashes considered above, this one had a different pattern: the crash was followed for about a year of slowly decreasing equity index prices (which peaked in October 2007) and a decline overall slower than those in 1929 and 1987. The total fall was huge with the index losing more than 57% of its value by March 2009. We refer to Chapter 3 and Lleo and Ziemba (2012) for a discussion of this crash and the application of the BSEYD model to predict it on June 14, 2007.

Table 9.4.   Exit points for S&P500 around the 2008 crash.

	Exit date (% of max. value)				
Entry	$\mu_2 = -\mu$ $\sigma_1 = \sigma_2$	$\mu_2 = -2\mu$ $\sigma_1 = \sigma_2$	$\mu_2 = -2\mu$ $\sigma_1 = 2\sigma_2$	$\mu_2 = -3\mu$ $\sigma_1 = \sigma_2$	$\mu_2 = -3\mu$ $\sigma_1 = 3\sigma_2$
	T = end of 2008				
2005-07-01	08-01-15 (88)	07-11-21 (91)	07-02-27 (89)	07-11-19 (92)	07-02-27 (89)
2006-01-01	08-01-08 (89)	07-11-09 (93)	06-06-15 (80)	07-08-14 (91)	07-02-27 (89)
2006-07-01	08-01-08 (89)	07-11-21 (91)	07-02-27 (89)	07-08-15 (90)	07-02-27 (89)
2007-01-01	08-01-08 (89)	07-11-21 (91)	07-02-27 (89)	07-08-15 (90)	07-02-27 (89)
2007-07-01	08-01-08 (89)	07-11-21 (91)	07-07-26 (95)	07-08-15 (90)	07-07-26 (95)
	T = end of 2009				
2005-07-01	08-03-06 (83)	08-01-17 (85)	07-02-27 (89)	08-01-15 (88)	07-02-27 (89)
2006-01-01	08-03-06 (83)	08-01-08 (89)	06-06-15 (80)	07-11-26 (90)	07-02-27 (89)
2006-07-01	08-03-06 (83)	08-01-16 (88)	07-02-27 (89)	08-01-08 (89)	07-02-27 (89)
2007-01-01	08-01-17 (85)	08-01-15 (88)	07-02-27 (89)	08-01-15 (88)	07-02-27 (89)
2007-07-01	08-01-17 (85)	08-01-15 (88)	07-07-26 (95)	08-01-15 (88)	07-07-26 (95)

Fig. 9.5.   The S&P500 index in 2005–2010 and the exit points for $\mu_2 = -\mu_1$, $\sigma_2 = \sigma_1$.

The changepoint model for any choice of the parameters detected the changepoint well before the actual crash in September 2008 though there were several too early detections (see Table 9.4). The results shown in Table 9.4 and Fig. 9.5 again support the choice of the post-crash volatility $\sigma_2 = \sigma_1$ and the post-crash drift $\mu_2 = -\mu_1$ or $\mu_2 = -2\mu_1$ (the shaded cells show exit points after the market peak).

9.4. Crashes in the Japanese stock and land markets

9.4.1. *The crash in the Nikkei stock average index*

The Japanese stock market was closed after World War II ended in 1945 until its reopening in 1948. From 1948 to 1988, there was a huge rise in the stock market measured by the Nikkei price weighted index of 225 stocks as well as the Topix value weighted index of more than 1000 stocks. A steady increase in quality and quantity of equipment and automobiles of various kinds led to an enormous inflow of financial assets. These in turn were invested primarily in Japanese stocks and land.

Low interest rates in the mid to late 1980s fueled the stock and land, and the Nikkei rose 220 times in yen and 550 times in US dollars from 1948 to 1988. There were however 20 corrections/declines of 10% or more from 1949 to 1988 as shown in Table 9.5.

Table 9.5. The 20 Corrections of 10% or more on the NSA from 1949 to 1988.

	Index Value			Date		
	Peak	Valley	% decrease	Peak	Valley	# Months
1	176.89	85.25	−51.8	01-Sep-49	06-Jul-50	11
2	474.43	295.18	−37.8	4-Feb-53	1-Apr-53	2
3	366.69	321.79	−12.2	6-May-53	3-Jun-53	1
4	595.46	471.53	−20.8	4-May-57	27-Dec-57	8
5	1,829.74	1,258.00	−31.2	18-Jul-61	19-Dec-61	5
6	1,589.76	1,216.04	−23.5	14-Feb-62	29-Oct-62	9
7	1,634.37	1201.26	−26.5	5-Apr-63	18-Dec-63	9
8	1,369.00	1,020.49	−25.5	3-Jul-64	12-Jul-65	13
9	1,588.73	1,364.34	−14.1	1-Apr-66	15-Dec-66	8
10	1,506.27	1,250.40	−17.0	1-Mar-67	11-Dec-67	9
11	2,534.45	1,929.64	−23.9	6-Apr-70	27-May-70	2
12	2,740.98	2,227.25	−18.7	13-Aug-71	20-Oct-71	3
13	5,359.74	3,355.13	−37.4	24-Jan-73	9-Oct-74	21
14	4,564.52	3,814.02	−16.4	12-May-75	29-Sep-75	5
15	5,287.65	4,597.26	−13.1	5-Sep-77	24-Nov-77	3
16	8,019.14	6,849.78	−14.6	17-Aug-81	1-Oct-82	14
17	11,190.17	9,703.35	−13.3	4-May-84	23-Jul-84	3
18	18,936.24	15,819.58	−16.5	20-Aug-86	22-Oct-86	2
19	25,929.42	22,702.74	−12.4	17-Jun-87	22-Jul-87	1
20	26,646.43	21,036.76	−21.1	14-Oct-87	11-Nov-87	1
Average			−0.224			6.5

Source: Yamaichi Research Institute.

Fig. 9.6.   The Nikkei stock average index, 1984–2016.

The Nikkei peaked at the end of December 1989 at 39,816. In Chapter 2, the bond–stock earnings yield model was shown to go into the danger zone in April 1989, based on too high interest rates relative to earnings yield. That model suggested that a large decline or crash was coming. The stock market started to fall on the first trading day of 1990. When the index bottomed, the market had fallen 48% from 38,916 at the end of December 1989 to 20,222 on October 1, 1990. Figure 9.6 shows the Nikkei stock average index from 1984 to 2014.

Interest rates increased 8 full months till August 1990. It took years and years to recover from this despite dropping interest rates after August 1990 for many years and in 2016, they were still low. Overall, the crash ushered in more than two decades of deflation, weak economic markets and a lost generation of young people. Various Japanese policies and regulatory constraints exacerbated the poor economic situation and never resolved the basic problem of overleveraging and excessive debt that was a major part of the 1980s buildup.

We tested the changepoint model on the Japanese crash of 1990 applying it to the Nikkei index with the results shown in Table 9.6 and Fig. 9.7. The meaning of the parameters is the same as in the previous section. For all the choices of the parameters, the model stopped well near the peak.

9.4.2.   The crash in the land market

While the Nikkei stock average in the late 1980s and its −48% crash in 1990 are generally recognized as a financial market bubble, a bigger bubble and crash were in the land market which started to fall in 1990. The land and stock markets were greatly intertwined as discussed by Ziemba (1991)

Table 9.6.   Exit points for the Nikkei stock average.

| Entry | Exit date (% of max. value) | | | | |
	$\mu_2 = -\mu$ $\sigma_1 = \sigma_2$	$\mu_2 = -2\mu$ $\sigma_1 = \sigma_2$	$\mu_2 = -2\mu$ $\sigma_1 = 2\sigma_2$	$\mu_2 = -3\mu$ $\sigma_1 = \sigma_2$	$\mu_2 = -3\mu$ $\sigma_1 = 3\sigma_2$
	$T =$ end of 1990				
1987-07-01	90-03-14 (83)	87-11-11 (54)	87-10-20 (56)	87-10-20 (56)	87-10-20 (56)
1988-01-01	90-02-26 (86)	90-02-23 (90)	90-04-02 (72)	90-02-23 (90)	90-04-02 (72)
1988-07-01	90-02-26 (86)	90-02-21 (92)	90-04-02 (72)	90-02-21 (92)	90-04-02 (72)
1989-01-01	90-02-23 (90)	90-02-23 (90)	90-02-21 (92)	90-02-23 (90)	90-02-21 (92)
1989-07-01	90-02-23 (90)	90-02-23 (90)	90-01-16 (95)	90-02-21 (92)	90-01-16 (95)
	$T =$ end of 1991				
1987-07-01	90-03-20 (79)	90-03-19 (80)	87-10-20 (56)	87-10-20 (56)	87-10-20 (56)
1988-01-01	90-04-02 (72)	90-03-20 (79)	90-04-02 (72)	90-03-19 (80)	90-04-02 (72)
1988-07-01	90-04-02 (72)	90-03-19 (80)	90-04-02 (72)	90-03-19 (80)	90-04-02 (72)
1989-01-01	90-02-26 (86)	90-02-26 (86)	90-02-23 (90)	90-02-26 (86)	90-02-23 (90)
1989-07-01	90-02-26 (86)	90-02-26 (86)	90-02-21 (92)	90-02-23 (90)	90-02-21 (92)

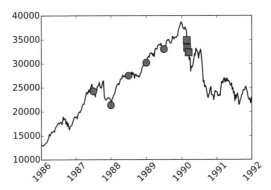

Fig. 9.7.   The Nikkei stock average in 1986–1991 and the exit points for $\mu_2 = -\mu_1$, $\sigma_2 = \sigma_1$.

and Stone and Ziemba (1993) and the discussion below. To get an idea of the price pressure on Japanese land prices, consider that in the late 1980s:

- some 120 million people lived in Japan in an area the size of Montana,
- only 5% of the land was used to house the people, buildings and factories because most of the land is mountainous,
- most of the land was owned by large corporations but 60% of Japanese families and 55% of those in Tokyo owned their own home,

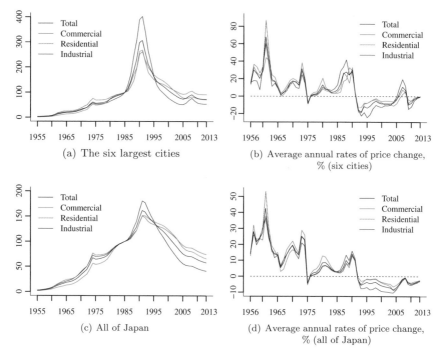

(a) The six largest cities

(b) Average annual rates of price change, % (six cities)

(c) All of Japan

(d) Average annual rates of price change, % (all of Japan)

Fig. 9.8.   Land price indices for industrial, residential, commercial and all land and annual rates of price change, 1955–2013.

Source: Japan Real Estate Institute.

- there was massive savings by households,
- only some 3% of Japanese assets were invested abroad despite great fear in the west and some very public purchases at inflated prices of expensive property such as the Pebble Beach golf course.

Figure 9.8 gives the Japan Real Estate Institute's land indices for the six largest cities, and for all of Japan for commercial, housing, industrial and total land for each 6-month period from 1955 to 2013. The graphs also give the yearly rate of changes. The six largest cities are Tokyo, Yokohama, Osaka, Nagoya, Kobe and Kyoto.

The countrywide indices are based on 140 cities. The data are appraisal based which tends to smooth the price levels and lag the market. Simple averages of samples of 10 lots in each city form the indices which were normalized at 100 as of 1985. The sampling procedure separates land into high, medium and low grades reflecting location, social circumstances, yield, etc.

Table 9.7.   Increase of land prices, 1955–1990, %.

	Nationwide				6 largest cities			
	Total	Com	Res	Ind	Total	Com	Res	Ind
1955 to 1990	65.5	59.6	81.2	56.7	178.8	127.7	219.1	150.8
1955 to 1970	15.1	14.5	15.5	15.8	18.7	11.0	20.2	23.6
1970 to 1990	4.3	4.1	5.2	3.6	9.6	11.6	10.8	6.4

Source: Japan Real Estate Institute.

The sampling procedure selects lots randomly and equally from each of these three classes.

Figure 9.8 and Table 9.7 indicate that the price increase has been largest in the six largest cities. Despite large rises in the 1980s, the relative gain in the period 1955–1970 was much larger than from 1970 to the circa 1990 peak. For land in the whole country, the 1955–1970 period produced gains of about 15 times the 1955 values. These prices then increased only about four-fold in the ensuing 20 years. In the six largest cities, the increase was also much larger in the 1955–1970 period versus the next two decades.

Land values in the six largest cities outpaced the Consumer Prices Index (CPI) by 20 times from 1955 to 1990. In the Ginza district of Tokyo each square meter of land was worth well over US$200,000 with some plots approaching $300,000. Choice downtown land in Tokyo sold for the equivalent of nearly a billion dollars an acre. At neighboring land prices, the value of land under the Emperor's palace and garden in Tokyo equaled that of all California or of Canada. The total land value in Japan in 1990 was about 4.1 times that of the whole US. The average acre of land in Japan was worth fully 100 times the average acre in the US. So even though the US has about 25 times more land than Japan, its 1990 total value was less than a fourth as much. Essentially half the world's land value at 1987–1990 prices was accounted for by Japanese land!

The price was kept up and bid higher because of the excess of demand over supply. Land turnover was very small as the Japanese believe in holding land whenever possible. This was reinforced by the tax system which encourages the purchase of more land and discourages land sales. High interest rates which led to a sharp fall in stock prices in 1990 did not lead to any decline in land prices until 1991 as shown in Fig. 9.8. However, there was a sharp decline in speculative land such as golf course membership and condos, see Stone and Ziemba (1993). As interest rates rise, land demand fell but in Tokyo, with virtually no new supply, demand still greatly exceeded supply. At the same time, supply declines with higher interest rates as development costs are curtailed. All the incentives favored holding land and not even developing it. As Canaway (1990) pointed out, land held for less than 5 years was taxed at fully 52% of its sale value. Meanwhile, yearly taxes paid to hold land were about 0.05 to 0.10% of its current value. Even upon death, it paid to borrow money which was deductible at full value while land was valued at about half its market value. Hence inheritance taxes are minimized. Canaway argued that in a major crash the stock market will go first, then the economy and finally the land markets. Our results confirm this.

9.4.3.   *The golf course membership index as a proxy for the land market*

Japanese land prices are difficult for a direct analysis since only low frequency time series are available. In part, this makes difficult to apply the changepoint model. Nevertheless, the overall land market can be well proxied by speculative land prices. In this section as such a proxy we use data on membership prices in Japanese golf courses.

In 1989 there were more than 400 golf courses in Japan with a total value of more than US$300 billion, a value larger than the Australian stock exchange capitalization of A$250 billion. Memberships, which cost as much as US$8 million, allowed play at a reduced cost plus the right to bring guests to play for a higher fee. However, their main value was not the ability to play golf but their share of the land occupied by the course and as an instrument to play the land market for relatively low stake with liquidity. These memberships were actively traded as speculative investments whose market was maintained by six market makers in Tokyo and Osaka. Weekly data were available in various areas of Japan since the beginning of 1982. These data were the best widely available data series on land prices in Japan and forms an ideal source for many types of analyses.

Rachev and Ziemba (1992) modeled the price changes as stable variants. The tails had considerable mass and the distributions were considered to have fat tails with a characteristic exponent about 1.4. This is consistent with the hypothesis that there was a speculative bubble in the late 1980s and the subsequent crash in 1990–1992.

Figure 9.9 shows the golf course membership (GCM) prices in various regions of the country: the western and the eastern parts of Japan, the

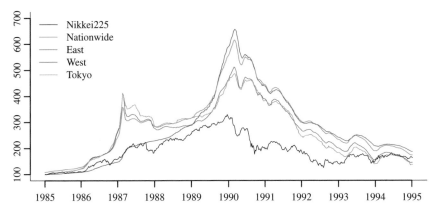

Fig. 9.9.   Graphs of the golf course membership prices in various areas of Japan and the Nikkei stock average, 1985–1995, with the 1985 values as 100%.

Table 9.8.   Exit points for the Golf Course Index crash.

	Exit date (% of max. value)				
Entry	$\mu_2 = -\mu$ $\sigma_1 = \sigma_2$	$\mu_2 = -2\mu$ $\sigma_1 = \sigma_2$	$\mu_2 = -2\mu$ $\sigma_1 = 2\sigma_2$	$\mu_2 = -3\mu$ $\sigma_1 = \sigma_2$	$\mu_2 = -3\mu$ $\sigma_1 = 3\sigma_2$
			$T = $ end of 1991		
1988-07-01	90-04-01 (95)	90-03-25 (98)	89-07-09 (62)	90-03-25 (98)	89-02-12 (54)
1989-01-01	90-03-18 (99)	90-03-18 (99)	89-07-09 (62)	90-03-18 (99)	89-02-05 (53)
1989-07-01	90-03-18 (99)	90-03-18 (99)	90-03-18 (99)	90-03-25 (98)	89-09-17 (72)
1989-10-01	90-04-01 (95)	90-04-01 (95)	90-04-01 (95)	90-04-01 (95)	90-04-01 (95)
			$T = $ end of 1992		
1988-07-01	90-04-01 (95)	90-04-01 (95)	89-07-09 (62)	90-03-25 (98)	89-02-26 (55)
1989-01-01	90-03-18 (99)	90-03-18 (99)	89-07-09 (62)	90-03-18 (99)	89-02-05 (53)
1989-07-01	90-03-25 (98)	90-03-18 (99)	90-03-18 (99)	90-03-25 (98)	89-09-17 (72)
1989-10-01	90-04-01 (95)	90-04-01 (95)	90-04-01 (95)	90-04-01 (95)	90-04-01 (95)

Tokyo area and the nationwide average. The golf course memberships market was a much bigger bubble than the stock market.

The results of applying the changepoint model are displayed in Table 9.8 with the same notation as the previous sections. We show only the nationwide index, although similar results and exit dates were obtained for the three other indices (the results can be found in Shiryaev, *et al.* 2015). In all the cases, the model exits well above 90% of the global maximum price, see Fig. 9.10. Compared with the stock market bubble, the changepoint model

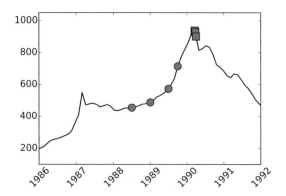

Fig. 9.10. The Japan GCM index and the exit points for $\mu_2 = -\mu_1$, $\sigma_2 = \sigma_1$.

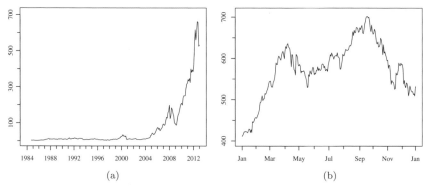

Fig. 9.11. The history of AAPL stock price (adjusted for dividends and splits). (a) From September 1984 to the end of 2012. (b) In 2009–2012.

applied to the golf course membership index exits almost immediately after the peak. One reason for that is much higher ratio μ_1/σ of the drift to volatility, which governs the statistic ψ_t from the model.

9.5. Other crashes: Apple stock, China and Iceland

9.5.1. *The crash in Apple computer stock in 2012*

AAPL stock had a spectacular run from the bottom of the 2007–2009 crash in March 2009, see Fig. 9.11 which shows the price history from September 1984 to the end of 2012; and the more recent period, from the beginning of 2009 to the end of 2012.

A sequence of valuable and easy to use products inspired by legendary visionary Steve Jobs created huge interest and sales around the world. All of these products had high margins which accumulated large cash levels. In November 2012 they had $121 billion in cash or $128 per share of the 941 million shares outstanding. The company has generated cash faster than any corporation in history. The stock was never at a high P/E ratio and was a favorite of hedge funds, open and closed mutual funds, ETFs and various small and large investors. It was traded as a proxy for the market with high liquidity. Its forward P/E ratio in November 2012 was 10.17 with estimated earnings per share of $49.28. The company had a quarterly dividend of $2.65 per share and a buy back of about $10 million in stock.

Steve Jobs left Apple in 1985 because of a power struggle with John Sculley who he brought over from Pepsi asking "do you want to sell sugared water all your life or change the world". Sculley came to Apple but he and Jobs had a disagreement on strategy and marketing which stagnated the company. The board favored the marketer over the genius. Jobs sold all but one of his AAPL shares. The company languished while he continued developing his ideas at NeXT and Pixar. When Jobs returned to Apple in 1996, he brought the new NeXT platform and ideas for user friendly products that had not yet been imagined by the market. He transformed the company into a winner. He held a lot of AAPL stock but more of Pixar which merged with Disney.

After his death on October 5, 2011, many feared that the sequence of great products would cease and that the pace of innovation could not be maintained and that the market cap of about $500 billion, various lawsuits for patent infringement, competition and labour and supply chain issues might slow it down. Some thought it was a bubble and others thought it would continue rallying because it was not expensive, not feeding on itself as in a typical bubble. The stock peaked at 705.07 on September 21, 2012 and then fell dramatically to the local low of 505.75 on November 16, 2012. Later, in pre-market trading on December 17, 2012, it fell to 499. On December 31, 2012, AAPL closed the year at 532; see Fig. 9.11.

The concentration of ownership by mutual funds (see Fig. 9.12) creates conundrum for Apple as regulations prohibit ownership to exceed a percentage of a fund's assets, so as AAPL rises relative to other stocks, funds often must sell shares. Some of the selling was tax loss selling in 2012 before expected higher capital gains and dividend rates in 2013 since more gains

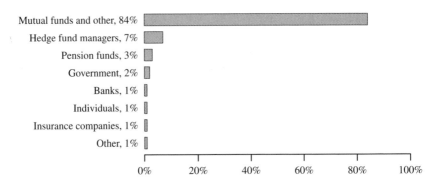

Fig. 9.12. Holders of Apple, April 17, 2012.

Source: Bloomberg via Eric Jackson.

are in AAPL than in any other stock. Despite the large decline in the latter part of 2012 the stock increased 30% in 2012.

Shiryaev, *et al.* (2014) applied the model to the Apple price bubble starting at the local low of 82.33 on March 6, 2009 and considering various entering dates for opening a long position in 2009–2012. It was assumed that the trend reversal will happen before the end of 2012. Higher tax rates on dividends and capital gains were expected in 2013, thus a sale in 2012 is suggested.

Table 9.9 and Fig. 9.13 present the result of the changepoint model application. Tests indicate that the choice $\mu_2 = -\mu_1$ is the optimal one, and for the 2012 time horizon works equally well both for early and late entering dates giving nearly 90% of the maximum price.

9.5.2. *The crash in Iceland in 2007–2009*

Iceland is a small country with only about 300 000 people. From 2002 to 2007, the economy and asset prices rose dramatically, with much leveraging of investments, especially by the banks. This led to high interest rates of about 10% long term and 16% short term. Eventually, it all collapsed in the wake of the 2007–2009 worldwide financial crisis. The decline was a massive crash of −95% in the equity index and a currency collapse.

The crash in Iceland is discussed in Section 3.2 with the BSEYD model prediction, the decline which occurred around the time of the Lehman Brothers collapse in the fall of 2008.

In Table 9.10 and Fig. 9.14, we show entries and exits using the changepoint model. We consider two entry points in April and June 2007,

Table 9.9.   Exit points for the Apple stock around the 2012 crash.

	Exit date (% of max. value)				
Entry	$\mu_2 = -\mu$ $\sigma_1 = \sigma_2$	$\mu_2 = -2\mu$ $\sigma_1 = \sigma_2$	$\mu_2 = -2\mu$ $\sigma_1 = 2\sigma_2$	$\mu_2 = -3\mu$ $\sigma_1 = \sigma_2$	$\mu_2 = -3\mu$ $\sigma_1 = 3\sigma_2$
	T = end of 2012				
2012-07-01	12-10-19 (87)	12-10-11 (89)	12-11-08 (77)	12-10-09 (91)	12-11-19 (81)
2012-01-01	12-10-11 (89)	12-10-05 (93)	12-04-17 (87)	12-05-17 (76)	12-01-25 (64)
2011-07-01	12-10-25 (87)	12-05-17 (76)	11-08-08 (50)	12-05-17 (76)	11-08-08 (50)
2011-01-01	12-11-02 (82)	12-10-26 (86)	11-08-09 (53)	12-10-26 (86)	11-08-09 (53)
2010-07-01	12-11-02 (82)	12-11-02 (82)	11-08-09 (53)	12-11-02 (82)	11-08-09 (53)
	T = end of 2013				
2012-07-01	12-12-14 (73)	12-11-08 (77)	13-01-24 (64)	12-11-08 (77)	13-01-24 (64)
2012-01-01	12-12-14 (73)	12-11-08 (77)	12-04-19 (84)	12-11-07 (79)	12-04-25 (87)
2011-07-01	12-11-08 (77)	12-11-07 (79)	11-08-08 (50)	12-11-07 (79)	11-08-08 (50)
2011-01-01	12-12-14 (73)	12-11-08 (77)	11-08-09 (53)	12-11-08 (77)	11-08-09 (53)
2010-07-01	12-12-14 (73)	12-11-15 (75)	11-08-10 (52)	12-11-08 (77)	12-04-25 (87)

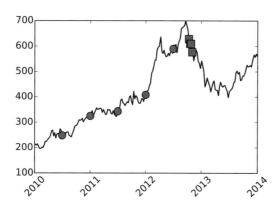

Fig. 9.13.   The Apple stock price in 2010–2014 and the exit points.

Table 9.10.   Exit points for the Iceland stock market crash in 2007.

	Exit date (% of max. value)				
Entry	$\mu_2 = -\mu$ $\sigma_1 = \sigma_2$	$\mu_2 = -2\mu$ $\sigma_1 = \sigma_2$	$\mu_2 = -2\mu$ $\sigma_1 = 2\sigma_2$	$\mu_2 = -3\mu$ $\sigma_1 = \sigma_2$	$\mu_2 = -3\mu$ $\sigma_1 = 3\sigma_2$
2007-04-01	07-08-10 (89)	07-08-09 (92)	07-08-10 (89)	07-08-09 (92)	07-08-10 (89)
2007-06-01	07-08-09 (92)	07-08-03 (93)	07-08-01 (94)	07-07-30 (94)	07-08-10 (89)

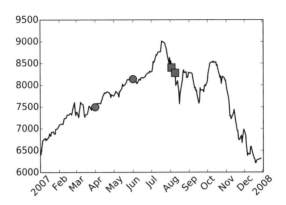

Fig. 9.14.   OMX Iceland 15 Index in 2007 and the exit points.

Table 9.11.   Exit points for the Chinese stock market crash in 2015.

	Exit date (% of max. value)				
Entry	$\mu_2 = -\mu$ $\sigma_1 = \sigma_2$	$\mu_2 = -2\mu$ $\sigma_1 = \sigma_2$	$\mu_2 = -2\mu$ $\sigma_1 = 2\sigma_2$	$\mu_2 = -3\mu$ $\sigma_1 = \sigma_2$	$\mu_2 = -3\mu$ $\sigma_1 = 3\sigma_2$
2015-04-01	15-06-26 (81)	15-06-19 (87)	15-05-11 (84)	15-06-19 (87)	15-05-28 (89)
2015-01-01	15-06-26 (81)	15-06-19 (87)	15-01-19 (60)	15-06-19 (87)	15-01-19 (60)
2014-08-01	15-07-03 (71)	15-06-26 (81)	14-12-02 (53)	15-06-19 (87)	14-12-04 (56)

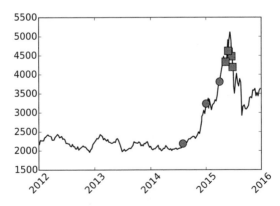

Fig. 9.15.   The SSEC Index in 2012–2015 and the exit point.

with the time horizon taken as the end of 2007. The model exits at about 90% of the index's maximum value.

9.5.3.   *The crash in China in 2015*

The growing Chinese economy has recently attracted many individual investors, whose actions are believed to fuel the bubble in the stock market. They borrowed heavily to buy equities, which resulted in stocks priced beyond their fundamental values. Thus a little decrease could potentially lead to a large sell-off due to investors facing margin calls, which is believed what has happened starting from the summer of 2015.

The Shanghai Stock Exchange Composite Index (SSEC) peaked in the middle of June 2015 showing about a 70% increase from the beginning of the year — of the bubbles considered in this chapter, the Chinese one is the sharpest. By the end of August, the index lost almost a half of its peak value. A local trough was also on July 2, with a loss of about 40% of the maximum value. In Chapter 3, we applied the BSEYD model to predict this Chinese stock market crash and the results are discussed there.

The changepoint detection model for all the parameters we consider signaled the changepoint before the July decline, in most cases being able to exit at more than 80% of the maximum value. There were, however, several false detections triggered by the temporary decline in the beginning of 2015. Table 9.11 and Fig. 9.15 illustrate the results. The shaded cells in the table mark the four highest exit points shown on the graph, all above 80% of the peak value.

Chapter 10

A Simple Procedure to Incorporate Predictive Models in Stochastic Investment Models

Stochastic optimization has found a fertile ground for applications in finance. One of the greatest challenges remains to incorporate a set of scenarios that accurately models the behavior of financial markets, and in particular their behavior during crashes and crises, without sacrificing the tractability of the optimal investment policy. This chapter shows how to incorporate return predictions and crash predictions as views into continuous time asset allocation models.

The greatest challenge in stochastic optimization is to incorporate a rich array of realistic scenarios that describes the behavior of financial markets without sacrificing the tractability of the optimal investment policy. While stochastic programming models show the greatest flexibility in incorporating scenarios, constraints and investment objectives, they do so at the expense of tractability and interpretability (we refer the reader to Ziemba, 2003b; Ziemba and Vickson, 2006, for a discussion of stochastic programming models applied to investment management). On the other hand, stochastic control often has tractable analytical or numerical solutions. However, most stochastic control models are constrained by unrealistic assumptions that fail to capture adequately the behavior of financial markets (we refer the reader to Davis and Lleo, 2014, for a discussion of stochastic control models applied to investment management).

The development of stochastic control models inspired by the Black–Litterman model (Black and Litterman, 1990, 1991b, 1992) is an important milestone, as it enables modelers to enrich the range of historical scenarios considered traditionally, with the addition of subjective scenarios provided by analyst views and expert opinions.

In fact, the predictive models presented in this chapter can be viewed as subjective scenarios. Here, we show how to incorporate return prediction and crash prediction models as views into the Black–Litterman model in continuous time proposed by Davis and Lleo (2013). The general idea is to treat the output of a predictive model as a view, and to model it with a stochastic differential equation of the same form as Eq. 10.6. We use the model's prediction to calibrate the drift of the view, and the model's error to estimate the diffusion term. Because the Kalman filter gives more weight to more credible observations and less weight to less credible observations, more accurate prediction models will have more influence on the asset allocation. These ideas can easily be generalised to more flexible stochastic programming models. This section is based on Davis and Lleo (2016).

10.1. Black–Litterman in continuous time: A primer

The Black–Litterman model in continuous time (Davis and Lleo, 2013) uses linear filtering to incorporate analyst views and expert opinions in a continuous time asset allocation. The key to the approach is that the filtering problem and the stochastic control problem are effectively separable. The model uses this insight to incorporate analyst views and non-investable assets as observations in the filter even though they are not present in the portfolio optimization.

The three key components of the model are: (i) the financial market, (ii) the views, and (iii) the linear filter.

10.1.1. *The financial market: Asset prices are driven by unobservable factors*

We start by considering an asset market comprising $m \geq 1$ risky securities S_i, $i = 1, \ldots, m$ and a money market account process S_0. The growth rates of the assets depend on n unobservable factors $X_1(t), \ldots, X_n(t)$ which follow the affine dynamics given in the Eq. 10.1. In this paper, we focus on a market with investable assets only in order to keep the discussion clear and concise. The extension to non-investable assets is straightforward, and we refer the reader to Davis and Lleo (2013) for the details.

Let $(\Omega, \mathcal{F}, \mathbb{P})$ be the underlying probability space. On this space is defined an $\mathbb{R}^N$-valued $(\mathcal{F}_t)$-Brownian motion $W(t)$ with components $W_j(t)$, $j = 1, \ldots, N$, and $N := n + m + k$. We are in an incomplete market setting with n sources of risks corresponding to the factors, m sources of risks related to the assets and k sources of uncertainty related to the analyst views.

The asset returns and risk premia are subject to the evolution of the n-dimensional vector of unobservable factors $X(t)$ modeled as an affine process:

$$dX(t) = (b + BX(t))dt + \Lambda dW(t), \qquad X(0) = x. \tag{10.1}$$

We derive an estimate $\hat{X}(t)$ for the factor process $X(t)$ using filtering. Once we have obtained the estimate, we can solve the optimization problem.

The dynamics of the money market asset S_0 is given by

$$\frac{dS_0(t)}{S_0(t)} = (a_0 + A_0' X(t))\, dt, \qquad S_0(0) = s_0, \tag{10.2}$$

and that of the m risky assets follows the SDEs

$$\frac{dS_i(t)}{S_i(t)} = (a + AX(t))_i dt + \sum_{j=1}^{N} \sigma_{ik} dW_k(t) \quad S_i(0) = s_i, \quad i = 1, \ldots, m. \tag{10.3}$$

We also assume that no two assets have the same risk profile:

Assumption 10.1: The matrix $\Sigma\Sigma'$ is positive definite.

The discounted asset price $\tilde{S}_i(t)$ are

$$\tilde{S}_i(t) = \frac{S_i(t)}{S_0(t)}, \quad i = 1, \ldots, m, \quad \tilde{S}_i(0) = \frac{s_i}{s_0},$$

and the dynamics of $\tilde{S}(t)$ are

$$\frac{d\tilde{S}_i(t)}{\tilde{S}_i(t)} = (\tilde{a} + \tilde{A}X(t))_i dt + \sum_{k=1}^{N} \sigma_{ik} dW_k(t) \quad \tilde{S}_i(0) = \frac{s_i}{s_0}, \quad i = 1, \ldots, m, \tag{10.4}$$

where $\tilde{a} = a - a_0 \mathbf{1}$, $\tilde{A} = A - A_0 \mathbf{1}$ and $\mathbf{1} \in \mathbb{R}^m$ denotes the m-element column vector with entries equal to 1.

Finally, we define the risk premium $\mathfrak{s}_i(t)$ as

$$\mathfrak{s}_i(t) = \log(\tilde{S}_i(t)), \quad i = 1, \ldots, m.$$

Hence, $\mathfrak{s}_i(t)$ solves the SDE:

$$d\mathfrak{s}_i(t) = \left[(\tilde{a} + \tilde{A}X(t))_i - \frac{1}{2}\Sigma\Sigma'_{ii} \right] dt$$

$$+ \sum_{k=1}^{N} \sigma_{ik} dW_k(t), \quad \mathfrak{s}_i(0) = \log \frac{s_i}{s_0}, \quad i = 1, \ldots, m \tag{10.5}$$

The dynamics of the risk premia is Gaussian (conditional on $X(t)$). We can use risk premia as an observation in a linear filtering.

10.1.2. *Analyst views*

We ask analysts to formulate views about risk premia or the spread between risk premia over a time horizon. A typical analyst statement would be: "*my research leads me to believe that the spread between 10-year Treasury Notes and 3-month Treasury Bills will remain low over the next year before gradually widening over the following two years to 200 basis points in response to improving macroeconomic conditions. I am 90% confident that the spread will be within a range of 180 bps to 220 bps in two years.*" Mathematically, we can translate the k views into a system of stochastic differential equations:

$$dZ(t) = (a_Z(t) + A_Z(t)X(t))dt + \Psi(t)dW(t), \qquad Z(0) = z, \qquad (10.6)$$

where $W(t)$ is the N-dimensional Brownian motion and Ψ is a $k \times N$ matrix with zeros on its first $(n+m)$ rows. We calibrate the drift $a_Z(t) + A_Z(t)X(t)$ to the central view, and the diffusion matrix Ψ to the confidence interval around the view. This entire construction takes place at initial time $t = 0$. We are neither modeling the arrival of new opinions nor the evolution of the views over time.

10.1.3. *Filter the views and asset prices to estimate the factors*

In this section, we outline a solution in the case where $A_0 = 0$. We refer the reader to Davis and Lleo (2013) for the general case $r(t) = a_0 + A_0 X(t)$.

We have two sources of observations for the risk premia:

(1) m investable risky assets $S_1(t), \ldots, S_m(t)$;
(2) k analyst views $Z_1(t), \ldots, Z_k(t)$.

The pair of processes $(X(t), Y(t))$, where

$$Y_i(t) = \begin{cases} s_i(t) = \log \dfrac{S_i(t)}{S_0(t)}, & i = 1, \ldots, m, \\[2mm] Z_{i-M}(t), & i = m+1, \ldots, m+k \end{cases}$$

takes the form of the 'signal' and 'observation' processes in a Kalman filter system, and consequently the conditional distribution of $X(t)$ is normal $N(\hat{X}(t), P(t))$ where $\hat{X}(t) = \mathbb{E}[X(t)|\mathcal{F}_t^Y]$ satisfies the Kalman filter equation and $P(t)$ is a deterministic matrix-valued function.

The dynamics of the elements $Y_i(t), i = 1, \ldots, m + k$ of the observation vector $Y(t)$ satisfy

$$dY_i(t) = \left[(\tilde{a} + \tilde{A}X(t))_i - \frac{1}{2}\Sigma\Sigma'_{ii} \right] dt + \sum_{j=1}^{N} \sigma_{ij}dW_j(t), \quad i = 1, \ldots, m,$$

(10.7)

$$dY_{i+m}(t) = (a_Z(t) + A_Z(t)X(t))_i dt + \sum_{j=1}^{N} \psi_{ij}(t)dW_j(t), \quad i = 1, \ldots, k.$$

(10.8)

We express the dynamics of $Y(t)$ succinctly as

$$dY(t) = (a_Y(t) + A_Y(t)X(t))dt + \Xi(t)dW(t), \quad Y(0) = y_0, \quad (10.9)$$

where the $(m + k)$-element vector a_Y, $(m + k) \times n$ matrix A_Y and the $(m + k) \times N$ matrix Ξ are given by

$$a_Y(t) = \begin{pmatrix} \tilde{a} - \frac{1}{2}\Sigma\Sigma \\ a_Z(t) \end{pmatrix}, \quad A_Y(t) = \begin{pmatrix} \tilde{A} \\ A_Z(t) \end{pmatrix}, \quad \Xi(t) = \begin{pmatrix} \Sigma \\ \Psi(t) \end{pmatrix}.$$

Next, we define two processes $Y^1(t), Y^2(t) \in \mathbb{R}^{m+k}$ as follows:

$$Y^1(t) = A_Y(t)X(t)dt + \Psi(t)dW(t), \quad Y^1(0) = 0, \quad (10.10)$$
$$Y^2(t) = a_Y(t) \cdot dt, \quad Y^2(0) = y_0, \quad (10.11)$$

so that $Y(t) = Y^1(t) + Y^2(t)$.

In the present case we need to assume that X_0 is a normal random vector $N(m_0, P_0)$ with known mean m_0 and covariance P_0, and that X_0 is independent of the Brownian motion W. The processes $(X(t), Y^1(t))$ satisfying (10.1) and (10.10) and the filtering equations, which are standard, are stated in the following proposition.

Proposition 10.1 (Kalman Filter). *The conditional distribution of* $X(t)$ *given* $\mathcal{F}_t^Y$ *is* $N(\hat{X}(t), P(t))$, *calculated as follows.*

(i) *The innovations process* $U(t) \in \mathbb{R}^{m+k}$ *defined by*

$$dU(t) = (\Xi\Xi')^{-1/2}(dY(t) - A_Y\hat{X}(t)dt), \quad U(0) = 0 \quad (10.12)$$

is a vector Brownian motion.

(ii) $\hat{X}(t)$ *is the unique solution of the SDE*

$$d\hat{X}(t) = (b + B\hat{X}(t))dt + \check{\Lambda}(t)dU(t), \qquad \hat{X}(0) = m_0, \qquad (10.13)$$

where $\check{\Lambda}(t) = (\Lambda\Xi' + P(t)A_Y')(\Xi\Xi')^{-1/2}$.

(iii) $P(t)$ *is the unique non-negative definite symmetric solution of the matrix Riccati equation*

$$\dot{P}(t) = \Lambda\mathfrak{s}^{\perp}(\mathfrak{s}^{\perp})'\Lambda' - P(t)A_Y'\left(\Xi\Xi'\right)^{-1}A_Y P(t)$$

$$+ \left(B - \Lambda\Xi'\left(\Xi\Xi'\right)^{-1}A_Y\right)P(t)$$

$$+ P(t)\left(B' - A_Y'\left(\Xi\Xi'\right)^{-1}\Xi\Lambda'\right), \qquad P(0) = P_0,$$

where $\mathfrak{s}^{\perp} := I - \Xi'\left(\Xi'\Xi\right)^{-1}\Xi$.

Now, the Kalman filter has replaced the initial state process $X(t)$ by an estimate $\hat{X}(t)$ with dynamics given in (10.13). To recover the asset price process, we use (10.7) and (10.8) together with (10.12) to obtain the dynamics of $Y(t)$:

$$dY(t) = dY_1(t) + dY_2(t)$$

$$= (a_Y + A_Y X(t))dt + (\Xi\Xi')^{1/2}dU(t), \quad Y(0) = y_0, \quad (10.14)$$

and from there, we recover the dynamics of $Z(t)$, $\mathfrak{s}(t)$, $\tilde{S}(t)$ and finally $S(t)$.

We observe that $\Xi\Xi' := \begin{pmatrix} \Sigma\Sigma' & \Sigma\Psi' \\ \Psi\Sigma' & \Psi\Psi', \end{pmatrix}$ and define the $(m+k) \times (m+k)$ matrix $(\Xi\Xi')^{1/2}$ as $(\Xi\Xi')^{1/2} := (\check{\Sigma}, \check{\Psi})'$. This implies that

$$\Xi\Xi' := \begin{pmatrix} \Sigma\Sigma' & \Sigma\Psi' \\ \Psi\Sigma' & \Psi\Psi' \end{pmatrix} = \begin{pmatrix} \check{\Sigma}\check{\Sigma}' & \check{\Sigma}\check{\Psi}' \\ \check{\Psi}\check{\Sigma}' & \check{\Psi}\check{\Psi}' \end{pmatrix},$$

and as a result

$$dZ(t) = (a_Z + A_Z X(t))dt + \check{\Psi}dU(t), \qquad Z(0) = z$$

$$d\mathfrak{s}_i(t) = \left[(\tilde{a} + \tilde{A}X(t))_i - \frac{1}{2}\Sigma\Sigma_{ii}'\right]dt + \sum_{k=1}^{m+k}\check{\sigma}_{ik}dU_k(t), \qquad \mathfrak{s}_i(0) = \log\frac{s_i}{s_0},$$

$$d\tilde{S}(t) = \left(\tilde{a} + \tilde{A}X(t)\right)_i dt + \sum_{k=1}^{m+k}\check{\sigma}_{ik}dU_k(t), \qquad \mathfrak{s}_i(0) = \frac{s_i}{s_0},$$

$$dS_i(t) = \left(a + \tilde{A}X(t)\right)_i dt + \sum_{k=1}^{M+k}\check{\sigma}_{ik}dU_k(t), \qquad S_i(0) = s_i. \qquad (10.15)$$

The filtering problem is unrelated to the subsequent stochastic control problem: the dynamics of $\hat{X}(t)$ will be the same for all investors regardless of their risk aversion or time horizon.

Solve the Stochastic Control Problem

We express and solve a stochastic control problem in which $X(t)$ is replaced by $\hat{X}(t)$ and the dynamic Eq. 10.1 by the Kalman filter. Optimal strategies take the form $h(t, \hat{X}(t))$.

Because the filter and the stochastic control problem are separable, we can apply the estimation method presented above to any continuous time investment problem. Davis and Lleo (2013) illustrate the procedure by solving a risk-sensitive asset management problem, where the investor's objective is to maximize the criterion

$$J(t, x, h; T, \theta) = -\frac{1}{\theta} \ln \mathbb{E} \left[e^{-\theta \ln V_T} \right] = -\frac{1}{\theta} \ln \mathbb{E} \left[V_T^{-\theta} \right]. \qquad (10.16)$$

This criterion relates the evolution of the investor's wealth, $V(t)$, with the investor's risk sensitivity $\theta \in (-1, 0) \cup (0, \infty)$.

The optimal asset allocation $h^*(t)$ for this stochastic control problem is

$$
\begin{aligned}
h^*(t) &= \frac{1}{1+\theta} \left(\check{\Sigma}\check{\Sigma}' \right)^{-1} \left[\hat{a} + \tilde{A}\hat{X}(t) - \theta \check{\Sigma}\check{\Lambda}'(t)D\Phi \right] \\
&= \frac{1}{1+\theta} \left(\Sigma\Sigma' \right)^{-1} \left[\hat{a} + \tilde{A}\hat{X}(t) - \theta \check{\Sigma}\check{\Lambda}'(t)D\Phi \right],
\end{aligned}
\qquad (10.17)
$$

where the value function Φ has the form

$$\tilde{\Phi}(t, x) = \frac{1}{2}x'Q(t)x + x'q(t) + k(t). \qquad (10.18)$$

Here, $Q(t)$ satisfies a Riccati equation, $q(t)$ solves a system of linear ODEs and we obtain $k(t)$ by direct integration.

10.2. Including the P/E

The P/E model is described in Chapter 4. We refer the reader to Section 4.1 for a description of the model. We can use the P/E to create a view about the future evolution of the equity risk premium. Using historical data, we perform a regression of the equity risk premium at an horizon h against the logarithm of the CAPE:

$$y_t^h = a + bx_t^n + \epsilon_t, \qquad (10.19)$$

where

- $y_t^h = \ln\left(\frac{\tilde{P}_{t,h}}{\tilde{P}_t}\right)$ is the risk premium at a horizon of h years;
- $x_t^{10} = \ln\left(\frac{P_t}{E_{t,-10}}\right)$ is the logarithm of the CAPE;
- $\tilde{P}_t = \frac{P(t)}{S_0(t)}$ and $\tilde{P}_{t,h} = \frac{P(t+h)}{S_0(t+h)}$ are respectively the discounted value of the S&P500 at time t and $t + h$.

For clarity, we drop the 'beg' superscript and consider the S&P500 with all dividends reinvested (S&P500 Total Return Index).

By varying the time horizon h from 1 year to 10 years, we can use the regressions to predict the evolution of the equity risk premium at various points over a 10 year horizon. The point estimates for $h = 1, \ldots, 10$ provide the data to fit the functions $a_Z(t)$ and $A_Z(t)$ in the view process (Eq. 10.6). Then we use the distribution of the error term ϵ_t to fit the diffusion term $\Psi(t)$.

10.3. Including the BSEYD

In Step 1 of Section 4.2, we saw that the S&P500 experienced 22 corrections, defined as declines of at least 10% peak-to-trough over a maximum of 1 year, between January 31, 1964 and December 31, 2014. On average, these downturns lasted for 199 days and resulted in a 20.3% decline in the index. Overall, the BSEYD produced 38 signals, of which 29 signals were followed by an equity market downturn. At 76.32%, the BSEYD's accuracy is statistically significant. Figure 10.1 displays the cumulative return on the S&P500 for the 2 years following a crash signal.

To illustrate the procedure, we consider the case where the BSEYD is currently producing a crash signal. Here, we model the view with a generalized Ornstein-Uhlenbeck process:

$$dZ(t) = (a_Z(t) - A_Z Z(t))\, dt + \Psi dW(t). \tag{10.20}$$

The solution to this SDE is

$$Z(t) = z e^{-A_Z t} + \int_0^t e^{-A_Z(t-s)} a_Z(s)\, ds$$

$$+ \Psi \int_0^t e^{-A_Z(t-s)} \Psi dW(s), \tag{10.21}$$

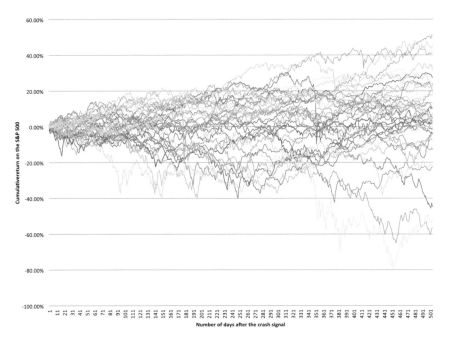

Fig. 10.1.   Cumulative return on the S&P500 after a crash signal.

with

$$\mathbb{E}\left[Z(t)\right] = z e^{-A_Z t} + \int_0^t e^{-A_Z(t-s)} a_Z(s) ds,$$

$$\mathrm{Var}\left[Z(t)\right] = \frac{\Psi^2}{2A_Z}\left(1 - e^{-2A_Z t}\right). \qquad (10.22)$$

This process gives us enough flexibility to incorporate crash predictions, while keeping the affine form necessary for an efficient resolution of the filtering and optimization problems.

A crash prediction model produces a binary signal: either it predicts a crash or it does not. As a result, we cannot map a crash prediction directly into a view. We need to turn the crash prediction into a return prediction by looking at the evolution of the risk premium conditional on the crash signal. The signals produced by the BSEYD provide us with 38 paths for the risk premium conditional on a crash signal. We can use these paths to calibrate the parameters of the view process by matching the moments of the stochastic process in (10.22) with the empirical moments inferred from these historical paths.

A typical downturn lasts for slightly more than one calendar year. Out of the 21 downturns, only four downturns lasted more than 2 years, and none lasted more than 2.5 years. To capture the evolution of the risk premium during these downturns, we need to consider at least a 2-year time horizon from the signal. On the other hand, we have 38 signals in 50 years, so we cannot have a time horizon of more than a couple of years without having a risk that the signals will interfere with each other. This leads us to concentrate on the evolution of the risk premium (conditional on a crash signal) over 2 years exactly.

If the horizon t of the optimization is longer, say $T = 5$ years, we will need to make an assumption on the behavior of the risk premium between the 2-year horizon of the crash prediction model and the 5-year horizon of the optimization. For simplicity, we assume in this chapter that the risk premium converges linearity to a long term average of 4%.

We calibrate the mean evolution of the view process to the mean path of the risk premium conditional on a crash signal. Figure 10.2 suggests that the sixth order polynomial function

$$\mathcal{P}(t) = 0.0006t^6 - 0.0107t^5 + 0.0671t^4 - 0.1994t^3$$

$$+ \, 0.2725t^2 - 0.1105t - 0.0406$$

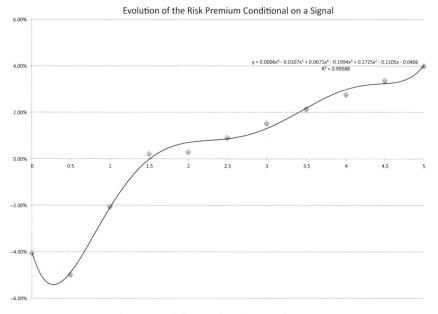

Fig. 10.2.   Polynomial calibration function.

provides a close fit to the actual data. To fit this polynomial function, we express the function a_Z as a order polynomial:

$$a_Z(t) = \beta_0 + \beta_1 t + \beta_2 t^2 + \beta_3 t^3 + \beta_4 t^4 + \beta_5 t^5. \tag{10.23}$$

Selecting $A_Z = \frac{1}{2}\ln 2 = 0.3466$, implies a half life of 2 years. To finish the calibration, we perform a Taylor expansion of $\mathbb{E}[Z(t)]$ around $t = 0$. Matching the terms of the Taylor expansion with the polynomial given in (10.23), we get: $z = -4.06\%, \beta_0 = -0.1246, \beta_1 = 0.5067, \beta_2 = -0.5038$, $\beta_3 = 0.1993, \beta_4 = -0.0302, \beta_5 = 0.0006$.

To get the diffusion parameter Ψ, we match the variance of $Z(t)$ to the highest annualized variance across the 38 historical paths, equal to 29.74%. From Eq. 10.22, we get $\Psi = 29.74\% \times \sqrt{\frac{2A_Z}{1-e^{2A_Z}}} = 31.82\%$.

Appendix A

Other Bubble-testing Methodologies and Historical Bubbles

A.1. Other bubbles and crash-testing methodologies

A.1.1. Bubble, crashes, dragon kings and black swans

Sornette (2003, 2004) studies bubbles and crashes extensively. Sornette (2009), and Sornette and Ouillon (2012) propose the concept of "Dragon-Kings" to refer to events that are both Dragons, born out of unique origins, and Kings, and have an extremely large magnitude or a very large impact. Dragon Kings occur in complex systems: phenomena, such as feedback, tipping points, bifurcations, phase transitions, tend to favor the occurrence of Dragon Kings.

Dragon Kings differ from Black Swans in a fundamental way. Black Swans are events that cannot be predicted based on existing data. On the other hand, Dragon Kings are predictable to some extent because they are generated by an underlying system, albeit a complex one.

A.1.2. Behavioral insights into bubbles and crashes

Goetzmann et al. (2016) used surveys of individual and institutional investors, conducted regularly over a 26-year period in the US, to assess the subjective probability of a market crash.

They observed that these probabilities are much higher than the actual historical probabilities. To understand this observation, the authors examined a number of factors that influence investor responses and found evidence consistent with an availability bias.

This research takes its roots in recent efforts to measure investor sentiment in financial markets (Fisher and Statman, 2000, 2003; Baker and Wurgler, 2006, 2007) and identify collective biases such as overconfidence and excessive optimism (Barone-Adesi et al., 2013)

The paper by Goetzmann *et al.* (2016) is just preliminary work, but it opens the way for a whole new research field by inviting sentiment, opinion and behavioral sciences into the debate.

A.1.3. *Modeling crashes as earthquakes*

Gresnigt *et al.* (2015) view the behavior of the stock market around the time of a crash as a seismic event. They develop an Early Warning System (EWS) based on an Epidemic-Type Aftershock Sequence (ETAS) model, proposed by [Ogata (1988)]. The ETAS is a branching model in which each event can trigger subsequent events. It is built on the mutually self-exciting Hawkes point process, a type of inhomogeneous Poisson process where the time t intensity depends on the history of events prior to time t.

The EWS works as a probability-based prediction over a short horizon of a few days. The authors tested their model on the S&P500 during the recent financial crisis with encouraging results.

A.1.4. *Bubbles as strict local martingales*

Jarrow, Protter and their co-authors propose an elegant mathematical bubble detection methodology hinging on the distinction between local martingales and strict local martingales. They define the value of a bubble as

$$\beta(t) := S(t) - FV(t) \geq 0,$$

where $S(t)$ is a stochastic process equal to the traded price of an asset at time t and $FV(t)$ is its fundamental value at time t. In plain English, the fundamental value equals the discounted cash flows received from holding the asset until its (possibly very distant) liquidation time and the discounted liquidation value. In other words, it is the price traders would pay if after purchase they had to hold the asset in their portfolio until liquidation.

A bubble reflects the notion that the resale value of the asset is higher than the price paid if it were to be held forever. A bubble is non-negative because a lower bound on its market price is its value obtained from buying the asset and not retrading.

The key insight into bubble detection model comes from the definition of the asset market price bubble. This definition reveals that the asset's price exhibits a bubble $\beta_t > 0$ if and only if its discounted gain process is a strict local martingale and not a martingale. The problem to test whether a price is a bubble then becomes the problem to distinguish a strict local martingale from a true martingale.

The key reference on the local martingale theory of bubbles include Loewenstein and Willard (2000a,b), Cox and Hobson (2005), Heston *et al.* (2007), Jarrow *et al.* (2007, 2010), as well as Jarrow (2016) and Protter (2016), Jarrow and Larsson (2012). Protter (2013) provides an excellent review of the mathematics of local martingale models.

A.1.5. *Economic regimes, market crashes and downside risk*

Financial markets tend to behave very differently in periods of calm and in periods of crisis. This simple observation has motivated the use of regime switching models to provide a more accurate representation of the evolution of financial markets. Mulvey and Liu (2016) use regime-switching model in the context of asset allocation and Asset and Liability management (ALM).

Although the idea of using regime switching models is not new in finance, most of the developments to date have focused on using either parametric models, estimated by standard econometric techniques, or Hidden Markov Models, estimated via the Baum–Welch algorithm, an application of the Expectation–Maximization (EM) algorithm. Mulvey and Liu suggest the use of trend filtering, a machine-learning algorithm closely related to the lasso estimator.

The trend-filtering algorithm identifies clearly conditions of financial stress, and the subsequent regime-based asset allocation outperforms a simple mean-variance optimization over the full period of the study and during financial crises.

A.1.6. *Bubbles and crashes on the credit market*

Bubbles and crashes occur across all asset classes, from stocks to commodities, real estate, bonds and even tulips. As each market is different in terms of microstructure and price behavior, detecting bubbles and crashes will require different assumptions, approaches and models.

Altman and Kuehne (2016) present evidences that a bubble has been inflating on the credit market. They start by comparing the current benign credit cycle to other benign cycles between 1971 and 2015. Then, they analyze the pattern of new issuance (volume, credit quality) before turning their attention to LBO financing.

Finally, they use Altman's Z and Z" score to compare the level of corporate risk in 2014 and 2012 with that observed at the start of the last credit crisis in 2007. Altman developed the Z score in 1968 to predict the probability that a firm will go into bankruptcy within two years based on five financial ratios: Working Capital/Total Assets, Retained Earnings/Total Assets, Earnings Before Interest and Taxes/Total Assets, Market Value of Equity/Book Value of Total Liabilities, Sales/Total Assets. Altman applied a discriminate analysis to a sample of 66 firms, half of which had filed for bankruptcy.

A.2. The changing nature of bubbles and crashes: A short history of bubbles and crashes

Table A.1 lists the main stock market crashes and bear markets since the 1600s. To be sure, stock market crashes, the focus of our book, are not the only type of financial disasters. Readers interested in financial history will find a list and a summary of banking crises that occurred worldwide since the early 1800 in Appendices A.3 and A.4 in Reinhart and Rogoff (2009). Jorion (2007), Lleo (2009), Lleo and Ziemba (2015a), Lleo and Ziemba (2014) and Wilmott (2013) discuss a long list of financial disasters.

In recent years, the replacement of human traders by algorithmic trading and the removal of circuit breakers on stock exchanges has led to an acceleration and an automation of trading, creating a new type of crash: the flash crash.

The first flash crash occurred on May 6, 2010, when the Dow Jones dropped nearly 1,000 points in a few minutes. An investigation later concluding that an algorithm employed by a trading house to handle a US$4.5 billion sell order of S&P500 futures was the leading cause. The faulty algorithm didn't specify a sell price or time frame and did not monitor market liquidity. Many trades were therefore placed at the market over a very short period of time, creating a liquidity chasm and propelling prices into a free fall. Market manipulations by individual traders also seemed to have worsened the situation.

Over the past 6 years since the original "flash crash", CNBC has documented another five mini crashes:

(1) "Four-digit drop" in Asia on August 24, 2015;
(2) Lunch-hour halt at the NYSE on July 9, 2015;
(3) Treasury Freeze on October 15, 2014;
(4) Flash Freeze on the NASDAQ on August 22, 2013;
(5) Facebook debut on the NASDAQ on May 18, 2012.

Table A.1.   List of stock market crashes and bear markets (Adapted from Wikipedia,   https://en.wikipedia.org/wiki/List_of_stock_market_crashes_ and_bear_markets, accessed on January 12, 2017).

Name	Dates	Country	Remarks
Kipper und Wipper	1623	Holy Roman Empire	A financial crisis caused by debased (fraudulent) foreign coins minted in the Holy Roman Empire from 1621 to 1623, done to raise funds at the start of the Thirty Years' War.
Tulip mania Bubble	1637	Netherlands	A bubble (1633–1637) in the Netherlands during which contracts for bulbs of tulips reached extraordinarily high prices, and suddenly collapsed.
The Mississippi Bubble	1720	Kingdom of France	Banque Royale by John Law stopped payments of its note in exchange for specie and as a result caused economic collapse in France.
South Sea Bubble of 1720	1720	United Kingdom	Affected early European stock markets, during early days of chartered joint stock companies.
Bengal Bubble of 1769	1769	United Kingdom	Primarily caused by the British East India Company, whose shares fell from £276 in December 1768 to £122 in 1784.
Credit crisis of 1772	1772	United Kingdom, United States	
Financial Crisis of 1791–1792	1791	United States	Shares of First bank of US boom and bust in August and September 1791. Groundwork of Alexander Hamilton's cooperation with the Bank of New York to end this event would be crucial in ending the Panic of 1792 next year.
Panic of 1796–1797	1796	—	
Panic of 1819	1819	United States	
Panic of 1825	1825	United Kingdom	
Panic of 1837	10 May 1837	United States	
Panic of 1847	1847	United Kingdom	The Panic of 1847 marks the end of "Railway Mania" in the UK.

(*Continued*)

Table A.1. (*Continued*)

Name	Dates	Country	Remarks
Panic of 1857	1857	United States	
Panic of 1866	1866	United Kingdom	
Black Friday	24 Sep 1869	United States	
Panic of 1873	9 May 1873		Initiated the Long Depression in the US and much of Europe.
Paris Bourse crash of 1882	19 Jan 1882	France	
Panic of 1884	1884		
Encilhamento	1890	Brazil	Lasting 3 years, 1890–1893, a boom and bust process that boomed in late 1880s and burst on early 1890s, causing a collapse in the Brazilian economy and aggravating an already unstable political situation.
Panic of 1893	1893	United States	
Panic of 1896	1896	United States	
Panic of 1901	17-5-1901	United States	Lasting 3 years, the market was spooked by the assassination of President McKinley in 1901, coupled with a severe drought later the same year.
Panic of 1907	1-10-1907	United States	Lasting over a year, markets took fright after US President Theodore Roosevelt had threatened to rein in the monopolies that flourished in various industrial sectors, notably railways.
Wall Street Crash of 1929	24-10-1929	United States	Lasting over 4 years, the bursting of the speculative bubble in shares led to further selling as people who had borrowed money to buy shares had to cash them in, when their loans were called in. Also called the Great Crash or the Wall Street Crash, leading to the Great Depression.
Recession of 1937–1938	1937	United States	Lasting around a year, this share price fall was triggered by an economic recession within the Great Depression and doubts about the effectiveness of Franklin D. Roosevelt's New Deal policy.

(*Continued*)

Table A.1. (*Continued*)

Name	Dates	Country	Remarks
Kennedy Slide of 1962	28-5-1962	United States	Also known as the 'Flash Crash of 1962'
Brazilian Markets Crash of 1971	7-1971	Brazil	Lasting through the 1970s and early-1980s, this was the end of a boom that started in 1969, compounded by the 1970s energy crisis coupled with early 1980s Latin American debt crisis.
1973–1974 stock market crash	1-1973	United Kingdom	Lasting 23 months, dramatic rise in oil prices, the miners' strike and the downfall of the Heath government.
Souk Al-Manakh stock market crash	8-1982	Kuwait	
Black Monday	19-10-1987	United States	
Rio de Janeiro Stock Exchange Crash	6-1989	Brazil	Rio de Janeiro Stock Exchange Crash, due to its weak internal controls and absence of credit discipline, that led to its collapse and of which it never recovered.
Friday the 13th mini-crash	13-10-1989	United States	Failed leveraged buyout of United Airlines causes crash.
Early 1990s recession	7-1990	United States	Iraq invaded Kuwait in July 1990, causing oil prices to increase. The Dow dropped 18% in three months, from 2,911.63 on July 3 to 2,381.99 on October 16,1990. This recession lasted approximately 8 months.
Japanese asset price bubble	1991	Japan	Lasting approximately 20 years, through at least the end of 2011, share and property price bubble bursts and turns into a long deflationary recession. Some of the key economic events during the collapse of the Japanese asset price bubble include the 1997 Asian financial crisis and the Dot.Com bubble. In addition, more recent economic events, such as the late-2000s financial crisis and August 2011 stock markets fall have prolonged this period.

(*Continued*)

Table A.1. (*Continued*)

Name	Dates	Country	Remarks
Black Wednesday	16-9-1992	United Kingdom	The Conservative government was forced to withdraw the pound sterling from the European Exchange Rate Mechanism (ERM) after they were unable to keep sterling above its agreed lower limit.
1997 Asian financial crisis	2-7-1997	Thailand Hong Kong Philippines South Korea Indonesia	Investors deserted emerging Asian shares, including an overheated Hong Kong stock market. Crashes occur in Thailand, Indonesia, South Korea, Philippines, and elsewhere, reaching a climax in the October 27, 1997 mini-crash.
October 27, 1997, mini-crash	27-10-1997		Global stock market crash that was caused by an economic crisis in Asia.
1998 Russian financial crisis	17-8-1998	Russia	The Russian government devalues the ruble, defaults on domestic debt, and declares a moratorium on payment to foreign creditors.
Dot.Com bubble	10-3-2000	United States	Collapse of a technology bubble.
Economic effects arising from the September 11 attacks	11-9-2001		The September 11 attacks caused global stock markets to drop sharply. The attacks themselves caused approximately US$40 billion in insurance losses, making it one of the largest insured events ever.
Stock market downturn of 2002	9-10-2002		Downturn in stock prices during 2002 in stock exchanges across the US, Canada, Asia, and Europe. After recovering from lows reached following the September 11 attacks, indices slid steadily starting in March 2002, with dramatic declines in July and September leading to lows last reached in 1997 and 1998.
Chinese stock bubble of 2007	27-2-2007	China	The SSE Composite Index of the Shanghai Stock Exchange tumbles 9% from unexpected selloffs, the largest drop in 10 years, triggering major drops in worldwide stock markets.

(*Continued*)

Table A.1.   (*Continued*)

Name	Dates	Country	Remarks
United States bear market of 2007–2009	11-10-2007	United States	Till June 2009, the Dow Jones Industrial Average, Nasdaq Composite and S&P500 all experienced declines of greater than 20% from their peaks in late 2007.
Financial crisis of 2007–2008	16-9-2008	United States	On September 16, 2008, failures of large financial institutions in the US, due primarily to exposure of securities of packaged subprime loans and credit default swaps issued to insure these loans and their issuers, rapidly devolved into a global crisis resulting in a number of bank failures in Europe and sharp reductions in the value of equities (stock) and commodities worldwide. The failure of banks in Iceland resulted in a devaluation of the Icelandic krona and threatened the government with bankruptcy. Iceland was able to secure an emergency loan from the IMF in November. Later on, US President George W. Bush signs the Emergency Economic Stabilization Act into law, creating a Troubled Asset Relief Program (TARP) to purchase failing bank assets. Had disastrous affects on the world economy along with world trade.
2009 Dubai debt standstill	27-11-2009	United Arab Emirates	Dubai requests a debt deferment following its massive renovation and development projects, as well as the Great Recession. The announcement causes global stock markets to drop.
European sovereign debt crisis	27-4-2010	Europe	Standard & Poor's downgrades Greece's sovereign credit rating to junk four days after the activation of a 45-billion EU-IMF bailout, triggering the decline of stock markets worldwide and of the Euro's value, and furthering a European sovereign debt crisis.

(*Continued*)

Table A.1.   (*Continued*)

Name	Dates	Country	Remarks
2010 Flash Crash	6-5-2010	United States	The Dow Jones Industrial Average suffers its worst intraday point loss, dropping nearly 1,000 points before partially recovering.
August 2011 stock markets fall	1-8-2011		Stock markets around the world plummet during late July and early August, and are volatile for the rest of the year.
2015–2016 Chinese stock market crash	12-6-2015	China	China stock market crash starts in June and continues into July and August. In January 2016, Chinese stock market experiences a steep sell-off which sets off a global rout.
2015–2016 stock market selloff	18-8-2015	United States	The Dow Jones fell 888 points during a 2-day period, 1300 points from August 18 to August 21. On Monday, August 24, world stock markets were down substantially, wiping out all gains made in 2015, with interlinked drops in commodities such as oil, which hit a six-year price low, copper, and most of Asian currencies, but the Japanese Yen, losing value against the US Dollar. With this plunge, an estimated 10 trillion dollars had been wiped off the books on global markets since June 3.
Aftermath of the United Kingdom European Union membership referendum, 2016	24-6-2016	United Kingdom, European Union, Australia, China, France, Germany, Hong Kong, India, Italy, Japan, South Korea, Spain, Sweden, Taiwan, United States	World Markets tumble after the UK voted to leave the European Union. Investors lost more than the equivalent of 2 trillion US dollars on 24 June 2016, making this day the worst single day drop in history according to data from S&P Global. The losses were extended to a combined total of the equivalent of US$3 trillion by additional selling on 27 June 2016 according to data from S&P Global.

(*Continued*)

Table A.1.   (*Continued*)

Name	Dates	Country	Remarks
Cryptocurrencies bubble	Ongoing (as of May 2017)	Worldwide, but mostly caused by China causes	The price of Bitcoin has rallied more than 100% during the first 5 months of 2017 with capitalization approaching USD40 billion. Among the reasons is the weakening of yuan which together with currency restrictions in China makes people look for alternative forms of protecting capital as well as to circumvent money laundering control.

The soaring interest for statistical learning, machine learning and artificial intelligence in trading and risk management will potentially cause more crashes, but it might also open new possibilities to prevent crashes, by, for example, designing new types of liquidity-based and trading-patter-based circuit breakers. Developments in this area will undoubtedly continue the transformation of trading activities from Amsterdam Coffee Houses, to US stock exchange pits and to fully computerized transactions. "Prediction is very difficult, especially about the future," a quote often attributed to Niels Bohr, summarizes the present situation aptly.

Mathematics of the Changepoint Detection Model

This appendix provides the mathematical details of the simple changepoint detection model used in Chapter 9. It should be noted that many more advanced models exist, we refer the reader to the specialized literature, see e.g. the book of Polunchenko and Tartakovsky (2012).

Recall that we model bubble-like prices by a random sequence S_t, t runs through $t = 0, 1, \ldots, T$. The probabilistic structure of the sequence is described by its log-returns $X_t = \log(S_t/S_{t-1})$ as follows:

$$X_t := \log \frac{S_t}{S_{t-1}} = \begin{cases} \mu_1 + \sigma_1 \xi_t, & t < \theta, \\ \mu_2 + \sigma_2 \xi_t, & t \geq \theta, \end{cases} \quad \text{for } t = 1, 2, \ldots, T,$$

where ξ_t are independent standard normal random variables, μ_1, σ_1 are some pre-changepoint parameters of drift and volatility, and μ_2, σ_2 are post-changepoint parameters. The moment θ is the moment of change.

The Bayesian nature of the model is represented by the fact that θ is a random variable independent of ξ_t and taking values in the set $\{1, 2, \ldots, T+1\}$ with known prior probabilities $p_t = P(\theta = t)$. The prior distribution function of θ will be denoted by $G(t) = \sum_{u \leq t} p_u$.

The fact that the moment of changepoint θ is directly unobservable is modeled by that only the information obtained from the sequence S_t can be used to make decisions. Namely, we deal with changepoint detection rules τ, which are defined as stopping times of the sequence S_t. Recall, the definition of stopping times says that τ is a random variable with values in the set $0, 1, \ldots, T$ such that for any t the random event $\{\tau \leq t\}$ belongs to the σ-algebra $\mathcal{F}_t = \sigma(S_0, \ldots, S_t)$ generated by S_u, $0 \leq u \leq t$. In other words, a decision to declare about a changepoint at time t should be made only based on the information available up to time t and not using any future information (which distinguishes this *online* model from *offline* models, where τ is not required to be a stopping time).

The goal of changepoint detection is to choose τ which is as close as possible to θ. Note that since θ is not a stopping time with respect to $\mathcal{F}_t$, one cannot put $\tau = \theta$. There are many optimality criteria for such closedness (see, e.g. Tartakovsky *et al.*, 2014; Poor and Hadjiliadis, 2009a). In view of our applications to bubble-like markets, we will use the criterion where τ is assumed to be the moment when one decides to exit the market. Namely, we think that a position is held open at $t = 0$ (in a rising market specified by μ_1, σ_1) and one wants to close it by $t = T$; if there is a change in the parameters μ, σ so that the market becomes falling, an earlier exit is desirable.

We identify the gain from closing the position at (stopping) time τ with expected utility $EU(S_\tau)$, where U is a utility function which is assumed to be either logarithmic or exponential, i.e.

$$U(x) = \alpha x^\alpha \text{ for } \alpha \leq 1, \; \alpha \neq 0 \qquad \text{or} \qquad U(x) = \log x.$$

Denoting by $\mathfrak{M}$ the class of all stopping times $\tau \leq T$, the problem of changepoint detection formulates as the *optimal stopping problem*

$$V = \sup_{\tau \in \mathfrak{M}} EU(S_\tau). \tag{B.1}$$

Its solution consists in finding the value V and the *optimal stopping time* τ^*, at which the supremum is attained (we'll show such a stopping time exists).

It will be always assumed that

$$\mu_1 > -\frac{\alpha \sigma_1^2}{2}, \qquad \mu_2 < -\frac{\alpha \sigma_2^2}{2}. \tag{B.2}$$

In this case, the sequence $(u_t)_{t=0}^T$, $u_t = U(S_t)$, is a submartingale[1] when the logarithmic returns of S are i.i.d. $\mathcal{N}(\mu_1, \sigma_1^2)$ random variables, and a supermartingale when they are i.i.d. $\mathcal{N}(\mu_2, \sigma_2^2)$ random variables. In the former case, the value of u_t increases on average as t increases, so it is profitable to hold the stock, and in the latter case the average value of u_t decreases meaning that one needs to sell the stock as soon as possible.

---

[1] A random sequence $(\zeta_t)_{t=0}^T$ is called a *submartingale* (resp., a *supermartingale* or a *martingale*) with respect to a filtration $(\mathcal{F}_t)_{t=0}^T$ if $E(\zeta_t \mid \mathcal{F}_{t-1}) \geq \zeta_{t-1}$ (resp., $E(\zeta_t \mid \mathcal{F}_{t-1}) \leq \zeta_{t-1}$ or $E(\zeta_t \mid \mathcal{F}_{t-1}) = \zeta_{t-1}$) for each $t = 1, \ldots, T$.

Consequently, the random variable θ represents the moment of time when holding the stock becomes unprofitable.

Remarks. (1) We consider only the case when S increases on average before the changepoint and decreases afterwards (according to (B.2)). This is interpreted as that one looks for a moment to *exit* a bubble-like market. However, by reverting the signs in the formulas appropriately, it is possible to consider the case when S first decreases on average, and then starts to increase. This would correspond to looking for a moment to enter a market.

(2) In Chapter 9, we consistently used the utility function $(-1/\sqrt{x})$. Other choices (which give identical results) can be found in the extended papers of Shiryaev *et al.* (2014, 2015).

B.1. The structure of the optimal stopping time

Now, we describe the solution of changepoint detection problem (B.1). As it is common for Bayesian changepoint models, the solution can be given in terms of the *posterior probability process*, or, equivalently, the *Shiryaev–Roberts statistic*. We use the latter as it results in somewhat simpler formulas.

The optimal stopping time τ^* will be described as the first moment of time when the Shiryaev–Roberts statistic exceeds some time-dependent threshold. In order to formulate corresponding results, we need to introduce auxiliary notation.

On the probability space $(\Omega, \mathcal{F}, P)$ which contains the random variables S_t and θ, define the filtration $\mathcal{F}_t = \sigma(S_u, u \leq t)$ generated by the sequence S. Introduce the family of probability measures P^u, $u = 1, \ldots, T+1$, generated by the sequence S with the value of the parameter $\theta \equiv u$. Following the standard notation of the changepoint detection theory, let[2] $P^\infty \equiv P^{T+1}$, and denote by $P_t = P \mid \mathcal{F}_t$, $P_t^u = P^u \mid \mathcal{F}_t$, the restrictions of the corresponding measures to the σ-algebra $\mathcal{F}_t$.

The *Shiryaev–Roberts statistic* is defined as the sequence $\psi = (\psi_t)_{t=0}^T$ by the formula

$$\psi_0 = 0, \qquad \psi_t = \sum_{u=1}^{t} \frac{dP_t^u}{dP_t^\infty} p_u \quad \text{for } t = 1, \ldots, T.$$

---

[2]Typically, P^∞ denotes the measure when there is no change in the probability law of the observable sequence on the whole time horizon (i.e. the change "occurs" at time $t = \infty$). Since in the problem considered, the time horizon is finite, this measure has the same meaning as P^{T+1}.

Using that the density dP_t^u/dP_t^∞ is given by the formula

$$\frac{dP_t^u}{dP_t^\infty} = \left(\frac{\sigma_1}{\sigma_2}\right)^{t-u+1} \cdot \exp\left(\sum_{i=u}^{t}\left[\frac{(X_i - \mu_1)^2}{2\sigma_1^2} - \frac{(X_i - \mu_2)^2}{2\sigma_2^2}\right]\right), \quad u \le t,$$

$$\frac{dP_t^u}{dP_t^\infty} = 1, \quad u > t,$$

it is possible to check that ψ_t satisfies the following recurrent equation:

$$\psi_t = (p_t + \psi_{t-1}) \cdot \frac{\sigma^1}{\sigma^2} \exp\left(\frac{(X_t - \mu_1)^2}{2\sigma_1^2} - \frac{(X_t - \mu_2)^2}{2\sigma_2^2}\right), \quad t = 1, \ldots, T.$$

$$(\text{B.3})$$

To state the expression for the value V_α of problem (B.1), define recurrently the family of functions $V_\alpha(t, x)$ for $\alpha \le 1$, $t = T, T-1, \ldots, 0$, $x \ge 0$ as follows. For $\alpha = 0$, let

$$V_0(T, x) \equiv 0,$$

$$V_0(t, x) = \max\{0, \ \mu_2(x + p_{t+1}) + \mu_1(1 - G(t+1)) + f_0(t, x)\},$$

where the function $f_0(t, x)$ is given by

$$f_0(t, x) = \int_{\mathbb{R}} V_0\left(t+1, \ (p_{t+1} + x) \cdot \frac{\sigma_1}{\sigma_2} \exp\left(\frac{(z - \mu_1)^2}{2\sigma_1^2} - \frac{(z - \mu_2)^2}{2\sigma_2^2}\right)\right)$$

$$\times \frac{1}{\sigma_1\sqrt{2\pi}} \exp\left(-\frac{(z - \mu_1)^2}{2\sigma_1^2}\right) dz.$$

For $\alpha \ne 0$, let

$$V_\alpha(T, x) \equiv 0,$$

$$V_\alpha(t, x) = \max\{0, \ \alpha\beta^t\left[(\gamma - 1)(x + p_{t+1})\right.$$

$$\left. + (\beta - 1)(1 - G(t+1))\right] + f_\alpha(t, x)\},$$

where

$$\beta = \exp\left(\alpha\mu_1 + \frac{\alpha^2\sigma_1^2}{2}\right), \quad \gamma = \exp\left(\alpha\mu_2 + \frac{\alpha^2\sigma_2^2}{2}\right),$$

and

$$f_\alpha(t, x) = \int_{\mathbb{R}} V_\alpha\left(t+1, \ (p_{t+1} + x) \cdot \frac{\sigma_1}{\sigma_2} \exp\left(\frac{(z - \mu_1)^2}{2\sigma_1^2} - \frac{(z - \mu_2)^2}{2\sigma_2^2}\right)\right)$$

$$\times \frac{1}{\sigma_1\sqrt{2\pi}} \exp\left(-\frac{(z - \mu_1 - \alpha\sigma_1^2)^2}{2\sigma_1^2}\right) dz.$$

The value $V_\alpha(t, x) + \alpha$ represents the maximal expected gain one can obtain from selling the asset if the observation starts as time t with the value of the Shiryaev–Roberts statistic equal to x. In particular, the value V_α in problem (B.1) is equal to $V_\alpha(0, 0) + \alpha$.

In the next section, we provide an algorithm how $V_\alpha(t, x)$ can be computed recursively, which, together with the following theorem, gives a solution to the changepoint detection problem.

Theorem B.1: *The following stopping time is optimal in problem* (B.1):

$$\tau_\alpha^* = \inf\{0 \le t \le T : \psi_t \ge b_\alpha^*(t)\}, \tag{B.4}$$

where the stopping boundary $b_\alpha^*(t)$, $t = 0, \ldots, T$, is uniquely defined by the relation

$$b_\alpha^*(t) = \inf\{x \ge 0 : V_\alpha(t, x) = 0\}.$$

The value V_α of problem (B.1) *is equal to $V_\alpha(0, 0) + \alpha$.*

B.2. A numerical algorithm

In order to compute the functions $V_\alpha(t, x)$ and $b_\alpha^*(t)$, which define the solution of the changepoint detection problem, we take a partition of $\mathbf{R}_+$ by points $\{x_n\}_{n=0}^\infty$, $x_n = n\Delta$, where $\Delta > 0$ is a small parameter, and compute the values $\bar{V}_\alpha(t, x_n)$, which approximate $V_\alpha(t, x_n)$, and $\bar{b}_\alpha^*(t)$, which approximate $b_\alpha^*(t)$, by (backward) induction over $t = T, T - 1, \ldots, 0$.

For $t = T$, let $\bar{V}_\alpha(T, x_n) = 0$ for each $n \ge 0$. Suppose $\bar{V}_\alpha(s, x_n)$, $n \ge 0$, are found for some $s > 0$. In order to find $\bar{V}_\alpha(s - 1, x_n)$, $n \ge 0$, define for any $x \ge 0$

$$\bar{V}_\alpha(s, x) = \sum_{n=0}^\infty \bar{V}_\alpha(s, x_n) \mathbb{I}\{x \in [x_n, x_{n+1})\},$$

and compute the values $\bar{V}_\alpha(s - 1, x_n)$, $n \ge 0$, by formulae on p. 262 with $\bar{V}_\alpha(s, x)$ in place of $V_\alpha(s, x)$ in the formulae for $f_\alpha(s, x)$. This can be done in a finite number of steps, since after we find n such that $\bar{V}_\alpha(s - 1, n) = 0$ then $\bar{V}_\alpha(s - 1, n') = 0$ for all $n' \ge n$. Proceeding by induction over $t = T$, $T-1, \ldots, 0$ we find all the values $\bar{V}_\alpha(t, x_n)$, $n \ge 0$. Then for each $t = 0, \ldots, T$ define $\bar{b}_\alpha^*(t) = x_{n_0(\alpha, t)}$, where $n_0 = n_0(\alpha, t)$ is the smallest number n_0 such that $\bar{V}_\alpha(t, x_{n_0}) = 0$.

The main result of this section is the following theorem which estimates the computational error of the method, i. e. the differences $\bar{V}_\alpha(t,x) - V_\alpha(t,x)$ and $\bar{b}^*_\alpha(t) - b^*_\alpha(t)$, and shows they are proportional to Δ. It will be assumed that the integral in the formulae for $f_\alpha(t,x)$ and the elementary functions in the formulae for $\bar{V}_\alpha(t,x)$ can be computed exactly (or with negligible errors), so the computational errors appear only due to the approximation of $V_\alpha(t,x)$ by the functions $\bar{V}_\alpha(t,x)$.

Theorem B.2: 1) *For all* $t = 0, 1, \ldots, T$, $x \geq 0$, *the estimate holds:*

$$0 \leq \bar{V}_\alpha(t,x) - V_\alpha(t,x) \leq C^\alpha_t \Delta,$$

where the constants C^α_t, $t = 0, 1, \ldots, T$ *are explicitly given by (with* β *and* γ *defined on p. 262)*

$$C^\alpha_t = \begin{cases} |\mu_2| \dfrac{(T-t)(T-t+1)}{2}, & \alpha = 0, \\[3mm] \alpha\left(\dfrac{\beta^{T+1} - \beta^t}{\beta - 1} - \dfrac{\beta^{T+1} - \gamma^{T+1}(\beta/\gamma)^t}{\gamma - \beta} \right), & \alpha \neq 0. \end{cases}$$

2) *For* $t = 0, 1, \ldots, T$, *the functions* $b^*_\alpha(t)$, $\bar{b}^*_\alpha(t)$ *satisfy the inequalities*

$$\bar{b}^*_0(t) - \left(\frac{C^0_t}{|\mu_2|} + 2 \right)\Delta \leq b^*_0(t) \leq \bar{b}^*_0(t),$$

$$\bar{b}^*_\alpha(t) - \left(\frac{C^\alpha_t}{\alpha\beta^t(1 - \gamma)} + 2 \right)\Delta \leq b^*_\alpha(t) \leq \bar{b}^*_\alpha(t), \qquad \alpha \neq 0.$$

B.3. Proofs of the theorems

Proof of Theorem B.1. The proof of Theorem B.1 will be given in two steps. First, problem (B.1) will be reduced to an optimal stopping problem for the Shiryaev–Roberts statistic ψ with respect to a new probability measure on $(\Omega, \mathcal{F}_T)$. Then we show that ψ_t is a Markov sequence with respect to this measure and use standard results about optimal stopping of Markov sequences.

Step 1. On the measure space $(\Omega, \mathcal{F}_T)$ introduce the family of probability measures Q^α, $\alpha \leq 1$, such that the logarithmic returns X_t, $t = 1, \ldots, T$, are i.i.d $\mathcal{N}(\mu_1 + \alpha\sigma_1^2, \sigma_1^2)$ random variables under Q^α. In particular, $Q^0 \equiv P^\infty$. For $t = 1, \ldots, T$, the explicit formula for the density dP_t/dQ^α_t, where

$Q_t^\alpha = Q^\alpha \mid \mathcal{F}_t$, is given by

$$\frac{dP_t}{dQ_t^\alpha} = \frac{dP_t}{dQ_t^0} \cdot \frac{dQ_t^0}{dQ_t^\alpha} = \left(\sum_{u=1}^{T+1} \frac{dP_t^u}{dP_t^\infty} p_u \right) \cdot \frac{dQ_t^0}{dQ_t^\alpha}$$

$$= \left(\sum_{u=1}^{t} \frac{dP_t^u}{dP_t^\infty} p_u + \sum_{u=t+1}^{T+1} p_u \right) \cdot \exp\left(\alpha \mu_1 t + \frac{\alpha^2 \sigma_1^2}{2} t - \alpha \sum_{u=1}^{t} X_i \right)$$

$$= (\psi_t + 1 - G(t)) \beta^t \cdot \exp\left(-\alpha \sum_{u=1}^{t} X_i \right).$$

Let us show that for any stopping time $\tau \le T$, it holds that

$$EU_0(S_\tau) = E^{Q^0} \left[\sum_{t=1}^{\tau} [\mu_2 \psi_t + \mu_1 (1 - G(t))] \right], \qquad \text{(B.5)}$$

$$EU_\alpha(S_\tau) = \alpha E^{Q^\alpha} \left[\sum_{t=1}^{\tau} \beta^{t-1} [(\beta - \beta/\gamma) \psi_t + (\beta - 1)(1 - G(t))] \right] + \alpha$$

$$\text{for } \alpha \ne 0, \qquad \text{(B.6)}$$

where E^{Q^α} denotes the expectation with respect to Q^α. Here and below, we define $\sum_{t=1}^{\tau} [\ldots] = 0$ if $\tau = 0$.

In order to prove (B.5), observe that

$$EU_0(S_\tau) = E \sum_{t=1}^{\tau} X_t = E^{Q^0} \left[\frac{dP_\tau}{dQ_\tau^0} \sum_{t=1}^{\tau} X_t \right] = E^{Q^0} \left[(\psi_\tau + 1 - G(\tau)) \sum_{t=1}^{\tau} X_t \right].$$

Using the "discrete version" of the integration by parts formula,

$$a_t b_t = \sum_{s=1}^{t} a_s \Delta b_s + \sum_{s=1}^{t} b_{s-1} \Delta a_s + a_0 b_0, \qquad \text{(B.7)}$$

valid for any sequences a_t and b_t with the notation $\Delta a_s = a_s - a_{s-1}$, $\Delta b_s = b_s - b_{s-1}$, we obtain

$$EU_0(S_\tau) = E^{Q^0} \left[\sum_{t=1}^{\tau} (\psi_t + 1 - G(t)) X_t + \sum_{t=1}^{\tau} \sum_{s=1}^{t-1} X_s (\psi_t - \psi_{t-1} - p_t) \right].$$

$$\text{(B.8)}$$

The sequence $\psi_t + 1 - G(t)$ is a martingale with respect to the measure Q^0 since it is the sequence of the densities dP_t/dQ_t^0. This implies that the expectation of the second sum in the above formula is zero. Indeed, we have

$$E^{Q^0}\left[\sum_{t=1}^{\tau}\sum_{s=1}^{t-1}X_s(\psi_t - \psi_{t-1} - p_t)\right]$$

$$= E^{Q^0}\left[\sum_{t=1}^{T+1}\sum_{s=1}^{t-1}E^{Q^0}\left[X_s(\psi_t - \psi_{t-1} - p_t)\mathbb{I}(t \leq \tau) \mid \mathcal{F}_{t-1}\right]\right] = 0,$$

where $\mathbb{I}(A)$ denotes the indicator of event A, and we use that X_s and $\mathbb{I}(t \leq \tau)$ are $\mathcal{F}_{t-1}$-measurable random variables, so they can be taken out of the conditional expectation, and

$$E^{Q^0}(\psi_t - \psi_{t-1} - p_t \mid \mathcal{F}_{t-1}) = 0, \quad t = 1, \ldots, T,$$

as it follows from that $\psi_t + 1 - G(t)$ is a martingale.

For the first sum in (B.8), we have

$$E^{Q^0}\left[\sum_{t=1}^{\tau}(\psi_t + 1 - G(t))X_t\right]$$

$$= E^{Q^0}\left[\sum_{t=1}^{T+1}E^{Q^0}\left((\psi_t + 1 - G(t))X_t\mathbb{I}(t \leq \tau) \mid \mathcal{F}_{t-1}\right)\right]$$

$$= E^{Q^0}\left[\sum_{t=1}^{\tau}\left[E^{Q^0}(p_t + \psi_{t-1})\mu_2 + \mu_1(1 - G(t))\right]\right]$$

$$= E^{Q^0}\left[\sum_{t=1}^{\tau}\left[\mu_2\psi_t + \mu_1(1 - G(t))\right]\right].$$

In the second equality, we use that $\mathbb{I}(t \leq \tau)$ is an $\mathcal{F}_{t-1}$-measurable random variable and it can be taken out of the conditional expectation, X_t is independent of $\mathcal{F}_{t-1}$, so $E^{Q^0}[(1 - G(t))X_t \mid \mathcal{F}_{t-1}] = (1 - G(t))E^{Q^0}X_t = (1 - G(t))\mu_1$, and, as follows from (B.3),

$$E^{Q^0}(\psi_t X_t \mid \mathcal{F}_{t-1})$$

$$= (p_t + \psi_{t-1})\frac{\sigma_1}{\sigma_2}E^{Q^0}\left[X_t \exp\left(\frac{(X_t - \mu_1)^2}{2\sigma_1^2} - \frac{(X_t - \mu_2)^2}{2\sigma_2^2}\right)\right]$$

$$= (p_t + \psi_{t-1})\mu_2.$$

In the third equality, we use the representation

$$E^{Q^0}\left[\sum_{t=1}^{\tau}(p_t + \psi_{t-1})\right] = E^{Q^0}\left[\sum_{t=1}^{T+1} E^{Q^0}\left(\psi_t \mid \mathcal{F}_{t-1}\right)\mathbb{I}(t \le \tau)\right]$$

$$= E^{Q^0}\left[\sum_{t=1}^{T+1} E^{Q^0}\left(\psi_t\mathbb{I}(t \le \tau) \mid \mathcal{F}_{t-1}\right)\right]$$

$$= E^{Q^0}\left[\sum_{t=1}^{\tau}\psi_t\right].$$

This proves formula (B.5).

Let us prove (B.6). We have

$$EU_\alpha(S_\tau)$$

$$= \alpha E \exp\left(\alpha\sum_{t=1}^{\tau}X_t\right) = \alpha E^{Q^\alpha}\left[\frac{dP_\tau}{dQ_\tau^\alpha}\exp\left(\alpha\sum_{t=1}^{\tau}X_t\right)\right]$$

$$= \alpha E^{Q^\alpha}\left[(\psi_\tau + 1 - G(\tau))\beta^\tau\right]$$

$$= \alpha E^{Q^\alpha}\left[\sum_{t=1}^{\tau}[(\psi_t + 1 - G(t))(\beta^t - \beta^{t-1}) + \beta^{t-1}(\psi_t - \psi_{t-1} - p_t)]\right] + \alpha,$$

where in the third equality, we use the formula for the conditional density dP_t/dQ_t^α, and in the last equality, we use formula (B.7). Using representation (B.3), it is possible to verify the following expression for the conditional expectation $E^{Q^\alpha}(\psi_t \mid \mathcal{F}_{t-1})$:

$$E^{Q^\alpha}(\psi_t \mid \mathcal{F}_{t-1}) = \frac{\gamma}{\beta}(\psi_{t-1} + p_t) \quad \text{for } t = 1, \ldots, T. \tag{B.9}$$

To check that the right-hand side (RH) of above expression for $EU_\alpha(S_\tau)$ coincides with the right-hand side $(\overline{RH})$ of (B.6), we show that their difference is equal to zero:

$$(RH) - (\overline{RH}) = \alpha E^{Q^\alpha}\left[\sum_{t=1}^{\tau}\beta^{t-1}(\psi_t\beta/\gamma - \psi_{t-1} - p_t)\right]$$

$$= \alpha E^{Q^\alpha}\left[\sum_{t=1}^{T+1}\beta^{t-1}(\psi_t\beta/\gamma - \psi_{t-1} - p_t)\mathbb{I}(t \le \tau)\right]$$

$$= \alpha E^{Q^\alpha}\left[\sum_{t=1}^{T+1}E^{Q^\alpha}\left[\beta^{t-1}(\psi_t\beta/\gamma - \psi_{t-1} - p_t)\mathbb{I}(t \le \tau) \mid \mathcal{F}_{t-1}\right]\right]$$

$$= \alpha E^{Q^\alpha} \left[\sum_{t=1}^{T+1} \beta^{t-1} (E^{Q^\alpha} (\psi_t \mid \mathcal{F}_{t-1}) \beta/\gamma - \psi_{t-1} - p_t) \mathbb{I}(t \le \tau) \right]$$
$$= 0,$$

where in the fourth equality we use that ψ_{t-1} and $\mathbb{I}(t \le \tau)$ are $\mathcal{F}_{t-1}$-measurable random variables, so their conditional expectations coincides with themselves, and apply (B.9). This proves (B.6).

Step 2. For convenience of notation, let $F_\alpha(t, \psi)$ denote the terms in the sums in (B.5)–(B.6):

$$F_0(t, x) = \mu_2 x + \mu_1 (1 - G(t)),$$
$$F_\alpha(t, x) = \alpha \beta^{t-1} [(\beta - \beta/\gamma)x + (\beta - 1)(1 - G(t))].$$

(B.10)

Representations (B.5) and (B.6) allow one to reduce problem (B.1) to the optimal stopping problems for the Shiryaev–Roberts statistic ψ

$$V_\alpha = \sup_{\tau \in \mathcal{M}} E^{Q^\alpha} \left[\sum_{u=1}^{\tau} F_\alpha(u, \psi_u) \right] + \alpha,$$

so that the optimal stopping times in these problems will also be optimal in problem (B.1).

Let $\mathcal{M}_t$ denote the class of all stopping times τ of the filtration $\mathcal{F}_t$ such that $\tau \le t$. In particular, $\mathcal{M}_T = \mathcal{M}$.

According to the results of [Shiryaev (2007), Ch. II, § 2.15], the Shiryaev– Roberts statistic is a Markov sequence with respect to the filtration $\mathcal{F}_t$ under each measure Q^α, $\alpha \le 1$, since ψ_t is a function of ψ_{t-1} and X_t, while X_t form a sequence of independent random variables. Following the general theory of optimal stopping of Markov sequences (see e. g. [Peskir and Shiryaev (2006), Ch. I]), introduce the family of the *value functions* $V_\alpha(t, x)$ for $t \in \{0, 1, \dots, T\}$, $x \ge 0$:

$$V_\alpha(t, x) = \sup_{\tau \in \mathcal{M}_{T-t}} E^{Q^\alpha} \left[\sum_{u=1}^{\tau} F_\alpha(t + u, \psi_u(t, x)) \right],$$

(B.11)

where $\psi(t, x) = (\psi_u(t, x))_{u=0}^{T-t}$ is a sequence of random variables defined by the recurrent formula

$$\psi_0(t, x) = x,$$

$$\psi_u(t, x) = (p_{t+u} + \psi_{u-1}(t, x)) \cdot \frac{\sigma_1}{\sigma_2} \exp \left(\frac{(X_u - \mu_1)^2}{2\sigma_1^2} - \frac{(X_u - \mu_2)^2}{2\sigma_2^2} \right)$$

with $X_1, X_2, \ldots$ being i.i.d. $\mathcal{N}(\mu_1 + \alpha\sigma_1^2, \sigma_1^2)$ random variables with respect to the measure Q^α. The sums in the definition of $V_\alpha(t, x)$ are equal to zero if $\tau = 0$, which, in particular, means that $V_\alpha(T, x) = 0$ for any $x \geq 0$.

The functions $V_\alpha(t, x)$ represent the maximal possible gain in the optimal stopping problem if the observation starts at time t with the value of the Shiryaev–Roberts statistic x. From formulae (B.5)–(B.6), it follows that original problem (B.1) corresponds to $t = 0$, $x = 0$, so the optimal stopping time for $V_\alpha(0, 0)$ will be the optimal stopping time in (B.1), and $V_\alpha = V_\alpha(0, 0) + a$.

The well-known result of the optimal stopping theory for Markov sequences (see Peskir and Shiryaev (2006), Theorem 1.8) states that the value functions $V_\alpha(t, x)$ satisfy the following *Wald–Bellman equations* for $t = 0, \ldots, T - 1$:

$$V_\alpha(t, x) = \max\{0, \; E^{Q^\alpha}[F_\alpha(t+1, \psi_1(t, x)) + V_\alpha(t+1, \psi_1(t, x))]\}. \quad \text{(B.12)}$$

Here, 0 is the gain from *instantaneous stopping* in the problems at hand. Using that X_t are i.i.d $\mathcal{N}(\mu_1 + \alpha\sigma_1^2, \sigma_1^2)$ random variables with respect to Q^α and computing the expectations $E^{Q^\alpha}[\ldots]$ in the above equation, we obtain that the functions $V_\alpha(t, x)$ satisfy the recurrent relations on p. 262.

From Peskir and Shiryaev (2006), Theorem 1.7, it follows that the optimal stopping time in problem (B.1) is the first moment of time when ψ_t enters the *stopping set* D_α:

$$D_\alpha = \{(t, x) : V_\alpha(t, x) = 0\}, \qquad \tau_\alpha^* = \inf\{t \geq 0 : (t, \psi_t) \in D_\alpha\}.$$

In order to prove representation (B.4), we show that for fixed t and α, the function $x \mapsto V_\alpha(t, x)$ is continuous and non-increasing, and there exists x such that $V_\alpha(t, x) = 0$. The non-increasing follows from that $\psi_u(t, x_1) \geq \psi_u(t, x_2)$ whenever $x_1 \geq x_2$, and the coefficients μ_2 and $\alpha\beta^t(1 - 1/\gamma)$ are negative in the formulae for $F_0(t, x)$ and $F_\alpha(t, x)$ respectively as it follows from the assumption $\mu_2 < -\alpha\sigma_2^2/2$ (see (B.2)).

In order to prove the continuity of $x \mapsto V_\alpha(t, x)$, we show by induction over $t = T, T-1, \ldots, 0$ that for arbitrary $0 \leq x_1 \leq x_2$ it holds that

$$V_\alpha(t, x_1) - V_\alpha(t, x_2) \leq c_t^\alpha (x_2 - x_1) \quad \text{(B.13)}$$

with the constants

$$c_t^\alpha = \begin{cases} |\mu_2|(T - t), & \alpha = 0 \\ \alpha\beta^t(1 - \gamma^{T-t}), & \alpha \neq 0. \end{cases}$$

For $t = T$, the claim is valid because $V_\alpha(T, x) = 0$ for all $x \geq 0$. Suppose it holds for some $t = s$ and consider $t = s - 1$. From the formulae on p. 262, it follows that

$$V_\alpha(s - 1, x_1) - V_\alpha(s - 1, x_2)$$

$$\leq \begin{cases} |\mu_2|(x_2 - x_1) + f_0(s - 1, x_1) - f_0(s - 1, x_2), & \alpha = 0, \\ \alpha\beta^{s-1}(1 - \gamma)(x_2 - x_1) + f_\alpha(s - 1, x_1) - f_\alpha(s - 1, x_2), & \alpha \neq 0. \end{cases}$$

Further, using the induction assumption for $t = s$, we find

$$f_\alpha(s - 1, x_1) - f_\alpha(s - 1, x_2)$$

$$\leq \int_{\mathbf{R}} \frac{c_s^\alpha(x_2 - x_1)}{\sigma_2\sqrt{2\pi}} \exp\left(\frac{(z - \mu_1)^2}{2\sigma_1^2} - \frac{(z - \mu_2)^2}{2\sigma_2^2}\right)$$

$$\times \exp\left(\frac{(z - \mu_1 - \alpha\sigma_1^2)^2}{2\sigma_1^2}\right) dz = c_s^\alpha(x_2 - x_1)\frac{\gamma}{\beta}.$$

Combining it with the previous inequality we find for $\alpha = 0$

$$V_\alpha(s - 1, x_1) - V_\alpha(s - 1, x_2) \leq (x_2 - x_1)(|\mu_2| + c_s^\alpha) = c_{s-1}^\alpha(x_2 - x_1)$$

and for $\alpha \neq 0$,

$$V_\alpha(s - 1, x_1) - V_\alpha(s - 1, x_2)$$

$$\leq (x_2 - x_1)(\alpha\beta^{s-1}(1 - \gamma) + c_s^\alpha\gamma/\beta)$$

$$= c_{s-1}^\alpha(x_2 - x_1),$$

which proves the claim. Since $0 \leq V_\alpha(t, x_1) - V_\alpha(t, x_2)$ because $x \mapsto V_\alpha(t, x)$ is a non-increasing function, we obtain that it is continuous.

Finally by induction over $t = T, T - 1, \ldots, 0$ we prove that there exists a root $r_{\alpha,t}$ of the function $x \mapsto V_\alpha(t, x)$. For $t = T$, this is true since $V_\alpha(T, x) = 0$ for all $x \geq 0$. Suppose there exists a root for $t = s > 0$. Then for $t = s - 1$ and $x \to +\infty$, we have

$$E^{Q^\alpha} V_\alpha(s, \psi_1(s - 1, x))$$

$$\leq \sup_{0 \leq y \leq r_{\alpha,s}} V_\alpha(s, y) \cdot Q^\alpha\{\psi_1(s - 1, x) \leq r_{\alpha,s}\} \to 0$$

since $y \mapsto V_\alpha(s, y)$ is a continuous function and, hence, bounded on the segment $[0, r_{\alpha,s}]$, while $Q^\alpha\{\psi_1(s - 1, x) \leq r_{\alpha,s}\} \to 0$ for $x \to +\infty$ as follows from the definition of $\psi_1(t, x)$. On the other hand, $F_\alpha(s - 1, x) \to -\infty$ as $x \to +\infty$, which follows from that, according to the assumption $\mu_2 < -\alpha\sigma_2^2/2$ (see (B.2)), the coefficients μ_2 or $\alpha\beta^{t-1}(\beta - \beta/\gamma)$ in front of x in formula (B.10) are negative respectively in the case $\alpha = 0$ or $\alpha \neq 0$. Then from (B.12), we obtain the existence of the root $r_{\alpha,s-1}$.

Proof of Theorem B.2. The proof of the first statement is conducted by induction over $t = T, T - 1, \ldots, 0$. For $t = T$, the estimate is true because $V_\alpha(t, x) = \bar{V}_\alpha(t, x) = 0$. Suppose it holds for $t = s$ and let us prove it for $t = s - 1$.

According to the recurrent formulae on p. 262, $0 \leq \bar{V}_\alpha(s-1, x) - V_\alpha(s-1, x)$ because $0 \leq \bar{V}_\alpha(s, x) - V_\alpha(s, x)$ for all $x \geq 0$ as it follows from the inductive assumption.

Let $n(x)$ denote the largest x_n not exceeding x. Then for $x \geq 0$, we have

$$\bar{V}_\alpha(s - 1, x) - V_\alpha(s - 1, x)$$
$$= \left[\bar{V}_\alpha(s - 1, x) - \bar{V}_\alpha(s - 1, x_{n(x)})\right]$$
$$+ \left[\bar{V}_\alpha(s - 1, x_{n(x)}) - V_\alpha(s - 1, x_{n(x)})\right]$$
$$+ \left[V_\alpha(s - 1, x_{n(x)}) - V_\alpha(s - 1, x)\right]$$
$$\leq 0 + C_s^\alpha \Delta + c_{s-1}^\alpha \Delta = C_{s-1}^\alpha \Delta,$$

where we use that the difference in the second line equals zero according to the definition of $\bar{V}_\alpha$, the difference in the fourth line, is estimated from above by $c_{s-1}^\alpha(x - x_{n(x)}) \leq c_{s-1}^\alpha \Delta$ according to (B.13), and for the third line, we use the inequality

$$\bar{V}_\alpha(s - 1, x_{n(x)}) - V_\alpha(s - 1, x_{n(x)})$$
$$\leq \bar{f}_\alpha(s - 1, x_n) - f_\alpha(s - 1, x_n)$$
$$\leq \int_{\mathbf{R}} \frac{C_s^\alpha \Delta}{\sigma_1 \sqrt{2\pi}} \exp\left(-\frac{(z - \mu_1 - \alpha\sigma_1^2)^2}{2\sigma_1^2}\right) dz = C_s^\alpha \Delta,$$

where the function $\bar{f}_\alpha$ is defined by the same formula as f_α, but with $\bar{V}_\alpha$ in place of V_α. The inequalities obtained prove the inductive step and, consequently, prove statement 1 of the theorem.

We proceed with the proof of statement 2. Fix $\alpha \leq 1$. Observe that $b_\alpha^*(t) \leq \bar{b}_\alpha^*(t)$ because $\bar{V}_\alpha(t, x) \geq V_\alpha(t, x)$ for all $t = 0, 1, \ldots, T$, $x \geq 0$.

Let us prove the lower inequalities. First, suppose for some $t \leq T$, there exists a non-negative integer number k such that

$$x_{n_0(t)-1} - x_k > \begin{cases} \dfrac{C_t^0}{|\mu_2|}\Delta, & \alpha = 0, \\[3mm] \dfrac{C_t^\alpha}{\alpha\beta^t(1-\gamma)}\Delta, & \alpha \neq 0 \end{cases} \tag{B.14}$$

(since α is fixed, it is omitted in the notation $n_0(\alpha, t)$). Let $k(t)$ denote the largest such integer number. Observe that for any $0 \leq k_1 \leq k_2 < n_0(t)$ it holds that

$$\bar{V}_\alpha(t, x_{k_1}) - \bar{V}_\alpha(t, x_{k_2}) \geq \begin{cases} |\mu_2|(x_{k_2} - x_{k_1}), & \alpha = 0, \\[2mm] \alpha\beta^t(1-\gamma)(x_{k_2} - x_{k_1}), & \alpha \neq 0, \end{cases} \tag{B.15}$$

as it follows from the definition of $\bar{V}_\alpha(t, x_k)$ by the formulae on p. 262. As a consequence,

$$V_\alpha(t, x_{k(t)}) \geq \bar{V}_\alpha(t, x_{k(t)}) - C_t^\alpha \Delta \geq \bar{V}_\alpha(t, x_{k(t)}) - \bar{V}_\alpha(t, x_{n_0(t)-1}) - C_t^\alpha \Delta > 0,$$

where in the first inequality, we use statement 1, in the second inequality, we use that $\bar{V}_\alpha \geq 0$, and in the last one, we apply (B.14) and (B.15). This implies $b_\alpha^*(t) > x_{k(t)}$. Using that $k(t)$ is the largest integer number satisfying (B.14), we see that

$$x_{k(t)} \geq \begin{cases} x_{n_0(t)-1} - \left(\dfrac{C_t^0}{|\mu_2|} + 1\right)\Delta, & \alpha = 0, \\[3mm] x_{n_0(t)-1} - \left(\dfrac{C_t^\alpha}{\alpha\beta^t(1-\gamma)} + 1\right)\Delta, & \alpha \neq 0. \end{cases}$$

Consequently, if for some $t \leq T$, there exists a non-negative integer number satisfying (B.14), the lower inequality in statement 2 holds for this t because $x_{n_0(t)-1} = \bar{b}_\alpha^*(t) - \Delta$.

In the opposite case, we have $x_{n_0(t)-1} \leq C_t^0\Delta/|\mu_2|$ if $\alpha = 0$ and $x_{n_0(t)-1} \leq C_t^\alpha\Delta/(\alpha\beta^t(1-\gamma))$ if $\alpha \neq 0$, which also implies the validity of statement 2, since $b_\alpha^*(t) \geq 0$. This finishes the proof.

Bibliography

Abreu, D. and Brunnermeier, M. K. (2003). Bubbles and crashes, *Econometrica* **71**, 1, pp. 173–204.

Allen, F. and Gorton, G. (1993). Churning bubbles, *Review of Economic Studies* **60**, 4, pp. 813–836.

Altman, E. I. and Kuehne, B. J. (2016). Credit market bubble building? A forming credit bubble could burst by 2017, *Quantitative Finance Letters* **4**, 1, pp. 14–18.

Anderson, K., Brooks, C., and Katsaris, A. (2013). Testing for speculative bubbles in asset prices, in A. R. Bell, C. Brooks, and M. Prokopczuk (Eds.), *Handbook of Research Methods and Applications in Empirical Finance*, (Edward Elgar, Cheltenham, UK), pp. 73–93.

Andrade, E. B., Odean, T., and Lin, S. (2016). Bubbling with excitement: An experiment, *Review of Finance* **20**, 2, pp. 447–466, doi:10.1093/rof/rfv016, http://rof.oxfordjournals.org/content/20/2/447.full.pdf+html, http://rof.oxfordjournals.org/content/20/2/447.abstract.

Bagnell, P. (1999). Shrinking breadth in a stock market danger, *Globe and Mail*, November 26.

Baker, M. and Wurgler, J. (2006). Investor sentiment and the cross-section of stock returns, *Journal of Finance* **61**, 4, pp. 1645–1680.

Baker, M. and Wurgler, J. (2007). Investor sentiment in the stock market, *Journal of Economic Perspectives* **21**, pp. 129–151.

Barone-Adesi, G., Mancini, L., and Shefrin, H. (2013). A tale of two investors: Estimating optimism and overconfidence, Technical Report.

Basseville, M. and Nikiforov, I. V. (1993). *Detection of Abrupt Changes: Theory and Application*, Vol. 104 (Prentice Hall Englewood Cliffs).

Berge, K., Consigli, G., and Ziemba, W. T. (2008). The predictive ability of the bond stock earnings yield differential, *Journal of Portfolio Management*, Spring, **34**, 3, pp. 63–80.

Berge, K. and Ziemba, W. T. (2003). *The predictive ability of bond versus stock earnings yield differences*, Working paper, Faculty of Commerce, University of British Columbia.

Bertocchi, M., Schwartz, S. L., and Ziemba, W. T. (2010). *Optimizing the Aging, Retirement and Pensions Dilemma* (Wiley (2nd Edn. 2015)).

Black, F. and Litterman, R. (1991). *Global asset allocation with equities, bonds and currencies*, Technical Report. Fixed Income Research, (Goldman Sachs & Co).

Black, F. and Litterman, R. (1991). Asset allocation: Combining investor views with market equilibrium, *Journal of Fixed Income* **2**, 1, pp. 7–18.

Black, F. and Litterman, R. (1992). Global portfolio optimization, *Financial Analysts Journal* **48**, 5, pp. 28–43.

Blanchard, O. J. and Watson, M. W. (1982). Bubbles, rational expectations, and financial markets, in P. Wachtel (Ed.), *Crisis in the Economic and Financial Structure*, Levington, MA: D.C. Heath, pp. 295–315.

Britten-Jones, M. (1999). The sampling error in estimates of mean-variance efficient portfolio weights, *Journal of Finance* **52**, 2.

Buffett, W. and Loomis, C. (1999). Warren Buffett on the stock market, *FORTUNE Magazine*.

Buffett, W. and Loomis, C. (2001). Warren Buffett on the stock market, *FORTUNE Magazine*.

Callen, J. and Fang, X. (2015). Short interest and stock price crash risk, *Journal of Banking & Finance* **60**, pp. 181–194.

Camerer, C. (1989). Bubbles and fads in asset prices, *Journal of Economic Surveys* **3**, 1, pp. 3–14.

Campbell, J. Y. and Shiller, R. J. (1988). Stock prices, earnings, and expected dividends, *Journal of Finance* **43**, 3, pp. 661–676.

Campbell, J. Y. and Shiller, R. J. (1989). The dividend ratio model and small sample bias: A Monte Carlo study, *Economic Letters* **29**, 4, pp. 324–331.

Campbell, J. Y. and Shiller, R. J. (1998). Valuation ratios and the long-run stock market outlook, *Journal of Portfolio Management* **24**, pp. 11–26.

Campbell, J. Y. and Shiller, R. J. (2001). Valuation ratios and the long-run stock market outlook: on update, Working paper W8221, NBER.

Canaway, P. (1990). Land prices in Japan: no cause for alarm, Baring Securities, May.

Comolli, L. R. and Ziemba, W. T. (2000). Japanese security market regularities, 1990–1994, in D. B. Keim and W. T. Ziemba (Eds.), *Security Market Imperfections in Worldwide Equity Markets* (Cambridge University Press).

Consigli, G., MacLean, L. C., Zhao, Y., and Ziemba, W. (2009). The bond-stock yield differential as a risk indicator in financial markets, *Journal of Risk* **11**, 3, pp. 3–24.

Cont, R. (2001). Empirical properties of asset returns: stylized facts and statistical issues, *Quantitative Finance* **1**, 2, pp. 223–236.

Corcos, A., Eckmann, J.-P., Malaspinas, A., and Malevergne, Y. (2002). Imitation and contrarian behaviour: hyperbolic bubbles, craches and chaos, *Quantitative Finance* **2**, pp. 264–281.

Corgnet, B., Hernán-González, R., Kujal, P., and Porter, D. (2015). The effect of earned versus house money on price bubble formation in experimental asset markets, *Review of Finance* **19**, 4, pp. 1455–1488.

Cox, A. M. G. and Hobson, D. G. (2005). Local martingales, bubbles and option prices, *Finance and Stochastics* **9**, 4, pp. 477–492.

Davis, M. and Lleo, S. (2013). Black-Litterman in continuous time: The case for filtering, *Quantitative Finance Letters* **1**, 1, pp. 30–35.

Davis, M. and Lleo, S. (2014). *Risk-Sensitive Investment Management, Advanced Series on Statistical Science and Applied Probability*, Vol. 19 (World Scientific Publishing, Singapore).

Davis, M. and Lleo, S. (2016). A simple procedure to incorporate predictive models in a continuous time asset allocation, *Quantitative Finance Letters* **4**, 1, pp. 40–46.

Delbaen, F. and Schachermayer, W. (1998). The fundamental theorem of asset pricing for unbounded stochastic processes, *Mathematische Annaler* **312**, 2, pp. 215–250.

Diba, B. T. and Grossman, H. I. (1988). The theory of rational bubbles in stock prices, *Economic Journal* **98**, 392, pp. 746–754.

Dimson, E., Marsh, P., and Staunton, M. (2014). *Global investment returns Yearbook 2014* (Credit Suisse Research Institute, Zurich).

Dzhabrov, C. and Ziemba, W. T. (2016). Sell in May and go away in the equity index futures markets, Working Paper. SSRN: https://ssrn.com/abstract= 2721068.

Estrada, J. (2006). The Fed model: A note, *Financial Research Letters* **3**, pp. 14–22.

Evanoff, D. D., Kaufman, G., and Malliaris, A. G. (Eds.) (2012). *New perspectives on asset price bubbles* (Oxford University Press).

Fama, E. F. and French, K. R. (1992). The cross-section of expected stock returns, *Journal of Finance* **47**, pp. 427–465.

Faugère, C. (2013). The fear premium and daily comovements of the S&P 500 E/P ratio and treasury yields before and during the 2008 financial crisis, *Financial Markets, Institutions & Instruments* **22**, 3.

Faugère, C. and Van Erlach, J. (2009). A required yield theory of stock market valuation and treasury yield determination, *Financial Markets, Institutions & Instruments* **18**, 1.

Ferguson, M. F. and Witte, H. D. (2006). Congress and the stock market, March 13. Available at SSRN: http://ssrn.com/abstract=687211 or http://dx.doi.org/10.2139/ssrn.687211

Fisher, K. and Statman, M. (2000). Investor sentiment and stock returns, *Financial Analyst Journal*, pp. 16–23.

Fisher, K. and Statman, M. (2003). Consumer confidence and stock returns, *Journal of Portfolio Management*, pp. 115–127.

Fisher, R. A. (1933). *Statistical Methods for Research Workers*, 5th Edn. (Oliver & Boyd, Edinburgh and London).

Fisher, R. A. (1955). Statistical methods and scientific inference, *Journal of the Royal Statistical Society, Series B* **17**, 1, pp. 69–78.

Flood, R. P., Hodrick, R. J., and Kaplan, P. (1986). An evaluation of recent evidence on stock market bubbles, NBER Working Paper No. w1971.

Frehen, R. G., Goetzmann, W. N., and Rouwenhorst, K. G. (2013). New evidence on the first financial bubble, *Journal of Financial Economics* **108**, 3, pp. 565–854.

Giot, P. and Petitjean, M. (2008). Short-term market timing using the bond-equity yield ratio, *European Journal of Finance*, April–June, pp. 365–384.

Glitnir (2006). List of available funds, May.

Goetzmann, W., Kim, D., and Shiller, R. (2016). Crash beliefs from investor surveys, Yale University Working Paper.

Goetzmann, W. N. (2014). Bubble investing, learning from history, NBER Working Paper W21693.

Gordon, M. J. (1959). Dividends, earnings and stock prices, *Review of Economics and Statistics* **41**, 2, doi:10.2307/1927792.

Graham, B. and Dodd, D. L. (1934). *Security Analysis*, 1st Edn. (New York: McGraw-Hill).

Gresnigt, F., Kole, E., and Franses, P. H. (2015). Interpreting financial market crashes as earthquakes: A new early warning system for medium term crashes, *Journal of Banking & Finance* **56**, pp. 123–139.

Grimmett, G. and Stirzaker, D. (2001). *Probability and Random Processes* (Oxford University Press, Oxford, UK).

Hensel, C. R. and Ziemba, W. T. (1995). US small and large capitalized stocks, bonds and cash returns during democratic and republican administrations, 1928–1993, *Financial Analysts Journal*, **51**, 2, March/April, pp. 61–69.

Hensel, C. R. and Ziemba, W. T. (2000). How did Clinton stand up to history? US stock market returns and presidential party affiliations, in D. B. Keim and W. T. Ziemba (Eds.), *Security market imperfections in world wide equity markets*, pp. 203–217. (Cambridge University Press, Cambridge, UK).

Herbst, A. F. and Slinkman, C. W. (1984). Political-Economic Cycles in the US stock Market, *Financial Analysts Journal*, **40**, pp. 38–44.

Heston, S., Loewenstein, M., and Willard, G. A. (2007). Options and bubbles, *Review of Financial Studies* **20**, 2, pp. 359–390.

Hobbs, G. R. and Riley W. B. (1984). Profiting from a presidential election *Financial Analysts Journal*, **40**, 2, pp. 46–52.

Huang, R. D. (1985). Common stock returns and presidential elections, *Financial Analysts Journal* **41**, 2, pp. 58–65.

Ibbotson Associates (1999). *Stocks, bonds, bills and inflation, 1999 Year Book* (Ibbotson Associates, Chicago).

Jacobs, B. I. and Levy, K. N. (1988). Disentangling equity return regularities: new insights and investment opportunities, *Financial Analysts Journal* **44**, pp. 47–62.

Jacod, J. and Protter, P. (2010). Risk neutral compatibility with option prices, *Finance and Stochastics* **14**, pp. 285–315.

Jarrow, R. (2016). Testing for asset price bubbles: three new approaches, *Quantitative Finance Letters* **4**, 1, pp. 4–9, doi:10.1080/21649502.2015. 1165838, http://dx.doi.org/10.1080/21649502.2015.1165838, http://dx. doi.org/10.1080/21649502.2015.1165838.

Jarrow, R., Kohia, Y., and Protter, P. (2011). How to detect an asset bubble, *SIAM Journal of Financial Math* **2**, pp. 839–865.

Jarrow, R. and Larsson, M. (2012). The meaning of market efficiency, *Mathematical Finance* **22**, 1, pp. 1–30.

Jarrow, R. and Protter, P. (2008). An introduction to financial asset pricing, in J. Birge and V. Linetsky (Eds.), *Handbooks in OR&MS*, Vol. 15 (Elsevier, Amsterdam).

Jarrow, R., Protter, P., and Shimbo, K. (2007). Asset price bubbles in a complete market, *Advances in Mathematical Finance* In Honor of Dilip B. Madan, pp. 105–130.

Jarrow, R., Protter, P., and Shimbo, K. (2010). Asset price bubbles in incomplete markets, *Mathematical Finance* **20**, 2, pp. 145–185.

Jorion, P. (2007). *Value-at-Risk: The New Benchmark for Managing Financial Risk*, 3rd ed. (McGraw-Hill, New York).

Kahneman, D. and Tversky, A. (1979). Prospect theory: An analysis of decision under risk, *Econometrica* **47**, pp. 263–291.

Kallberg, J. G. and Ziemba, W. T. (1983). Comparison of alternative utility functions in portfolio selection problems, *Management Science* **29**, 11, pp. 1257–1276.

Kandel, S. and Stambaugh, R. F. (1996). On the predictability of stock returns: An asset allocation perspective, *Journal of Finance* **51**, pp. 385–424.

Kindleberger, C. and Aliber, R. (2011). *Manias, Panics and Crashes*, 6th Edn.

Koivu, M., Pennanen, T., and Ziemba, W. T. (2005). Cointegration analysis of the fed model, *Finance Research Letters* **2**, pp. 248–256.

LeFevre, E. (2014). Reminisces of a stock operator, creative space, Independent Publishing Platform.

Livermore, J. (1940). *How to Trade in Stocks* (Duell, Sloan and Pearce).

Lleo, S. (2009). Risk management: A review, http://www.cfapubs.org/doi/abs/10.2470/rflr.v4.n1.1.

Lleo, S. (2010). *Risk Management: Foundations for a Changing Financial World*, Chap. Risk Management: a Review, Reserach Foundation of CFA Institute (John Wiley & Sons), pp. 73–112, http://www.cfapubs.org/doi/abs/10.2470/rflr.v4.n1.1.

Lleo, S. and Ziemba, W. (2012). Stock market crashes in 2007–2009: were we able to predict them? *Quantitative Finance* **12**, 8, pp. 1161–1187.

Lleo, S. and Ziemba, W. (2014). How to lose money in the financial markets: Examples from the recent financial crisis, *Alternative Investment Analyst Review* **3**, 3, pp. 22–35.

Lleo, S. and Ziemba, W. (2015a). How to lose money in derivatives: Examples from hedge funds and bank trading departments, in A. Malliaris and W. Ziemba (Eds.), *The World Scientific Handbook of Futures Markets* (World Scientific Publishing Co., Singapore).

Lleo, S. and Ziemba, W. T. (2015b). Some historical perspectives on the bond-stock yield model for crash prediction around the world, *International Journal of Forecasting* **31**, 2, pp. 399–425.

Lleo, S. and Ziemba, W. T. (2016a). The bond-stock earnings yield differential model: additional applications and other models for stock market crash prediction, *Quantitative Finance Letters* **4**, 1.

Lleo, S. and Ziemba, W. T. (2016b). Can Warren Buffett also predict equity market downturns? Technical Report.

Lleo, S. and Ziemba, W. T. (2016c). Predicting Chinese stock market crashes, Technical Report.

Lleo, S. and Ziemba, W. T. (2017). Does the bond-stock earning yield differential model predict equity market corrections better than high P/E models? *Financial Markets, Institutions and Instruments*, **26**, 2, pp. 61–123.

Loewenstein, M. and Willard, G. A. (2000). Local martingales, arbitrage and viability: free snacks and cheap thrills, *Economic Theory* **16**, pp. 135–161.

Loewenstein, M. and Willard, G. A. (2000). Rational equilibrium asset-pricing bubbles in continuous trading models, *Journal of Economic Theory* **91**, 1, pp. 17–58.

Lucca, D. O. and Moench, E. (2011). The Pre-FOMC announcement drift. Federal Reserve Bank of New York Staff Reports No. 512. September.

Lucca, D. O. and Moench, E. (2015). The Pre-FOMC announcement drift. *The Journal of Finance*, **70**, pp. 329–371. doi: 10.1111/jofi.12196.

Maio, P. (2013). The "Fed Model" and the predictability of stock returns, *Review of Finance* **17**, 4, 1489–1533.

Maudlin (2008). Thoughts from the frontline.

Meyer, M. and Booker, J. (2001). *Eliciting and Analyzing Expert Judgment: A Practical Guide*, ASA-SIAM Series on Statistics and Applied Probability (Society for Industrial and Applied Mathematics).

Modigliani, F. and Richard, A. C. (1979). Inflation, rational valuation and the market, *Financial Analysts Journal*, pp. 24–44.

Montier, J. (2011). The seven immutable laws of investing, in John Mauldin's *Outside the Box*, March 11.

Mulvey, J. and Liu, H. (2016). Identifying economic regimes: Reducing downside risks for university endowments and foundations, *Journal of Portfolio Management* **43**, 1, pp. 100–108.

Neyman, J. (1934). On the two different aspects of the representative method, in *Royal Statistical Society*.

Neyman, J. (1937). Outline of a theory of statistical estimation based on the classical theory of probability, *Philosophical Transactions of the Royal Society A* **236**, 767, pp. 333–380.

Neyman, J. and Pearson, E. (1933). The testing of statistical hypotheses in relation to probabilities a priori, in *Mathematical Proceedings of the Cambridge Philosophical Society*, Vol. 29, pp. 492–510.

Ogata, Y. (1988). Statistical models for earthquake occurrences and residual analysis for point processes, *Journal of the American Statistical Association* **83**, 401, pp. 9–27.

O'Hagan, A. et al. (2006). *Uncertain Judgments: Eliciting Expert's Probabilities* (Wiley, Chichester, UK).

Peskir, G. and Shiryaev, A. (2006). *Optimal Stopping and Free-Boundary Problems* (Birkhäuser Basel), ISBN 978-3764324193.

Phillips, P. C. B., Shi, S.-P., and Yu, J. (2013). Testing for multiple bubbles 1: Historical episodes of exuberance and collapse in the S&P500, *New Economics Papers*, October.

Polunchenko, A. S. and Tartakovsky, A. G. (2012). State-of-the-art in sequential change-point detection, *Methodology and Computing in Applied Probability* **14**, 3, pp. 649–684.

Poor, H. V. and Hadjiliadis, O. (2009). *Quickest detection*, Vol. 40 (Cambridge University Press, Cambridge).

Protter, P. (2005). *Stochastic Integration and Differential Equations: A New Approach, Stochastic Modeling and Applied Probability*, Vol. 21, 2nd Edn. (Springer-Verlag, Berlin).

Protter, P. (2013). A mathematical theory of financial bubbles, *Paris-Princeton Lectures on Mathematical Finance* **2081**, pp. 1–108.

Protter, P. (2016). Mathematical models of bubbles, *Quantitative Finance Letters* **4**, 1, pp. 10–13, doi:10.1080/21649502.2015.1165863, http://dx. doi.org/10.1080/21649502.2015.1165863, http://dx.doi.org/10.1080/21649 502.2015.1165863.

Rachev, S. and Ziemba, W. T. (1992). The distribution of golf course membership prices in Japan. Presentation at ORSA-TIMS Meeting in San Francisco, November.

Rajan, R. and Zingales, R. L. (2003). The politics of financial development in the 20th century, *Journal of Financial Economics* **69**, 1, pp. 5–50.

Reese, J. P. and Forehand, J. M. (2009). *The Guru Investor: How to Beat the Market using History's Best Strategies* (Wiley, Hoboken, New Jersey).

Reinhart, C. M. and Rogoff, K. S. (2009). *This Time is Different: Eight Centuries of Financial Folly* (Princeton University Press, Princeton, New Jersey).

Riley, Jr, W. B. and Luksetich, W. A. (1980). The market prefers Republicans: myth or reality, *Journal of Financial and Quantitative Analysts* **15**, 3, pp. 541–59.

Ritter, J. R. and Warr, R. S. (2002). The decline of inflation and the bull market of 1982–1999, *Journal of Financial and Quantitative Analysis* **37**, 1, pp. 29–61.

Sato, Y. (2016). Fund tournaments and asset bubbles, *Review of Finance* **20**, 4, pp. 1383–1426.

Savage, L. (1972). *The Foundations of Statistics*, 2nd Edn. (Dover, New York).

Scheinkman, J. and Xing, W. (2003). Overconfidence and speculative bubbles, *Journal of Political Economy* **111**, 6, pp. 1183–1219.

Schroder (2002). Schroder Investment Management Ltd,.

Schwartz, E. S. and Moon, M. (2000). Rational pricing of internet companies, *Financial Analysts Journal* **56**, 3, pp. 62–75.

Schwartz, S. L. and Ziemba, W. T. (2000). Predicting returns on the Tokyo stock exchange, in D. B. Keim and W. T. Ziemba (Eds.), *Security Market Imperfections in World Wide Equity Markets* (Cambridge University Press, Cambridge, UK), pp. 492–511.

Shepherd, C. (2008). S&P500 ratio is now at 723, www.trendinvestor.info.

Shiller, R. (2000). *Irrational Exuberance* (Princeton University Press, Princeton, New Jersey).

Shiller, R. (2009). *Irrational Exuberance*, 2nd Edn. (Princeton University Press, Princeton, New Jersey).

Shiller, R. J. (1996). Price earnings ratios as forecasters of returns: The stock market outlook in 1996, Technical Report. http://www.econ.yale.edu/shiller/data/peratio.html, http://www.econ.yale.edu/shiller/data/peratio.html.

Shiller, R. J. (2006). Irrational exuberance revisited, *CFA Institute Conference Proceedings Quarterly* **23**, 3, pp. 16–25.

Shiller, R. J. (2015). *Irrational Exuberance*, 3rd Edn. (Princeton University Press).

Shiryaev, A. N. (1963). On optimal methods in quickest detection problems, *Theory of Probability and Its Applications* **8**, 1, pp. 22–46.

Shiryaev, A. N. (2002). Quickest detection problems in the technical analysis of the financial data, in *Mathematical Finance — Bachelier Congress 2000*, Geman, H., Madan, D., Pliska, S. R. and Vorst, T. (eds.) (Springer, Berlin), pp. 487–521.

Shiryaev, A. N. (2007). *Optimal stopping rules* (Springer, Berlin).

Shiryaev, A. N. (2010). Quickest detection problems: fifty years later, *Sequential Analysis* **29**, 4, pp. 345–385.

Shiryaev, A. N. (2010). Quickest detection problems: fifty years later, *Sequential Analysis* **29**, 4, pp. 445–385.

Shiryaev, A. N., Zhitlukhin, M. V., and Ziemba, W. T. (2014). When to sell Apple and the Nasdaq? Trading bubbles with a stochastic disorder model, *Journal of Portfolio Management* **40**, 2, pp. 54–63.

Shiryaev, A. N., Zhitlukhin, M. V., and Ziemba, W. T. (2015). Land and stock bubbles, crashes and exit strategies in Japan circa 1990 and in 2013, *Quantitative Finance* **15**, 9, pp. 1449–1469.

Siegel, J. J. (2008). *Stocks for the Long Run: The Definitive Guide to Financial Market Returns and Long-Term Investment Strategies*, 4th Edn. (McGraw-Hill, New York).

Siegel, J. J. (2014). *Stocks for the Long Run: The Definitive Guide to Financial Market Returns and Long-Term Investment Strategies*, 5th Edn. (McGraw-Hill, New York).

Sornette, D. (2002). Predictability of catastrophic events: material rupture, earthquakes, turbulence, financial crashes and human birth, *Prof. Nat. Acad. Sci. USA* **99**, pp. 2522–2529.

Sornette, D. (2003). Critical market crashes, *Physics Reports* **378**, 1, pp. 1–98.

Sornette, D. (2004). *Why Stock Markets Crash: Critical Events in Complex Financial Systems* (Princeton University Press, Princeton, New Jersey).

Sornette, D. (2009). Dragon-kings, black swans and the prediction of crises, *International Journal of Terraspace Science and Engineering* 1(3), 1–17 **1**, 3, pp. 1–17.

Sornette, D. and Ouillon, G. (2012). Dragon-kings: mechanisms, statistical methods and empirical evidence, *The European Physical Journal Special Topics* **205**, 1, pp. 1–26.

Sornette, D. and Zhou, W.-X. (2002). The US 2000–2002 market descent: how much longer and deeper? *Quantative Finance* **2**, pp. 468–481.

Stiglitz, J. E. (Ed.) (1990). *Symposium on Bubbles* (Journal of Economic Perspectives), Vol. 4, No. 2, pp. 13–18.

Stone, D. and Ziemba, W. T. (1993). Land and stock prices in Japan, *Journal of Economic Perspectives*, Summer, pp. 149–165.

Stovall, R. (1992). Forecasting stock market performance via the presidential cycle, *Financial Analysts Journal* **48**, 3, pp. 5–8.

Swensen, D. W. (2000). *Pioneering portfolio management: an unconventional approach to institutional investments* (The Free Press, New York).

Tartakovsky, A., Nikiforov, I., and Basseville, M. (2014). *Sequential analysis: Hypothesis testing and changepoint detection* (CRC Press).

Thaler, R. H. (1997). Irving fisher: Modern behavioral economist, *The American Economic Review* **87**, 2, pp. 439–441, papers and Proceedings of the Hundred and Fourth Annual Meeting of the American Economic Association.

Weigand, R. A. and Irons, R. (2007). The market p/e ratio, earnings trends, and stock return forecasts, *Journal of Portfolio Management* **33**, 4, pp. 87–101.

Wells, N. and Chemi, E. (2016). A short history of stock market crashes. http:// www.cnbc.com/2016/08/24/a-short-history-of-stock-market-crashes.html.

Wilmott, P. (2013). *Paul Wilmott on Quantitative Finance*, 2nd edn. (John Wiley & Sons).

Wong, W. K. and McAleer, M. (2000). Financial astrology: mapping the presidential election cycle in US stock markets. Available at SSRN.

Yan, W., Woodard, R., and Sornette, D. (2012). Detection of crashes and rebounds in major equity markets, *International Journal of Portfolio Analysis and Management* **1**, 1, pp. 59–79.

Yan, W., Woodard, R., and Sornette, D. (2012). Role of diversification risk in financial bubbles, *Journal of Investment Strategies* **1**, 4, pp. 63–83.

Yardeni, E. (1997). Fed's stock market model finds overvaluation, Technical report, US Equity Research, Deutsche Morgan Grenfell.

Ziegler, A. and Ziemba, W. T. (2015). Returns from investing in S&P500 futures options, in A. Mallaris and W. T. Ziemba (Eds.), *Handbook of Futures Markets* (World Scientific, Singapore), pp. 643–688.

Ziemba, W. T. (1991). The chicken or the egg: land and stock prices in Japan, in W. T. Ziemba, W. Bailey and Y. Hamao (Eds.), *Japanese Financial Market Research* (North Holland, Amsterdam).

Ziemba, R. E. S. and Ziemba, W. T. (2007). *Scenarios for Risk Management and Global Investment Strategies* (Wiley).

Ziemba, R. E. S. and Ziemba, W. T. (2013). *Investing in the Modern Age* (World Scientific Publishing,).

Ziemba, W. T. and Vickson, R. G. (Eds.) (2006). *Stochastic optimization Models in Finance* (World Scientific Publishing, Singapore).

Ziemba, W. T. (2003). *The Stochastic Programming Approach to Asset Liability and Wealth Management* (AIMR, Charlottesville, VA).

Ziemba, W. T. (2012). *Calendar Anomalies and Arbitrage* (World Scientific Publishing, Singapore).

Ziemba, W. T. (2015). Presentation, in *Fourth International Conference on Intelligent Finance, Chongqing*.

Ziemba, W. T. (2016a). Nonpredictable stock market declines, *Quantitative Finance Letters* **4**, pp. 53–59.

Ziemba, W. T (2016b). *Great Investment Ideas.* (World Scientific Publishing).

Ziemba, W. T. (2017). *The adventures of a modern renaissance academic in investing and gambling Travels with Dr Z:* (World Scientific, Publishing in press).

Ziemba, W. T. and Schwartz, S. L. (1991). *Invest Japan* (Probus, Chicago).

Ziemba, W. T. and Schwartz, S. L. (1992). *Power Japan* (Probus, Chicago).

Ziemba, W. T. and Schwartz, S. L. (1992). *Invest Japan: The Structure, Performance and Opportunities of Japan's Stock, Bond and Fund Markets.* (Probus Publishing Co).

Zweig, M. (1986). *Winning on Wall Street* (Warner Books, New York).

Zweig, M. (1987). *Winning with the new IRAs* (Warner Books, New York).

Index